W9-ABI-611

POETRY AND CHANGE

POETRY
AND
CHANGE

Donne, Milton, Wordsworth,
and the Equilibrium of the Present

JOSEPHINE MILES

UNIVERSITY OF CALIFORNIA PRESS

Berkeley / Los Angeles / London

DALE H. GRAMLEY LIBRARY
SALEM COLLEGE
WINSTON-SALEM, N. C.

PR
502
M49

University of California Press
Berkeley and Los Angeles, California
University of California Press, Ltd.
London, England

Copyright © 1974, by
The Regents of the University of California

ISBN: 0–520–02554–7
Library of Congress Catalog Card Number: 73–84387
Designed by Jim Mennick
Printed in the United States of America

❧ *Contents*

I. PATTERNS

✷ *Introduction*

ACCUSTOMED as we are to change, or unaccustomed, we think of a change of heart, of clothes, of life, with some uncertainty. We put off the old, put on the new, yet say that the more it changes the more it remains the same. Every age is an age of transition. We even think of speedups of change, a dizzying whirl of newness; we speak of complete new revelation and then find it written in notes of ten years back. As we never step twice into the same river, it is difficult to discover where the water has gone, what flood control will do, and all the metaphors of "influence."

Literature especially among the arts provides a fine frame for the study of change. Over many centuries, writing is published at a steady rate, forms of language agreed on, emphases of subject and order emphasized, a steady stream of values observable in all their sensory shapes and forms. The poet is a person in place and time, sharing in a language, participating in a culture. Also he is an artist, accepting and explaining the sensory values of the aesthetic for his time; also he is a poet using in various ways the competencies of his language, his society, his profession. In change is the sense of choice of what to use from available norms, what to discard as outworn, what to initiate or emphasize as a new essential to the norm. An individual works with availabilities, some so conditioning he can scarcely recognize them, some so *outré* he trembles at their presence.

The clue in art is the patternings, the limited and repeated ways of combining materials available in the medium; in language, the uses of sound, sense, structure to reinforce each other; the vogues of choice, the sequences of agreement into which burst radians of variation; or, sequences of variation into which flash illustrations of agreement.

In the twentieth century, a great age for qualification, certain clear frequencies have been attributed to all the most-used words, as indicated by concordances, for example, or to characteristic sound patterns discerned by careful analysis. But increasingly as the century has gone on, these simple linearities of repetition have taken on depth. As Kenneth Burke early suggested, it is the clusters of usage, the combinations of chords, that more deeply serve to characterize; and linguistic studies have helped literature as they have discriminated the chords; the classic alternatives in syntactic as well as phonological and semantic structures which allow readers to recognize categories, not merely elements, of usage, and thereby to simplify the many individual practices to a few major kinds, there being after all not so many fundamentally different ways to order and transform the language.

Two recent collections of essays have been particularly helpful in their relating of language to literature: New Literary History, ed. Ralph Cohen, 4, no. 1 (autumn 1972), and Daedalus, ed. Stephen R. Graubard, "Language as a Human Problem" (summer 1973). Note the wisdom of Dell Hymes in his statement that "we have not thought through new ways of seeing how linguistic resources do, in fact, become organized in the world"[1] and his question about frequencies of occurence in relation to qualitative role.[2] Also the guess of Calvert Watkins[3] either that language "flees" what it perceives consciously as old-fashioned or archaic; or else that the language moves by extrapolation in the direction indicated by what it preserves. And thus "this awareness of the past history in the present structure."[4] Edward L. Keenan in "Logic and Language" makes clear what I have tried to emphasize as a matter of choice among repertoires of transformations, the embedded clause as a matter of predisposition[5] or what I have called assumption, like modification also, in contrast to assertion. And Paul Kiparsky's "The Role of Linguistics is a Theory of Poetry" is much more helpful than many such essays in the past, as in his reference[6] to use of awareness of parallelisms even in reordered constituents.

Modern linguistic studies have helped a great deal in defining the parts of language in terms of its functions, and in clarifying alternatives for similar functions. The concept of "in other words" helps with the selections and arrangements made by literature. Attention to the movability and interchangeability of parts enables characterization of differing wholes. In the first two chapters of this book I relate present concepts of parts and wholes in their linguistic and artistic structures and in their assumption of linguistic and artistic norms. In the third, with borrowings and adaptations of tables and text from earlier work, I relate both individual and group to temporal development by the agreements and variations they maintain in language. The following chapters, on individuals and eras, attempt to make certain specific illustrations of how such relations work, in the eccentricity or adaptability of a writer to his time, with some sense for the present of where we are moving.

Many ideas and questions which have come to me from others are dealt with in individual chapters, and acknowledgment is made to publication in earlier forms. Acknowledgment too, to the Committee on Research of the University of California for its unfaltering aid, even in terms of cents when the dollars ran out, and to Rita Fattaruso, John Crawford, and Elin Stetz for unfaltering and skillful aid beyond monetary definition.

New Literary History, 4, no. 1 (Fall, 1972): 35–45, first printed "Forest and Trees: The Sense at the Surface." *Literary Style: A Symposium,* ed. and (in part) trans. Seymour Chatman (London and New York: Oxford University Press, 1971), pp. 24–28, "Style as *Style.*" *Style,* 5 (fall 1971): 226–230, "Styles in Lyric." *Eras and Modes in English Poetry* (Berkeley and Los Angeles: University of California Press, 1964) and *Style and Proportion: The Language of Prose and Poetry* (Boston: Little, Brown and Company, 1967), the tables and text revised in "Sequences of Change." *Just So Much Honor,* ed. Peter Amadeus Fiore (University Park and London: Pennsylvania State University Press, 1972), pp. 273–291, "Ifs, Ands, and Buts for the Reader of Donne." *Milton's Lycidas: The Tradition and the Poem,* ed. C. A. Patrides (New York: Holt, Rinehart and Winston, 1961), pp. 95–100, "The Language of *Lycidas.*" *Eighteenth Century Studies,* 2 (1968): 35–44, "A Change in the Language of Literature." *William Blake. Essays in Honor of Geoffrey Keynes,* ed. Morton Paley and Michael Phillips. (Oxford: Clarendon Press, 1973), pp. 86–95, "Blake's Frame of Language." *Edwin Arlington Robinson: A Collection of Critical Essays,* ed. Francis Murphy (Englewood Cliffs, N.J.: Prentice-Hall, 1970) pp. 110–116, "Robinson and the Years Ahead." *Twentieth Century Literature in Retrospect,* ed. Reuben A. Brower, *Harvard English Studies* 2 (Cambridge: Harvard University Press, 1971), pp. 205–224. "Twentieth Century Donne." *Massachusetts Review,* 7 (Spring 1966): 321–355, and 12 (Autumn 1971): 689–708, "In Camera, 1965" and "The Home Book of Modern Verse, 1970," now parts of "Mid-Century."

NOTES TO INTRODUCTION

1. *Daedalus,* p. 59.   2. Ibid., 71.   3. Ibid., p. 110.
4. Ibid., p. 110.   5. Ibid., p. 192.   6. Ibid., p. 242.

✎ 1. The Sense at the Surface

TREE-DIAGRAMS which branch out sentence structures from root subject-predicates to twiggy subordinations and modifications are disconcerting to the literary critic interested more in structures of plot and character than in grammar. While paradigm and syntax, the choice and arrangement of words, *invention* and *distribution* in the terms of an older rhetoric, make a useful frame for analysis in both vertical and horizontal dimensions of synonymity and sequence, the critic as artist wishes not to be so analytically scientific that he must generalize about what are individual processes of involvement.

Patterns of artistry, on the other hand, make the linguist uneasy because they seem extraneous to his stabilized forms. He tries to build art somehow into language by calling it pseudostatement or deviant, parasitic, say, as mistletoe. The older metaphor of flowers, or "colors," came closer to catching the relation, because it called attention to the affecting forms of the aesthetic, as distinguished from the numb or anesthetic, surface of art.

An artist carries cognitive meanings into sensory meanings by the processes of patterning, by the setting up and confirming or disappointing, delaying or hastening, suspending or strengthening of expectations by sensory patterns; and so moves, by knowledge and delight.

In literature, questions of "meaning" relate to how words signify, how they compose concepts, how by maintaining appropriateness to situation they imply special characteristics of situation, how kinds of propositions establish relations of expectation, and how similarities of items not only phonologically and semantically but also grammatically, especially transformationally, make possible repetitions which work not only in sequence but by implications from depths to surfaces. All of these are then available to artistic usage, that is, to organization by sensory pattern, and some suggest not only surface design but the possibilities of design from depth, by the latent as well as the manifest. If design does not cause, it confirms, what is in the language.[1]

Perception of how the selective process of design can work to involve the reader is made more vivid by perception of transformation in grammar: the relating of statement to question and imperative, the relating of active to passive, the relating of word to phrase to clause; not only the articulatable parts of speech but their alternative relations to each other become more available to a sense of design. With awareness of the artist's repetitions in patterning we can see deeper into the nature of his repetitions, not only the simplest of sound alliterations, not only the refrains of words and phrases, not only the many uses of synonymity in restatement and further restatement, but also the types or -*emes* of these elements, the classes of sound and referents, and the substitutabilities of question for command, or adjective for clause. We enjoy patternings of such elements even at their simplest, and have a fine sense of appropriateness.

When we write the correction / / *str.* in the margin beside such a statement as "I like swimming, hunting, and to fish," we are resting upon a set of assumptions about the arts of grammar, logic, and rhetoric which take sensory design to be a useful aid in the absorption of meaning. Specifically, in this instance, we assume that unless fishing is very different from hunting and swimming, it should not be given a different form, that sensory parallelism should support cognitive parallelism. How easily we respond to the difference between the random beat of wind and branch, a regular natural beat as a wave, and an intention-laden beat in the pattern of an identi fying knock or whistle.

In basic forms like nursery rhymes, we see just how much pattern we can absorb. In "Peter Piper picked a peck of pickled peppers," there is even challenge to pronunciation. Further, in these pickled peppers there is more than simple repetition of *p*'s; there is repetition of a type called plosive sounds, the *k*'s along with the *p*'s; "Peter Piper purchased a pound of pungent peppers" would be a softer and differently loaded line. It is at such a point that linguists help by listening, by discriminating classes of sounds more relevant to ear than eye.

It is at such a point that linguistic study is helpful in discriminating the elements for design—not merely obvious visual surfaces but auditory echoes, semantic associations, structural similarities which may work below the surface but are also implied in the surface richness. As *p* relates to *k*, and assonance to off-rhyme, so synonym to synonym, and a way of saying to implied other ways. Surface questions or imperatives may suggest basic statements; adjectives may call up kernel sentences from which they have been transformed. In Chomsky's example from *Cartesian Linguistics*,[2] the sequence *"God is invisible. God creates the world. The world is visible"* says in three basic sentence-forms what may also be presented with differing tone and effect as *God, who is invisible, creates the world, which is visible.* Or, adjectivally, *Invisible God creates the visible world.* Is the last more "economical" in that it uses fewer words? More assumptive, because it states less? More "decorative" because it qualifies? These questions may be asked more simply if they are seen in relation to the many other grammatical choices the poet tends to make in certain steady connections. The great virtue of present-day language study for art is that it shows language to be truly and effectively analyzable in its articulations and thus in its power to be both variably patterned at its aesthetic surface and implicative of alternatives beneath the surface. So sensory meaning can corroborate cognitive. So "The House that Jack Built" can be seen to make a fine step in design when it moves from the clauses of *This is the house that Jack built, This is the malt that lay in the house that Jack built* to the double clauses of *This is the rat that ate the malt . . . / This is the cat that chased the rat . . .* and then to the participial alternatives— *This is the maiden all forlorn / That milked the cow with the crumpled horn . . .* (not *that is crumpled,* not *is forlorn*). The choice of alternatives between *Jack built the house, the house that Jack built, the house built by Jack,* even a Hopkinsian *by-Jack-built house,* parallels the choices within other modes of grammar in treating the reader with various degrees of assumption.

Even prose exemplifies, everyday prose, as in this sample at random from the news. The spacing separates the auxiliary elements of connected phrases and clauses from the other basic functioning parts of statement and modification.

Mexican police   Friday   asked the U.S. Federal Bureau of Investigation to arrest a 42-year old New York murder convict   who escaped   aboard a helicopter   from federal penitentiary   last Wednesday.

Cognitively this passage is ordered; aesthetically it's random. *Méxican* and *féderal* are potential units of like stress, but they do not recur, *Fríday ásked the, Ú.S. Búreau,* are stronger but are not made much of; they might be in the concluding *Wédnesday,* but are prevented by the use of *last.* In sound quality as well, the alliterations or assonances do not function to pattern; *Mexican . . . murder, asked . . . to arrest, from federal,* are potentials not developed by arrangement or emphasis. If they were, they'd create attention to their own sensory qualities, which in this message we'd take as a distraction, a "poetic" overload. In the following paragraph, in contrast, is a small design, a repetition which we may take as a sensory aid to the cognitive message:

The police chief in Ciudad Victoria reported he had information from police in Brownsville, Tex., that Kaplan had boarded yet another small plane in Brownsville for Sausalito, Calif.

The parallel of *police . . . in Ciudad Victoria* with *police in Brownsville, Tex.* and then again *in Brownsville*, tastefully accentuated by *yet another*, gives us a sequence in structure aesthetically supportive of the sequence in meaning; Kaplan's actions are seen to be repeated, and similar agencies are aware of this procedure.

In Shakespeare's sonnets, the *When . . . When . . . When . . . Then* repeated structure of the quatrains and couplet provide a strong basis for strong variation within. In Donne's and Milton's sonnets, on the other hand, less sensorily obvious guides are given, more exaggeration or more intricacy. To look at such poems with a sense of the articulatable parts of language—not merely of simple sound at one extreme and sonnet tradition on the other, but also of the central working grammar in its relation to the poem's logic and rhetoric, is to see and hear more, to feel more, of the poem's entity. Linguistic study helps by recognizing what characteristics are groupable and repeatable in certain recurrent ways, that is, by giving us classes of qualities to work with instead of innumerable items.

Consider, for example, the elements of design in Milton's sonnet "When I consider." The traditional forms are there, the repeated measures and lines, but we see very little else at the outset to give shape to the thought: *world and wide, patience . . . prevent, either . . . or, best . . . best,* and a few other such parallels. At the end, these unfold into what turns out to be the triumphant pattern of both sound and structure in the last line, " 'They also serve who only stand and wait.' "

DALE H. GRAMLEY LIBRARY
SALEM COLLEGE
WINSTON-SALEM, N. C.

When I consider how my light is spent,
  Ere half my days, in this dark world and wide,
  And that one Talent which is death to hide,
  Lodg'd with me useless, though my Soul more bent
To serve therewith my Maker, and present
  My true account, lest he returning chide;
  "Doth God exact day-labor, light denied,"
  I fondly ask; But patience to prevent
That murmur, soon replies, "God doth not need
  Either man's work or his own gifts; who best
  Bear his mild yoke, they serve him best; his State
Is Kingly. Thousands at his bidding speed
  And post o'er Land and Ocean without rest:
  They also serve who only stand and wait."

Seemingly the poem only slowly develops into pattern. But a closer look shows pattern at the beginning also: the piling up of elements to be recognized as descriptive phrases: *how, ere, in,* then moving into their transformations *which* and *Lodg'd.* The poem is at first situational and modificatory, then becomes inner dialogue in superlatives; and finally in the last three lines the verbs of action take over in *speed* and *post* paralleled cumulatively by *stand and wait* and joined by *They also serve.* In other words, the sonnet is deeply contrastive in forms below the superficial surface but not below the surface of sensory linguistic attention.

Donne works another way. In the last of the Holy Sonnets, surface design is a steady tool throughout: line-ends enforced by rhymes; the rhymes parallel in meaning as in *would not, soone forgott, cold and hott;* a structure shifted between octave and sestet.

Oh, to vex me, contraryes meet in one:
Inconstancy unnaturally hath begott
A constant habit: that when I would not
I change in vowes, and in devotione.
As humorous is my contritione

As my prophane Love, and as soone forgott:
As ridlingly distemper'd, cold and hott,
As praying, as mute; as infinite, as none.
I durst not view heaven yesterday; and to day
In prayers, and flattering speaches I court God:
To morrow I quake with true feare of his rod.
So my devout fitts come and go away
Like a fantastique Ague: save that here
Those are my best dayes, when I shake with feare.

There are many kinds of parallels: *in . . . in, Inconstancy . . . constant, in, and in, as . . . as . . . as, yesterday . . . to day, come* and *go,* and many more. These are persistently, structurally contrastive, and they are not resolved. Actions lead to counteractions through repeated subordinate clauses, *So, Like, save, when;* and move into the figure of *fantastique Ague,* with the exception, further, that the ague is health; *best dayes* and *shake* bridge sound across the caesura in an irony of identification. For Donne a tight design is part of the air he breathes, the art he works in. It does not become, but *is.* In several final lines the pattern settles. In the evident triumph of "And thou like Adamant draw mine iron heart," the rigor of *d—d* is belied by the sad relation of the suitable *iron* to the unsuitable *heart.* The endings of many of the Holy Sonnets likewise design the middle-ground conclusion in doubleness: *lov'st . . . loth,* in II; *red . . . white,* in IV; *house . . . heale,* in V; the *ls* ending VI; *repent . . . pardon,* in VII; *remember . . . forget,* and *debt . . . mercy,* in IX; *sleepe . . . wake, eternally . . . die,* in X; *Creator . . . Creatures,* in XII; *chast . . . ravish,* in XIV, and so on. Donne accepts and plays upon design as bondage enforcing the limitations of flesh; it is not emergent in Milton's way.

In his own way, Wordsworth moves toward the present, even in his most traditional sonnets, by untangling the logic, unsuspending the vision, and making general statements of observation and affection very straightforwardly. Actions bal-

ance qualifications. Declaration and exclamation and question
in octave lead to further generalization in sestet.

> I grieved for Buonaparté, with a vain
> And an unthinking grief! The tenderest mood
> Of that Man's mind—what can it be? what food
> Fed his first hopes? what knowledge could *he* gain?
> 'Tis not in battles that from youth we train
> The Governor who must be wise and good,
> And temper with the sternness of the brain
> Thoughts motherly, and meek as womanhood.
> Wisdom doth live with children round her knees:
> Books, leisure, perfect freedom, and the talk
> Man holds with week-day man in the hourly walk
> Of the mind's business: these are the degrees
> By which true Sway doth mount; this is the stalk
> True Power doth grow on; and her rights are these.

The serious links of thought and association are punctuated
by sound as well as by shape: the internal accents and repetitions of *grieved* . . . *grief*; *mood* . . . *mind*; *Governor* . . . *good*;
man . . . *week-day man*; *true Sway* . . . *True Power*; *these* . . .
these. Not merely alliterative, these deeper verbal and phrasal
repetitions give assurance to question and to answer directly
made. Figuration is gentle—a little of womanhood, a little of
natural growth in the stalk of Power; figure is helpful but
not essential to the step-by-step meditation. Many of Wordsworth's sonnets are more Miltonically artful than his *Prelude*
measures; some are as deliberative and plain as his simplest
lyrics; but most have taken the step into modernity by their
literal progressive motions of association between sight or
concept and feeling or response.

Modern poets like Pound have abjured Wordsworth; his
literal statements of feeling for scenes and people have of-
fended poets seeking objects withdrawn from scenes and people to carry, nevertheless, a symbolizing force. Yet the image

tradition, the classical tradition of natural objects as norms of nature, has persisted under symbolism and has emerged in much of the poetry of the present as implicit rather than explicit: the photography of experience. Not all the poets in the present agree at this center. Pound and Thomas pull away toward Miltonic or Whitmanic revelation, as do Ginsberg and Snyder; Lowell, like Joyce and many of the younger poets, moves toward multiplicities of action, like Donne but not with Donne's subordinating connectives. But many seem to seek a kind of essentializing function. In the famed first poem of Williams's "Spring and All," the first dozen lines are Pound-like in their suspension—*the scattering of tall trees*—but then *dazed spring approaches*—it quickens for the birches—*rooted they / grip down and begin to awaken*. For Williams, the shift from one grammatical mode to another, from suspensive participles to active verbs, is itself a part of the poetry, as we saw it also in Milton's sonnet. Not always do such shifts function poetically in a single poem. More often, en masse, they may indicate shifts in preference from one stage to another of a poet's life, as for Stevens away from the qualifying epithets of *Harmonium*; or from one era of poetry to another, as from eighteenth-century explicit qualification to nineteenth-century implication.

In almost every era, or poet's work, or poem, sections in one mode may work beside sections in another. So it is possible to observe shared ways of poetizing for whole eras and kinds of writing. I have pointed out, for example, in *Eras and Modes* (1964) and *Style and Proportion* that under the textures of single poems and passages lie the contextures of whole agreements of usage, based upon preferences for certain choices of form and vocabulary, certain characterizing proportions of the materials of language. In the sixteenth and seventeenth centuries there were many poets and prosaists of root sentences, using many verbs, few adjectives and connectives: Ballads, Wyatt, Herbert, Vaughan, with Sidney and Lyly experimenting in prose. In prose more strongly the subordinating art of clauses, the Bible's, Bunyan's, Jonson's and Donne's, with Donne's poetry in close alliance. In eighteenth-century poetry and nineteenth-century prose, a spectacular increase of poetic and scientific arts of phrases, of qualifications.

A style in the use of language is built up, along with a style of moral judgment, a style of attitude toward reader, and so on, by a number of small recurring selections and arrangements working together. Along with his time and his particular type, the poet keeps using certain main terms because they signify what he wants to consider; then also he arranges them in certain recurrent ways, so that the quality of his text, his moving surface of statement, will convey, in addition to the sheer signifying, part of his feeling and sense about what he is saying. The artist adds to the qualities of his materials the qualities of design, the control of patterns of repetition, of likeness in differences, which will guide the audience to respond to the total effects as he wishes. In the interaction of a barn being "represented," red color being "selected," lines and masses being "arranged," viewer being led into the scene, we see the process of creating and reshaping of expectations which design contrives.

A poet's language has its leaf or hand print, the whorls that make it singular, the individuality in its style of engagement. But these do not work in isolation; they are part of the forest, part of the *langue*, part of the competence of poetry. The strands of common usage which hold poems together in any time, and from time to time, seem of such strength and predictable duration that one can see, in literature especially among the arts, the commonalty provided by the medium itself as well as by shared cultural values and interests. So the individual is to be read in the context of the language and literature he shares, that is, of his profession in time, his acceptances, his assumptions, and what he does with them. A leaf is unique not because there are no other leaves, but because of its singular variations upon the commonplace of leaf in its particular part of the forest.

Patterning, that is, is more than the work of a single author in a single poem or in an *oeuvre*, it is also the work of a profession, a craft, a making or seeing in language, over history. Not only specific word choices, or *topoi*, but also form-class choices, or technical forms, cluster by certain intentions or habits into discernible styles which embody, express, reveal, convey, whatever the metaphor of the ideology of art, part of the attitude and message of a view wider than person. The predictable regularities of vocabulary change, the close identifiability of terms of structures within periods, the limits of invention in any one poetic, all attest to the cultural and professional determinations within which individuals freely work. So the reader, even as the listener in oral tradition, comes to the work with many expectations for form and expression, which are then fulfilled, frustrated, played upon, by the author as part of his way of guidance. A young poet today, for example, is tuned to expectations of fragmentations, to participial constructions, to an "image" vocabulary in ways that can be deeply disturbed by a counter set of abstractions or stanzaic forms. Not only the context of situation makes for certain choices of signification; also the context of the literary tradition helps to establish the especial texture, both cognitive and sensory, of a literary text.

Consciousness of texture of language has not been lacking in writers of the past. Demetrius as a rhetorician was elegant on the subject of textures, noting the power of adjectives with minimization of connectives to achieve the smooth surface, the seamless marble, of Pindar's poetry. So too Isocrates' prose. Contrasting Isocrates' suspensions to the tensions of Cato's *quod* clauses, W. R. Johnson writes,[3] "Here as almost everywhere in Greek, it is largely a matter of participles, those marvellous aspectual proteans, half-noun, half-adjective, that can, without regard for space or time, impersonate or describe what-

ever phenomena a Greek sentence wants to sketch." The tone
of a Latin sentence, Johnson says, depends much on its proportioning of subordinate and subjunctive clauses. He traces
Cicero's conscious change from a subordinative style to a
simpler one.

In the seventeenth century, Lancelot[4] wrote to similar
analytic effect:

For it is observable that the parts of speech may be connected together, either by simple construction, where the several terms are
arranged in their natural order, so that you see, at a single glance,
the reason why one governs the other; or by a figurative construction, where, departing from that simplicity, we use some particular
turns and forms of expression, on account of their being either more
nervous, more concise, or more elegant, in which there are several
parts of speech not expressed but understood.

With detailed historical perspective, Edward L. Surtz in
"Epithets in Pope's *Messiah*"[5] shows extended debate from
Aristotle to Trapp and Kames, whether adjectives were to function *pro hic et nunc* or as universal, the crystallization of an
essential property. Should an adjective add new information
or confirm an old assumption? Again in the twentieth century
attention was brought to adjectives by Pound and the Imagists.
Fighting statements of universality, they opposed adjectival
generalizations as nonpoetic; they opposed the eighteenth century and Keats and Tennyson as if they were their immediate
predecessors and claimed as preferable the more colloquial
syntactics of Browning.

Other senses of syntactic contrast continued also. For example, note what the preface to Max Weber's *Essays in Sociology*[6] has to say about a contrast in German:

The genius of the German language has allowed for a twofold
stylistic tradition. One tradition corresponds to the drift of English
towards brief and grammatically lucid sentences. Such sentences
carry transparent trains of thought in which first things stand first.

Friedrich Nietzsche, Georg Christoph Lichtenberg, and Franz Kafka are eminent among the representatives of this tradition.

The other tradition is foreign to the tendency of modern English. It is often felt to be formidable and forbidding, as readers of Hegel and John Paul Richter or Karl Marx and Ferdinand Tönnies may testify.

. . . They use parentheses, qualifying clauses, inversions, and complex rhythmic devices in their polyphonous sentences. Ideas are synchronized rather than serialized. At their best, they erect a grammatical artifice in which mental balconies and watch towers, as well as bridges and recesses, decorate the main structure. Their sentences are Gothic castles. And Max Weber's style is definitely in their tradition.

Similarly, it is said of Mayakovsky in Russian:[7] "He was most ingenious in coining new verbal forms with, as he called it, the small change of suffixes and flections." He called rhyme the dynamite which exploded the fuse of the line. So, on the other hand, George Oppen and other Objectivists stressed not the rhymes and connectives, not even verbs, but bare nouns: "substantives for their own sakes," "little words that I like so much like 'tree,' 'hill,' and so on. . . ."[8]

Even more explicitly, John Crowe Ransom describes in *The New Criticism*[9] how the poet moves among the possible alternative articulations in language to make his choices:

A given word will probably have synonyms. The order of words in a phrase may be varied. A transitive predication may be changed to a passive; a relative clause to a participial phrase. In the little words denoting logical connections and transitions a good ideal of liberty may be taken without being fatal; they may be expanded into something almost excessively explicit, or they may be even omitted, with the idea that the reader can supply the correct relations.

So against the *thingness* of some phenomenologists, the field dynamics of Charles Olson can come into play.

The aesthetic of surface design serves to carry the reader in a direction of expectation and also to support by coinciding with the manifest meanings of the work. It is most obviously seen as we have seen it in the treatment of easily recognizable phonological, lexical, or structural elements. Much more can be done by critics, as Burke, Boyd, Chatman, Ohmann, Hill, and others have begun, by sensitivity to the basic units and then to their patterns and effective use. Alliteration is simple enough; then what about alliteration overused or used ironically? Repetitions of syllables for stress or timbre, for sound or sense, need first to be discerned, then related; or perhaps first felt, then discerned. The parallels and antitheses of syllable to syllable and syllable to sense, as in the realm of onomatopoeia, render the dimension of surface texture vivid to response. W. K. Wimsatt's essay on "Rhyme and Reason"[10] is a model of a kind which needs much further to be emulated.

Charles Fillmore's question,[11] "What do I need to know to use appropriately?" is not just a pragmatic but also an aesthetic question, in tune with Zellig Harris's early stress on the principle of controlled substitution, a principle adaptable to art.[12] Merleau-Ponty[13] quotes Bergson that we decipher life as a painter does a face—by rediscovering the intention through the lines. "We are capable of this kind of reading because we carry in our incarnate being the alphabet and the grammar of life, but this does not presuppose an achieved meaning either in us or in it."

Aristotle's idea of probability in art is given modern expression in Leonard Meyer's *Music, the Arts, and Ideas*[14] "In fine, a musical style is a probability system. It changes by its own internal dynamic process. . . . a finite array of interdependent melodic, rhythmic, harmonic, timbral, textural, and formal relationships and processes." Whether we agree with Morse Peckham that art creates its expectations in order to destroy them, or with Allen Tate and others that the rage for order itself drives art, the interplay is plain. What we do not need is an atomism which drives critics to the connotative inexpressibilities of symbolism on the one hand, or on the other, an absolutism which tries to collapse art into language or language into art, or, on a third hand, a dualistic view of the *what* and the *how* as binary, in a semiobjectivity. *What* and *how* persist independently in order that they may work together.

Language means by signs; art means by designs. In literature, signs and designs work together in ways we have yet fully to explore. The statement "It's cold outside" offers greater potentialities of sound and sense than just a repeated sibilant or a concept of temperature. It may suggest a semantic range of synonymity all the way to "It's freezing"; it may imply a form of perlocution in "He says that it's cold"; it may hint its double root in "The weather is outside; the weather is cold"; it may take on the figure of *pure ice*; it may "really" mean, as some pragmatists would like to say, "Close the door"; it may locate itself in a world of poetic choice, like the present, where *cold*, like *door*, is a term of high frequency in design. What is done to the word or the sentence to shade or strengthen its force in context is part of what is done for the whole work and the reader's role in it. Part has already been done in the language, alive with assumptions and expectancies before the poet comes to it, so that he may find in it various clear alternatives for construction. Will he make statements, or turn them to questions or imperatives? Will he choose to practice the objective impersonal passive forms which years of pseudoscience have tended to advocate or require? Will his doubts be reflected in conditionals and subjunctives, or rather in parenthetical disclaimers? Will he issue strings of simple assertions, or subordinate one to another in complex structures, or relegate many assertions to the assumptive powers of qualification? Here pivot the multiple relations of materials of statement to their possible sorts of transformation, and, as these sorts are not unlimited, they provide certain nuclei of usage within the language, familiar to reader as to author. Their shared sense of the potentialities of language, its range in alternatives of form, its centers of variation, makes the more possible their shared sense of the aesthetic surface where signs take new shape in designs, where roots and branches of sentence structure attain freshly signifying surfaces in the *sylvae*, in the leafy forests of literature.

NOTES TO CHAPTER 1

1. John Langshaw Austin, *How to Do Things with Words* (Cambridge: Harvard University Press, 1962).
2. Noam Chomsky, *Cartesian Linguistics* (New York: Harper & Row, 1966).
3. W. R. Johnson, *Luxuriance and Economy* (Berkeley and Los Angeles: University of California Press, 1971), p. 26.
4. Quoted in *Language*, 45 (1969): 348.
5. *Philological Quarterly*, 27 (1948): 209–218.
6. Max Weber, *Essays in Sociology* (New York: Oxford University Press, 1946).
7. *The Bedbug and Selected Poems*, ed. Patricia Blake (New York: Meridian Books, 1960).
8. *Contemporary Literature*, 10 (spring 1969).
9. John Crowe Ransom, *New Criticism* (New York: New Directions, 1941), pp. 303–304.
10. In W. K. Wimsatt, *The Verbal Icon: Studies in the Meaning of Poetry* (New York: Noonday Press, 1958).
11. Charles Fillmore, "Verbs of Judging," *Studies in Linguistic Semantics* (New York: Holt, Rinehart and Winston, 1970).
12. Zellig Harris, *Methods in Structural Linguistics* (Chicago: University of Chicago Press, 1947–1951).
13. Maurice Merleau-Ponty, *In Praise of Philosophy* (Evanston: Northwestern University Press, 1963), p. 123.
14. Leonard Meyer, *Music, the Arts, and Ideas* (Chicago: University of Chicago Press, 1967), pp. 115, 116.

✹ 2. *Style as* Style

I F W E describe what is before us in a text, what we perceive as objectively and neutrally as possible, we start out with one of those thorough phoenetic-syntactic-semantic-generic-social-thematic analyses of a poem that may give us more sheer data than we know how to use. We assume some basis for selection—say occurrence—and this enables us to bring to light some salient linguistic facts in the poem. It is interesting, for example, to note the steady co-occurrence, in alternate lines or stanzas, of plosive sounds with polysyllabic words with complex clausal structures and with a content of reference to a certain person in a tone of anger. We can then proceed to explain the reasons, linguistic, biographical, or artistic, for this co-occurrence; or we can attempt to estimate its extent, assess its effects, and so on.

A frequent danger lies in the fact that the principles for selection not only are established prior to thorough observation but are based on the reader's interest, with the result that the two elements of material and effect are immediately confused. To say, for instance, that the selection of doublets is an obvious feature of an author's style runs the risk of implying criteria of selection without exploring them. Why, and to whom, after all, is the feature "obvious"? Obviousness can arise not only from the nature of the text but from the nature of the reader; it could, for example, be the result of a strong sensitivity to a trait lacking or present in his own style or culture.

Many cautions have been made against giving excessive weight to co-occurrences, which, rather than being determined by aesthetic criteria, are simply made obtrusive by the particular set of linguistic or cultural conventions present behind the work. Brooks and Warren,[1] for example, have pointed out the danger of overrating the value of onomatopoeia in s sounds, or in the "murder of innumerable beeves," and Yvor Winters has dealt with what he calls the fallacy of imitative form.[2]

On the other hand, without a basis for selection in personal interest or some externally derived concern for harmony, truth, and effect, we can be submerged in a welter of data. Many years ago the aesthetician David Prall tried objectively to describe all the qualities and interqualities of one painting, and gave it up as an impossible job. The solution is, I think, simply to have and to state a criterion of selection, so that data and measure of data are kept separate, and interests of author not necessarily identified with interests of reader.

But to get at the identifying, the sufficient as well as the necessary, features for the description of an individual literary text, a further basis of selection seems necessary, one that will separate identifying traits of interest not only from readers' interest but from other writers' interest, that is, from the common styles established by the language and culture and not just by the individual work. Rostrevor-Hamilton's study[3] of the word *the* in English poetry is illuminating of *the* not just as an obvious word of the poetry and not just as a word of interest to him, but as cultural vehicle of a kind of attitude, a weighted structure present in the language and made use of by certain specific poets to certain specific effect.

Such distinctions, based upon such extensions of interest from text to readers and to other texts, remind us why close study of the describable elements of text, however cautiously selected and correlated, does not provide the complete story of style. As manner in the treatment of matter, style chooses and discards matter as well as arranging it; it works within the category of *invention* as well as within those of *disposition* and *elocution*. Therefore we need to know not only disposition or arrangement of what materials, but also choice *from* what materials—the prior givens, the limits and potentialities of thought and attitude already weighting the available materials as well as the accustomed manners. The loaded materials and manners are met and confirmed or counteracted by the specific loadings of the specific artistic structure of the specific artist work. A word weighted with a dull repetitive convention can be, for example, confined in that dull conventionality by the structure and sound of the line it is used in, or brightened by the shock of a new context; an alliterative pattern can be used inertly and neutrally, or comically, or with portentous grace. So we have the confluence in a literary text of ready-made forms and associations from the language, with those from the literature in general, and with those from specific genres of usage in particular, including the author's own; and all of these will be given the compacting force of an individual artistic entity in pattern and design.

It is at this point of individual entity that it is least possible to talk about style, unless with reference to the resources from which the work has been drawn. This poet's "way of writing," this poem's "way of writing" can be discerned chiefly by comparison and contrast, by relation to other works. The very concept of manner suggests that the way is separable from the material and thus may be followed in extension from material to material, that treatment is discernible across things treated. So if we are talking about a single work or entity we will probably not talk about its style, but if we relate it to other entities, and its elements to other elements, we necessarily do so.

Some critics elect to consider certain features in a text in their extension and intension or interrelation, in order to be able to say that this work's or this author's or this genre's style can be characterized by certain describable elements—in other words, a partial intensive or necessary definition of their participation in a style. Others elect to consider the potentialities, the store of availabilities, or code, from which any text may be shaped; that is, an observation of what is not, as well as what is, drawn upon, and thus a sufficient as well as necessary definition, a setting apart of the entity as well as a focusing upon its central features.

Our own language structure gives us a clue to how these two perspectives need to be related and interplayed. A dimension of reference often ignored at a time when connotativeness and figurativeness are considered is the dimension of the normative or intensive, where a word is used to label a good or bad example of a kind rather that just any example. Without any further modification except perhaps intonation, the word *cat* may vary its reference from "There's a cat," meaning animal, to "There's a cat," meaning woman, to "There's a *cat*," meaning a specially good example of either. A phrase that helpfully plays one of these meanings against the other is "out in the west where men are men." The necessary or extensive *men*, all we could call *men*, is made sufficient and intensive, implying what we would not. Such a linguistic usage, and I do not know whether it characterizes just English, or some, or all languages, makes for much cultural confusion in the discussion of any concept, including that of style. If we may be assuming the normative, we may be suddenly dropped into the descriptive, as in H. H. Munro's use of the verb *go* in "She was a good cook as cooks go, and as good cooks go, she went." It is exactly in mere elements that the values reside; *cat* is both *a cat* and *the cat*, eighteenth-century poetry is not only a collection of poems written in the eighteenth century, but a norm of poetry for some, of non-poetry for others. The relation of norm to non-norm, of poetry to non-poetry, for example, is not merely evaluative, not merely of good to bad, because for many speakers to exclude by definition is a prior sort of evaluation, and to be bad or to fail, very different from not "really" representing a category at all. So, at least in English, evaluation is built into words as well as being a modification of them.

Some speak of style descriptively, noting and relating elements of styles; some normatively, trying to see its full reference to value. The two emphases can profitably come together, but probably not all in one way, for the reason that the basic relation differs from one philosophy to another. For formal idealism, I suppose the whole shape controls the parts. For organic idealism, I suppose the details emerge and develop from the germ or seed of the norm. For materialism, on the other hand, details build up to the norm. For much present-day existentialism, one vivid detail may establish the character of the whole. It is my thought that beyond all these, or implicit in them, is the concept of working back and forth between part and whole, with neither fully established, but always open to new effects from the other; so that ever-new details may be seen to be relevant, and ever-new relevances be discerned in constant interplay. In this sense, for style, every detail of usage is relevant; if we can show it to be so, so much the merrier. From plosives and fricatives to the frictions and explosions of mankind and the universe is a not impossible way, though never a way to be assumed. For the literary scholar the way is mediated twice, through the patterns of language as distinct from art and through the patterns of art as distinct from language, and thus through the two together.

We can explicitly relate certain linguistic features or codes to a writer's own style, just as we may set one text against another in a certain canon. It will be possible to speak descriptively of different stages or phases of an author's style and of the artistic principles relating them to other features of manner. It will also be possible to speak normatively, saying, for example, that such features show us certain qualities of coherence, consistency, relevance, and other evaluative criteria; or in the negative, that the writer has *no* style because he uses these features in such a muddled way that no clearly characterizing manner can be discerned.

The danger in either way lies in ignoring the grounds of artistic and linguistic relevance which make connection possible between the necessary and the sufficient, the descriptive and the normative aspects of reference. To assume that a describably dense sound structure makes for a highly valuable poem, that is, "necessarily establishes high poetic quality" would be as foolish as some critics make it seem. On the other hand, it may not be foolish to say "I like dense sound structure so I am pretty sure to like this poem which has it," or, even more resoundingly, "For me a good poetic style requires a dense sound structure, so this style which lacks it is not really a good style; indeed, not really a style at all." It seems to me that we must allow for such common normative slides from descriptive characteristics, because they are easily and well made by certain philosophical procedures, notably the mechanist or existentialist in some forms. But the most philosophical, as most encompassing, of procedures is that which accepts the difference between, and thus the relation between, traits descriptive and traits normative, and so can relate not only specific message to specific code, and specific poem to specific school, and specific judgment to specific philosophy of values, but also, within any work itself, its own center to the periphery of its style; explaining its necessity and sufficiency, and the interplay between identity and possibility.

Style is what it is; what it is has deep involvement with what, linguistically, artistically, evaluatively, individually, it is not.

Making use of the concept of normative language, we can look to the word *lyric* as a guide to style in poetry as history. More than extended narrative which carries all the furnishings of action, more than drama which must be faithful to a variety of characterizations, lyric intensively concentrates on the values of words as music upholds them. Through closer repetitions, smaller units of melody, it makes the insistences on values which by their ongoing presence tell us what to care for.

To distinguish lyrical style from other poetic styles, the word *lyre* provides its guiding syllable, giving the concept of language musically accompanied, measure marked by musically pitched accents. It serves as contrast to the term *foot*, common in the descriptions of poetry in many languages as a unit of measure more durational, more ground-covering, and so more spatial, than the lyre's pitched string. The hand-pluck or strum is as formal as the foot beat, equally external, but not progressively moving; it may stress a pattern of circularity or repetition or simultaneity or various kinds of thoughtful relation other than linear action. Narrative and dramatic forms both cover ground; they march and confront. The lyrical air too moves in time, from note to note to note; but its motion is less durational, less spatial, more relational in terms of musical pitch. The lyre makes shorter intervals than narrative and drama require, and makes closer relations of these intervals, one to another. Of the dimensions of a tone, pitch or height, duration or breadth, stress or intensity, and timbre or quality, it is the deepening rather than the widening forces which are most at play. The lyric is an art of time in sound, both tonal and referential, which plays across the fabric of temporal sequence the material of atemporal relations; or accents its atemporal materials with a temporal design not only of word sequence but of formal timing by measure.

The heart of the lyric, its essential voice is, for instance, a three-note exclamation: three-tone to establish the minimum of temporal direction. In larger forms, the three tones establish themselves in structure: Shakespeare's *when, then, ever*; Donne's change *from, through, to*, Wordsworth's response of thought and feeling to image, Williams's "so much depends," Stevens's third world. Minimal or maximal, the measure accentuates a temporal melody, a temporal form, for materials and structures of feeling less temporal than in other verbal forms.

To distinguish lyrical styles one from another is to observe how poets play upon one or another of the emphases open to them within the nucleus of the genre. Traditionally, types have been distinguished by the subject of reference, by the word or occasion, as in elegy, epitaph, epigram, morning song; or by certain habits of forms which cohere, as in ballad, ode, or sonnet. But if we hold together the lyric coherences of reference and tone as they are lyrically conceived, we need to consider what kinds of tonal-referential emphasis are possible to basic choice. One would be song, the fullest use of patterns of pitch, of melody; one would be stress measures, as in the more deliberative and level verse of blank verse, couplet, cadence, in a Stevens fashion. A third would be the strong uses of timbre, or tone quality, with less emphasis on outer stresses for meter and line, and more on inner patterns of assonance and consonance, even of onomatopoeia; a development of the potential harmonies of the tone. Variations on these three possibilities have been named by Pound—*logopoeic, phanopoeic,* and *melopoeic*: the accentuating of the forms of speech, including song; or of forms of stressed tonal presentation; or of inner harmonies. When Northrop Frye writes of these distinctions, I think he confuses them by a confusion of melody and harmony; the root of *mel* is sweetness, honey, sensuous accord, euphony not melody; less temporal than speech and melody, it builds the patterns of sound into the line and the language rather than marking the external points of measure. As *phanopoeia* pulls away from the interworking of sound and sense toward sense, *melopoeia* pulls toward sound, color; the force of relation, the precarious combination, is most fully held by *logopoeia* when its measures are marked by melody as in song. When Eliot writes mock lyric in *The Waste Land* and part serious in *Four Quartets*, he uses and mocks all these kinds.

The strum of *good night ladies* and *the wounded surgeon*, the consonance of river and garden, the phanopoeia of Cleopatra's barge, Pound had already used and mocked, as he had thoughtfully discriminated.

The idea of style brings us to some repeated ways of use, with some relevance, maybe as expression or disguise or objectification, to the lyric writer. Many of what we would call lyrical styles are styles of the times in which they are written; or styles relevant to certain subject matters. Most truly we can speak of styles in lyrics when we think of recurrent clusters of those traits particularly characteristic of the lyric. A good example is the contrast between eighteenth-century and nineteenth-century styles—the first highly involved with choral music, the harmony of melopoeias as Dryden specifically noted, and the sudden return to the song "melodies" of Moore and Byron. Some of the same contrast we see today between the two poetry anthologies of Allen and of Hall, or, in the first of these, between Snyder and Creeley. All the potentialities of language are drawn on—kind of word, sentence structure, dramatic tone and character, narrative voice, figurative or symbolic formations, degrees of abstraction, and so on.

Differing and changing concepts of lyrical function have modified the concepts of its essentials. Greek classification was by subject, by meter, by accompanying instrument, and, obliquely, by point of view, the first-personal. For Dante, it was a compact statement of ideas in contrast to the more extended epic movement. For the Renaissance, its bent, its trope, was vital. For Romanticism, the temporality of personal memory, and thus the back-and-forth between psyche and object, spatial yet nonspatial in romantic ambiguity. A way of knowing. Then how song? Song is a way of knowing. The great historical mass of the lyric allows for remarkably stable variations on this remarkably stable theme. To speculate on what all the variations share is to heighten our sense of the possibilities within lyric styles as intrinsic rather than extrinsic—the variations made possible by the *lyre* itself—that is, the point at which musical note and verbal tone interact—the point of pitch. The three or four pitch-stresses of spoken language are enriched by the octave ranges; the pitch varieties of melody are held in check by the relative monotones of speech; the interplay makes for, in the lyric, an essentially more vertical pattern of sound than in other forms of poetry and of spoken art. Vital varieties in lyric styles then are based upon variations in the use of verticality of sound, of pitch-stress in relation to the essential temporal duration in speech patterns. The meaning, the feeling, of the lyric goes up or down as well as along. It can take on the high cry of jubilance or wailing, the low note of meditation or mourning, as well as the steady stichic or linear motion of narration and argument. Its measures are in time but not by time. They effect a simultaneity because they combine two significances in one: the quality of meaningful accent, as we would say *foréver* not *fórever*, and the quality of musical accent that pitches *ever* high or low. If the two concur, they confirm; if conflict, set up reverberations.

In language, the medium: sound, syntax, and reference; the structures of each separately and together. In art, the means, the uses of these structures by designs of repetition and interrelation. In poetry, the most closely measured art, the pacing of the meaningful syllables in time, by the tonal qualities of stress and duration and by the tonal qualities of pitch and color. In lyric, most closely measured of poetries, the closest use of both quantity and quality of sound, the nearest spoken approximation to music in its use of vertical as well as durational properties of tone, the force of melody, of pitch variety as intrinsic to design of form and meaning.

In lyrical styles, the various possible combinations of tonal traits: a strong rhythm or beat; a strong melody either confirming of, or indifferent to, or in conflict with the sense-measure and the reference; accentuating either external boundaries or internal focal points. Or strong overtones, stressing tone color, carrying into depth the implications of the melody and often superseding it, again possibly in conflict with, possibly confirming, the sense. The more lyric the poem, the more its full meaning needs to be discerned in the many different possible relations of its sense to its sound, and the more the richness of its powers of sound conveys that sense in their multiplications of tonal design. In the chief characteristics of tone itself reside the chief characteristics of spoken sound for poetry. Stress provides measure, making for chant at its simplest, making possible the monotone in which much poetry is read aloud; providing the frame for such ongoing measures as the blank verse which has been called "the dear damned cradle of us all." Timbre and duration together provide in English the tone color of euphony, the harmonic and chordal qualities, the built-in music, of patterned consonant and especially vowel sounds. Finally, pitch, so much more important to song than to speech in English, leaves its song-like residue in the lyre's lyric, with its potentiality of tuned accompaniment. It is here, if we want to essentialize, that we may look to the life-voice of the lyric—above its foot-beat and heart-beat and cadenced breath, the modulations of pitch which make for melody even in words, the spoken power of implied tune, implying also the expressive and signifying powers of tune to carry a motion of language even beyond measure or reference. This is what the *fa - la - las* are about: they sound simple, they are at the pitch of lyricism.

Different eras hear these simplicities differently. Ben Jonson, a master of subtly easy measure in "Charis"—"See the chariot at hand here of love"—was duly troubled by Donne's submission of sound to the complexities of argument; Milton worked to complicate in another way, by the internal loading of euphonies, before which the stringed instrument would have wavered. So too today, the ear which delights in the sustained and broken tensions of Robert Creeley honors "the sound of silence" more than do those who press a heavy beat beneath the verbal fragmentations. What comes right to a listening ear is a whole cluster of traits of language—simple sentences and repetitions for accompaniment, as by Jonson, subordinations, as by Donne, for a reasoning tone.

NOTES TO CHAPTER 2

1. Cleanth Brooks and Robert Penn Warren, *Understanding Poetry* (New York: Henry Holt and Co., 1938).
2. Yvor Winters, *The Anatomy of Nonsense* (Norfolk, Conn.: New Directions, 1943).
3. Rostrevor-Hamilton, George, *The Tell-Tale Article* (New York: Oxford University Press, 1950).

❧ 3. Sequences of Change

IF WE can see how the process of art in language, as well as the process of language itself, has an order to it, a stability and regularity, then we may accept change more readily, move with it more easily. Pattern shows us how. It does not crack, shatter, and reform; rather, like a texture of existence, it lets some strands go as it takes up others, and takes up none so many that the continuity of old sustaining new cannot be maintained. The chief vocabulary of English poetry at any one time reveals persistent strands, recent losses, incipient gains. Chief words waver and die away from the work of one poet and of many, perhaps return again for a few but in the main subside, while at the same time new words appear in major emphasis, tentatively or in large bursts of assurance. The stock of words is, one supposes, open-ended; yet simplicity and common usage have reason, and as some words in the most common stock in prose start to fade, we may not unwisely seek their successors from the common stock again.

Structural proportionings too develop and decline in certain lines of agreement, as if choice of sentence structure were based not only on whim, subject matter, mystery of ear, but also on needed functions in the time: crisp assertiveness in one era, complex subordinations in another, qualifying assumptions in another, none ever in complete control of the literary language, but each often dominating for a while as if to set clear certain relations, in certain vocabularies, and in certain sound patterns.

Proportion is a concept important for the analytical study of an art because it concerns not only the structure in the discernible parts of the material and not only the content or reference of the parts but also the relation between material and structure, the relation between *what* and *how* in *how much what?* So, for example, an architect will care not only about the character or function of the room he is designing and not only about its links to other rooms but also about its own proportions and its proportionate relations, in shape, size, and arrangement. Or a cook will care not only about the order of combination of salt and sugar in a sauce but also about the amounts of salt and sugar, the proportion of one to the other for very different effects.

Proportion is, so to speak, an aesthetic, a sensory interest, as this relates to interest in identity and function. It is the relation of the old *quadrivium* of geometry, music, architecture, astronomy, with its patterns in numbers, to the *trivium* of grammar, rhetoric, logic, with its patterns in letters. The figures 235 can mean a sum checkable in fact or a sum functionable for a purpose, or within itself have an aesthetic relevance of shape, an ascending pattern of 235 as distinguished, for example, from a balanced one of 232. Many theories of beauty have their basis, as they did for Pythagoras and for Leonardo da Vinci, and still do today, in a consciousness of "right" proportions. So in language, for the Romans, a recommended proportion for language in verse was the two nouns and two adjectives to one verb, which they called the "golden line" and which still very well represents the "high style" in English. Interest in the interworking of parts in structure leads also to interest in proportioning of parts.

Modern grammar, with its emphasis on functioning parts, aids in the discerning of proportions in the use of language and thus in the discerning of some of the choices in prose and poetry as arts of language. Asking such questions as whether prose is similar to poetry in its uses and whether the histories of the two run parallel in continuity and change, I have found more and more illumination in their grammars as well as in their vocabularies, in the ways that proportionings of materials reflect proportionings of structures.

An important objection to the literary relevance of proportion is that it is not specific, that it is expressible as an average or norm, not as descriptive of actualities. The important answer is that it is both general and specific; that is, I have not yet found a text of which the general proportions are alien to central specific passages. Of course, no writer is apt to write in monotone without variation. But if a proportion shows many connectives, for example, then paragraphs illustrating just this ratio of connectives come immediately to view. The most fundamental part of the objection is that proportion is abstracted from order, from context. True, it is by such abstraction that I hope to follow out certain main lines of emphasis; but these abstractions need ultimately to be seen in order and context again, the specific adjectives with their specific nouns, the emphasis and choices in their correlative progressing.

The advantage of thinking about grammar, logic, and rhetoric together is to see their interconnections more plainly. This *trivium* of letters, as distinguished from the *quadrivium* of numbers, establishes the full relations of letter to letter, letter to reference, and letter to intent and effect, which a system of symbols makes pertinent. As representing sound and syllable, unit of meaning from morpheme to word and utterance, the letter of *logos* conveys spirit in the signs of speech. Each specialist sees the proliferations of complexity in the process, the exceptions and ambiguities that make the borderlines of distinctions; the subtle differences between one verb form and another, the habits of tautology, the artifices of rhetoric as device. But the contemplation of lettered, of literary, language in general can afford to blur these distinctions for the sake of focusing upon the whole use of the medium in a paragraph or stanza, to learn how one sentence, one word, one syllable fits with another, and how all fit the pattern of their intent. Not a geometer, musician, astronomer, or architect, I nevertheless think that proportion, the basis of the *quadrivium*, is pertinent to language as well as to structural forms. Properties of sound, syllable, grammatical unit, and rhetorical scheme in composed language are just as significant as properties of perceived design in stone or constellation.

Specifically, the changing pattern of proportions I present in concentrated form on pp. 41–42 is that of adjectives, nouns, verbs, and connectives used by sixty poets and sixty prose writers in English in the past five centuries. Because my earlier interest was in frequencies of reference in the major vocabulary of poetry, I paid little attention in *Eras and Modes* and the *Continuity of Poetic Language* to questions of syntactic proportion, to connectives, and to prose structures. Then, when I recognized the close relations between syntactic structures and the proportioning of parts of speech, I supposed that prose would differ in its uses especially by an emphasis on connectives. As can be seen, this idea did not turn out to be wholly true. But it led to the selective emphases upon certain parts of speech and upon poetry and prose in parallel through the centuries.

First, to be more specific about the parts of speech: the terms commonly called terms of reference or content are nouns, adjectives, verbs. Words used chiefly for linking and connecting, prepositions and conjunctions, then are usually grouped as "grammatical terms." These two kinds of terms, referential and grammatical, constitute the language of our study. Of the other parts of speech, the pronouns, and the articles or determiners so neatly treated by Rostrevor-Hamilton, both are so closely related to the noun that they belong to a fuller study of the noun itself; their absence here limits the validity of what is indicated about the noun's functions in other forms as the absence of adverbs limits the view of the verbs.

The chief specific pattern then is the proportion, in a sequential text of one thousand lines of poetry (six to eight thousand words) and eight thousand words of prose, of adjective to noun to verb, the referential pattern; and of these to connectives, the grammatical pattern. These proportions, simply established, allow us to see the overall structure of the text—its dominant subordination or its dominant qualification, for example—more easily than a close structure-by-structure scrutiny would do. It allows us to see the trees within the forest.

Note needs to be made of inclusion in categories: in a simpleminded way, all nouns and gerunds as nouns; numerical or limiting adjectives and present and past participles as adjectives when used so, as in *sparkling broken glass*; infinitives as verbs; all connectives, prepositional and conjunctival, together as connectives. As Jespersen says, "The difference between the various functions of one and the same word, e.g., *before* in . . . 'using this before my marriage,' and 'many times before I was married,' is not important enough to cause it to be placed in different categories."[1] Of the seventy most used connectives, half, like *before*, are used as either prepositions or conjunctions, so that the tendency of the language seems to relate the two; and this relation simplifies the habit of the reader to note all connective material as of a kind, whatever the further possible subdivisions. In the distinguishing of verbs, it seems to me that the forms *I go, he goes, he is going, he has gone, he hopes to go* all share a predicative force which the assumptive form, a *going* or *gone concern*, lacks. At any rate, it has turned out that adjectival writers are the large users of participial adjectives, so that they seem to concur in my feeling of affinity in such parallelism as that of *England's green and pleasant land*.

The two tables which follow (tables 1a and 1b) give an overview of English poetry and English prose in their pattern of structural variation. Most immediately visible is the similarity of the two patterns. In both tables, the writers cluster first at lower left, then at upper center, then at middle right, with an effect of motion through five centuries from one extreme through midpoints to another extreme and then back to midpoint. The great difference between the two is that the prose motion first leads, then follows the poetic, developing a middle style earlier than poetry, but then not moving into the adjectival heights until a century later, coming in the twentieth century to much the same agreement with which it had begun, though closer to mid level.

In closer detail, the reader may note, starting at the left, that each century-column contains the names of the ten writers publishing in that century, in order, from bottom to top, of the dominance of verb over adjective: strongest verbs at bottom, balance in the middle, least verbs at top. So in prose Tyndale's Bible, More, Sidney, and others, like the Ballads, Wyatt, and Sidney in poetry, use the active English of three verbs to every one or two adjectives; while a few experimenters, Bacon and Ascham in prose, like Spenser, Shakespeare, and Sylvester in poetry, try a stronger set of attributions. Connectives, somewhat more numerous for prose, tend to follow nouns in number; that is, to relate to the extra noun called for in phrase or clause. The average sixteenth-century proportion for prose is 2–4–3–5, for poetry 2–4–3–4, as these numbers represent reduction by the least common denominator of four hundred, of proportions such as 800–1,600–1,200–2,000 adjectives, nouns, verbs, connectives in 6,000–8,000 cursive words of text.

If read across the bottom of the page, the averages reflect the similarities of tendencies in the two forms: for prose, the seventeenth-, eighteenth-, and nineteenth-century decrease of verbs with increase of nouns; the nineteenth-century increase of adjectives; the twentieth-century increase of verbs, which with lessening of connectives would seem to be not clausal but independent. Nearly the same pattern for poetry: a similar

TABLE 1a. PROPORTIONS IN ENGLISH POETRY

	British					American
	16th Century	17th Century	18th Century	19th Century	20th Century	19th & 20th Centuries
	A-N-V-C	A-N-V-C	A-N-V-C	A-N-V-C	A-N-V-C	A-N-V-C
Adjectival			Thomson 4-5-2-4p	Keats 4-6-2-5cp	Thomas 3-6-2-4p	Whitman 3-7-2-5p
		Blackmore 3-5-2-4	Blake 3-6-2-6cp	Swinburne 4-6-3-6crp	Spender 3-5-2-4p	Crane 3-5-2-4
			Bowles 3-5-2-4			Dwight 3-5-2-4
			Collins 3-5-2-4			
	Sylvester 3-5-2-3p	Milton 3-4-2-4	Gray 3-5-2-3			
			Cowper 3-4-2-4c	Tennyson 3-4-2-3		
Balanced	Shakespeare 3-4-3-4cr		Pope 3-5-3-4	Shelley 2-5-2-4p	Lawrence 3-4-2-4c	Bryant 2-4-2-4
	Spenser 3-4-3-4r	Waller 3-5-3-4r	Johnson 2-5-2-3	Hopkins 2-5-2-3	Sitwell 2-6-2-5cp	Emerson 2-4-2-3
	Dunbar 1-3-1-3	Dryden 2-5-2-4	Wordsworth 2-4-2-4	Yeats 2-4-2-4c	Nicholson 2-5-2-4p	Eliot 2-4-2-3
			Crabbe 2-4-2-3		Graves 2-4-2-3	Roethke 2-4-2-2
						Robinson 2-3-2-2
Predicative	Sidney 2-5-3-4r	Jonson 2-4-3-4cr		Coleridge 2-4-3-4c	Jennings 2-4-2-4	Lowell 2-5-3-3
	Gascoigne 2-5-3-4cr	Herrick 2-4-3-4c		Byron 2-4-3-4	Gunn 2-4-2-3	
	Surrey 2-4-3-4r	Herbert 2-4-3-3		Browning 2-4-3-3	Muir 2-4-2-3	
	Wyatt 2-3-3-3	Donne 2-3-3-6cr			Auden 2-4-2-3	
	Coverdale 1-2-2-3	Marvell 2-3-3-3		Hardy 1-3-2-3		Dickinson 1-3-2-2
	Ballads 1-3-3-3	Vaughan 2-3-3-3				
	2-4-3-4	2-4-3-4	3-5-2-4	2-5-2-4	2-5-3-4	2-4-2-3

A-N-V-C Adjective-Noun-Verb-Connective   c clausal or phrasal   p phrasal   r relative

NOTE: Proportions for Pindar's Odes (Olymp. 1,2; Plyth. 1,8,9; Ist. 5,6,7) are 1260-2050-760-970. For other proportions in other languages, see Appendix, Eras and Modes, rev. ed. 1964. It may be noted also that there is a correspondant motion of sound structures, from sixteenth and seventeenth century regular stanzaic and linear, to eighteenth century irregular stanzaic and regular linear, to nineteenth century regular stanzaic and linear, to twentieth century irregular and regular linear and stanzaic.

TABLE 1b. PROPORTIONS IN ENGLISH PROSE

	British 16th Century (A-N-V-C)	17th Century (A-N-V-C)	18th Century (A-N-V-C)	19th Century (A-N-V-C)	20th century (A-N-V-C)	American 19th & 20th Centuries (A-N-V-C)
Adjectival	Ascham 3-4-2-5c	Browne 3-5-2-4p	Gibbon 3-6-2-5p Smith 3-5-2-5p	Macaulay 3-5-2-5p Ruskin 3-5-2-6cpr Pater 3-5-2-5 Carlyle 3-4-2-4 Darwin 3-4-2-3p De Quincey 2-4-1-3p	Huxley 3-5-2-4	Whitman 3-5-2-5p
Balanced	Bacon 2-4-2-5cpr	Hobbes 2-5-2-5 Burnet 2-5-2-5 Clarendon 2-4-2-5 Milton 2-4-2-5cr Locke 2-3-2-5cr	Alison 2-5-2-5p Burke 2-5-2-5p Godwin 2-4-2-4p Swift 2-4-2-4	Arnold 2-5-2-4 Shaw 2-5-2-4	Russell 3-5-3-5p Orwell 3-4-3-4 Churchill 2-5-2-4 Read 2-5-2-4p Wain 2-5-2-4	Twain 3-5-3-4 Eliot 3-4-3-4 Paine 2-5-2-4 Lardner 2-6-3-4
Predicative	Holinshed 2-5-3-5p Hooker 2-4-3-5c Dekker 2-4-3-5c Sidney 2-4-3-4 Lyly 2-4-3-4 More 2-4-3-4c Latimer 1-4-3-4c Tyndale 1-4-3-5cpr	Donne 2-4-3-5 Johnson 2-4-3-5 Dryden 2-4-3-4 Bunyan 1-4-3-5cpr	Addison 2-5-3-5 Jonson 2-5-3-4 Shaftesbury 2-4-3-4p Berkeley 2-4-3-4	Hazlitt 2-5-3-5 Frazer 2-5-3-4p	Connolly 2-5-3-4 Lawrence 2-5-3-3 Joyce 2-4-3-4 West 2-4-3-4	Emerson 2-5-3-4 Baldwin 2-5-3-4 Edwards 2-4-3-5 Santayana 2-4-3-4 Hemingway 2-4-3-4
	2-4-3-5	2-4-2-5	2-5-2-5	3-5-2-4	2-5-3-4	2-5-3-4

A-N-V-C Adjective-Noun-Verb-Connective   c clausal or phrasal   r relative   p phrasal portioning at first and last, and in between a later lessening of verbs, an earlier gain and then loss of adjectives, a persistently smaller number of connectives except in the present day; in America, more oddity of meagerness in poetry than in prose.

Our writing has moved in good array from much clausal subordination to much phrasal subordination to much adjectival assumption, through three standard styles—plain, middle, and high. Our present day has made the change, noted by many commentators, toward a variant, a lessening of connectives while the referential forms are at their height: a device of juxtaposition, it would seem, in relation to strong statement and assumption. Through the temporal stages of general usage, the types are to be found, whether in general favor or not, in individual practice. For example, in prose the simpler statement in favor now, as in the work of Lawrence, was early emphasized by Hazlitt and still earlier by Lyly and Sidney. In the midst of the early predicative stress we yet find Ascham's complex modificational bent, notable in the prose of Sir Thomas Browne, before its cumulative force in Gibbon in the eighteenth century. The balanced choice too has its range of use, early in the work of Bacon and of Milton, as well as late in Orwell; for all of whom the poise of adjective and verb, of phrase and clause, presents equivalent emphases before and after the chief time of classical strength. As a whole we may say that about half the writers favor the early clausal qualification; a fifth, the nineteenth-century phrasal qualification; and the rest, between and at present, some variety of balance, now tending toward the simple. Yet again we may note writers who move out from any of these possibly generalizable types to further extremes. Ben Jonson is such a one, who, even in literary criticism, employs such a variety of verbs that one might think he was writing the narrative of Bunyan or Joyce; while many more actual narrative writers, as in the histories, do not so predicate.

The material itself, the chief language of poetry, for example, also may be shown in tabular form (tables 2a, 2b), as new main words first appear in one decade (defined as new because they achieve major uses by at least four writers less than a century apart) and are dropped in another, not to be used again in a century. Again the rhythmic steadiness of flow is apparent. (See basis in *Eras and Modes*, rev. ed., p. 223.) Change, both positive in innovations and negative in rejections of major words, moves with fair regularity even into the twentieth century, within a frame of slower change in structure and sound. (See also table 1a and note 2, chapter 12.) The basic vocabulary of poetry was established by the Elizabethan era. Poets agreed largely on the emphasized terms for their religious, courtly, and pastoral worlds. Then Spenser, Sidney, Sylvester, Campion contributed an abundance of rich emotions and values in newly stressed words like *muse, virtue, joy, new, sad, happy,* so that those who wrote in the first years of the new century, Ben Jonson, John Donne, George Sandys, Fletcher, Wither, Herrick, Quarles, Herbert, Carew, Shirley, were able to look about them and to discard and add frugally as they wished. They added a few verbs, *meet, appear, praise, write;* and discarded some courtly trappings from the past: *gold, fortune, hell, knight, lady, cruel, desire.* Their successors in turn dropped the formal feelings of the pastoral: *gentle, shepherd, faith, grief, woe,* and so on, to add a more classical vocabulary of *care, fate, soft, sense, shine.* Two early conventions were thus dropped by a sort of wearying and rejection, and more general action and sensation were added, with a sense of freer choice. An equilibrium was established by mid-century.

Then the poets born in mid-century and publishing toward its end, after the Restoration, set a new tone. They dropped little, but added much, a whole new set of meanings: Roscommon's *wild,* Oldham's *vain,* Blackmore's *human, various, land, sky,* Pomfret's *charm, mighty, delight.* Here, perhaps, prepared for by the classic sensory terms, we have the beginnings of men's, of poets', sense of and response to the natural world in its scope and variety. The new tendency moves quickly.

TABLE 2a. MAIN USES ADDED BY POETS IN SUCCESSIVE GENERATIONS

	1470	1500	1530	1570	1600	1630	1670	1700	1730	1770	1800	1830*	1870*	1900*
Basic ANV 96 + 26 (Initial major uses)			new	meet	care	cloud	nymph	green	foot	strange	shadow	dead	small	bone
			proud	appear	fate	hour	fool	sing	home	bird	last	bed	clear	window
			sad	pride	wind	age	seem	breathe	hold	body	house	watch	[living]	room
			happy	voice	wake	wild	pass	leave	own	moon		red	road	
			long	praise (v)	soft	vain	maid	golden	child	water		rain	people	
			muse	write	sense	human	deep	silent	pleasure	dream		stone	walk	
			sight		shine	various	behold	truth	feel	star				
			virtue		poet	land	mountain	dark	black	woman		flesh		
			bright			sky		field	pale	blue		pain		
			sacred			charm		shade	morning	dim		wall		
			grow			mighty			sleep	the dead		street		
			divine			delight			turn	wing		cry		
			air						weep	word		run		
			earth						mother					
			sea						cold					
			joy						white					
			part						ear					
			fly						snow					
			move						wave					
									gray					
									memory					
									young					
									tree					
									pray					

* Confirmed by four or more American poets of the 1930s and 1940s

TABLE 2b. MAIN USES DROPPED BY POETS IN SUCCESSIVE GENERATIONS

1470	1500	1530	1570	1600	1630	1670	1700	1730	1770	1800	1830	1870*	1900
		law	knight	gentle	look	word	work	fame	noble	woe	wise	king	
		people	gold	shepherd	grace	wit	flame	foe	muse	proud	teach	son	
		ground	lady	faith	face	fall		please	sacred	divine	virtue	poor	
		father	fortune	woe	show	true		move	meet	fly	sense	hope	
		fame	cruel	seek	place	common		bold	pride	appear	mighty	art	
			desire	grief	part	begin		praise (v)	care	wake	nymph	silent	
			hell			town		various	fate	scene	fool	dim	
						sin			age	wide	maid	sleep	
						prince			vain	shade	behold	weep	
						kind			charm	pleasure	ear		
						sight			mountain		pray		
						write							

* Confirmed by four or more American poets of the 1930s and 1940s

Within a generation, *sky*, for example, will become a term of major importance for half a dozen poets or more. Yet Blackmore, the innovator, was berated by the men of his age as a bad poet with foolish ideas. Is there not here a sense of the future, felt, derided, yet accepted and moving forward?

The next generation, turning into the eighteenth century, confirms this feeling by dropping more than it adds, as if clearing the way, ex post facto, for materials already initiated —very concisely and critically now abandoning the terms of intellect, representing an outmoded faith, which Blackmore has supplanted. In the face of the rich new natural vocabulary, the old terms of human concept and action go: *common, true, sin, town, sight, word, wit, begin, write,* these and others are lost to poetry—not so many to be lost again for a hundred years. It is a milestone of change, this abrupt abandoning of a conceptual vocabulary in favor of a sensory descriptive one. There is room in poetry now, through the eighteenth century, for new words of two main kinds: more of the words of nature which we have already seen begun, like *deep, wide, green, golden, dark, silent, mountain, field, shade, song, breathe, pass,* many of which will persist into the present, and words of an artifice in nature which will last no more than a century: *fool, maid, nymph, scene, behold.*

Now again in the late eighteenth century, in the generation born in the 1730s to 1760s, we have the phenomenon, as in the two preceding late centuries, of addition before subtraction; of a minimum of discarding of major terms, preceding and accompanying a maximum of additions. First Sidney and Spenser, then Blackmore and Pomfret, now Crabbe, Bowles, Blake, make the step forward—this time into a new inner world: *cold, pale, black, white, grey, own, home, child, mother, morning, memory, foot, ear, pleasure, sorrow, wave, wood, feel, hold, sleep, turn, weep.* It is in this world, with its more recently added outward counterparts like *moon, star, water, body, bird, wing, shadow, house,* and especially with the innovations of mid-nineteenth century *dead, red, rain, stone,* that we still reside. For again, since this great period of innovation, the process has been one of a relieving loss of words—all through the nineteenth century the abandoning of the formalism and enthusiasm of the eighteenth: the *noble, sacred, divine, gentle, proud, wise, woe, pleasure, fame, virtue, sense, scene, mighty, appear, behold,* which we have not so long ago seen introduced. In like manner, American poets abandoned their eighteenth-century *shore, stream, strong, beautiful, holy,* in favor of *snow* and *leaf* and *stone* and the English *nothing.*

· With the beginning of a new poetic generation in America,[2] writers born in the 1930s and 1940s and beginning to publish in the 1970s, we can see new materials as well as the strengthening of past traditions by confirmation in the present. By definition,[3] innovation needs to persist. Strong uses in the poetry of those born in the 1930s therefore reveal latent powers of innovation in the 1830s—Wilde's *wall,* Hopkins's *flesh,* Henley's *street,* and de la Mare's and Muir's *road,* and especially the power of Yeats with his haunting verbs *break, cry, run.* Usage within the century has carried these words forward to their major import now for poets like McClure in San Francisco and Cruz in eastside Manhattan. These current poets also reveal the powers of the generation we have just seen, that of Pound and Eliot, the 1870s. Words dominating newly from this time are *small, clear, window, people, walk,* and a new structure represented by Lawrence's *living* and Snyder's *going*—the present participle as adjective in major use. Agreed-on use of Barker's *bone, kiss, summer.* Nicholson's *window,* Jennings's *room,* even perhaps Nicholson's *finger,* Thomas's *lip* and *tongue,* Snyder's *touch,* show strong new possibilities in even one generation.

At the same time, words fall away in the leadership of the 1870s. *King* is lost again, *son, poor, dim, silent, art, hope, sleep, weep;* human relation, human feeling, withdrawn from the romantic nineteenth century. This was the change for which

Pound pleaded, the giving up of emotional statement and general *dimness* for objective exactitude; and he and his confrères relied on already present vocabulary for this in the sensory nature of Wordsworth and Coleridge—*bird, body, man, water, star, tree,* stemming from the natural world of the Sylvester-Milton tradition, then of Swinburne, de la Mare, Muir, Nicholson, finally into the newest American poets, the *black, white, leaf, water, light, love, night.* This is *the* poetic tradition, rather than the Donne tradition which has survived more obliquely. And this tradition now too is changing, with the bodily specificities of *bone, ear, flesh, finger, hair, mouth, skin, tongue* in the world of *door, room, glass, sound, street, road, wall, window,* with its values of *small* and *clear,* and its newly active verbs of *break, run, touch, walk, watch, want* of the present generation.

Tables 3 and 4 list the major words of some poets discussed here, in order to show by selective example how changes develop from mode to mode and era to era. As reminder, a major word is one used ten times or more in a specific 6,000–8,000 word text. Fuller data are available in *Eras and Modes* (1964) and *Style and Proportion.*

What we see in proportion and reference we see also in connective terms (table 5, from *Style and Proportion,* p. 90): steady agreement by both poetry and prose on major connectives like *by, from, in, of, on, to, with, and, as, but, for, or, when, who, where;* some losses and declines as of *which, so, unto, nor, therefore, without, yet, though;* the recent gains of *after, around, beneath, between, above, beyond,* plus prose *thus;* some returns from earlier times like *how, yet, out,* prose, *what.* The presence in this table of some words like *neither* with no early major uses listed for poetry, and of others for prose, should raise questions. The checking I have done verifies these data, but many large errors probably go deeper than a superficial check can discover. At any rate, in both poetry and prose the major kinds of additions are clear. In both poetry

TABLE 3. EXAMPLES OF MAJOR VOCABULARIES OF POETS OF THREE DIFFERENT MODES IN THREE DIFFERENT ERAS

Poet Birth Date	Work and Edition (first 1,000 lines)	Measure	Total Words	Adjectives	Nouns	Verbs	Connectives
John Milton † 1608	Nativity, L'Al., Il P., Lyc., Comus. (Minor Poems, ed. M. Y. Hughes, 1939.)	5'–4'	6,720	1,200 (12)* dark fair good great high holy old sad sweet	1,550 (16) air day ear eye god heaven light night star sun wind	770 (8) bring come (20) give go hear (20) keep know lie live make see sing sit	1,420 (14)
John Dryden ‡ 1631	Absalom and Achitophel, 1,030 lines. (Ed. Noyes, 1950.)	5' couplets	7,800	1,020 (10) bad good high long old public true wise	1,950 (19) arm day eye fate father friend god hand heart heaven (40) king (40) law (20) life love man (20) name time nature people (20) power (20) prince soul (30) youth	1,060 (10) bring find give (20) know love make (30) please rise see think	1,500 (15)
John Donne § 1576	Songs and Sonets, 1,010 lines. (Random House.)	5'–4' stanzas	7,100	660 (7) bad false good new poor true	1,300 (13) day death eye face fear heart love (110) man name soul sun tear thing world year	1,230 (12) come die fall find give go keep know love make see show take (20) tell think	2,380 (24)
William Blake † 1757	America, etc. (Poetry and Prose, 1939.)	5' lines	7,700	1,200 (12) beautiful black bright dark divine eternal (20) gentle golden great happy human little (20) old pale red silent soft starry sweet terrible wild	2,400 (24) air bosom child cloud (30) daughter day (30) death (30) earth eye fire flower foot furnace god hand head heaven (20) joy (20) lamb land life love (20) man (20) morning mountain night (20) son sun time valley (20) voice wheel worm	1,030 (10) awake bring come fall find give go know hear hide live look love make pass rise see sing sit sleep smile stand take turn walk weep	2,380 (24)
William Wordsworth ‡ 1770	Lyrical Ballads, omitting groups between "Anecdote" and "Old Man." (Complete Poetical Works, Cambridge ed., 1904.)	5'–4' stanzas	6,596	940 (9)* cold dear deep green little old poor sweet warm wild young	1,560 (16) day heart joy love mountain nature pain spirit sun thing thought tree wood year	940 (9) love pray stand weep	1,400 (14)

Samuel Taylor Coleridge § 1772	*Ancient Mariner and Christabel*, 1,300 lines (Rhinehart ed.)	4' stanzas 8,170	790 (6) black bright holy little poor sad strange sweet white	1,750 (13) air bird body cloud day eye love mist moon (20) night rock sail sea ship sky sun water wind wood	1,200 (9) blow fly love pray sing	1,500 (12)
Dylan Thomas † 1914	*Selected Writings*, first 29 poems. (New Directions, 1946.)	5' stanzas 7,960	1,020 (10) black dead golden green red white	2,300 (23) bell bird blood (20) bone boy child day death (20) eye (20) face grave hand (20) head heart (20) heaven house land light love (30) man (40) moon mouth night sea (30) sky sleep stone summer sun (20) time (30) tongue tower tree voice water weather wind (20) word world	790 (8) break drive d op fall hold lie make (20) turn	1,540 (15)
D. H. Lawrence ‡ 1885	*Pansies*, through "Touch," 1,030 lines. (*Complete Poems*, London, 1957.)	5'–3' lines, stanzas 7,200	1,000 (10)* black dark dead dear dirty gold good great (20) little (30) living long new (20) old superior white wild young (20)	1,560 (15) beast bird body bourgeois child creature day the dead (20) death eye flame flesh foot god (20) hand heart house life (50) machine man (60) mill mind mist money moon night people (20) sea sex sin soul sun swan thing water woman (20) work world worm	1,120 (11) come (20) die feel fight find get (20) give go (30) know (20) leave live look make (20) put rise ee think turn want work	1,470 (14)
W. H. Auden § 1907	*Poems*, through "Trouble," 630 lines (*Collected Poetry*), and *In Time of War*, 380 lines (Random House, 1945.)	5' stanzas 7,220	750 (8) good great last little new old	1,590 (16) child (20) day death earth (20) eye father fate heart home life (20) love (20) man (20) mother nothing thing time truth word world	1,030 (10) come fall fee find give go grow know (10) learn look make (20) see (20) seem speak take	1,370 (14)

* 30 percent or over participial adjectives   † Adjectival mode   ‡ Balanced mode   § Predicative mode

Poet Birth Date	Work and Edition (first 1,000 lines)	Measure	Total Words	Adjectives	Nouns	Verbs	Connectives
Gary Snyder 1930	Riprap (Origin, 1949) 600 lines; Myths & Texts (Totem, 1961) 400 lines	lines	5,630	870 (9) all (30) no one thousand two going big black cold high little long old small thin white wild young	1,800 (18) air cat child cloud cave creek day eye feet fire girl hand head heat hill home land leaf man mind mountain night one pine (20) road rock sea seed shadow ship summer sun time tree woods year	600 (6) come go live make see think	1,040 (10)
Jerome Rothenberg 1931	White Sun, Black Sun (Hawks Well, 1960) 550 lines; The Seven Hells (Trubar, 1962) 390 lines	lines	5,640	580 (6)* all no some lost burning black (20) blue dark (20) full red old small white (20)	1,710 (7) arm ashes blood bone chair city cry darkness death (20) door earth eye (30) face (20) fire (20) flesh flower (20) hair hand (20) Hell grove key love (15) man mirror neon (20) night (30) pain rain (20) river sand sea (20) sky silence sorrow skin shadow (20) sun (20) thief voice (30) wind window	760 (8) cry (20) cover die grow fall (20) hear leave (30) pity run rise stand see sleep tell throw think turn wait walk	1,180 (12)

Michael McClure 1932	*New Book* (Grove, 1961)	lines	7,500
Robert Sward 1933	*Kissing the Dancer* (Cornell, 1964)	lines	7,230

Michael McClure — *New Book* (Grove, 1961) — lines 7,500

900 (9)
all no (40) black (20) blue brown clear cold (30) dark empty free huge light open pure real (20) sick strong white

1,880 (19)
air (20) all (20) animal (20) arm beauty (20) blackness blood body breath cloud cry desire dream edge eye (40) face (30) feeling (20) figure fire flame flower form god hand (20) head hell heart instant leaf lie light (30) matter memory man net night nothing pain (20) room rose (30) shape sight skirt skin smoke space star table thing (30) wall water world

1,080 (11)
feel (20) fill hate hear know (20) love (20) make (30) move (30) remember see (60) speak stand touch turn

1,500 (15)

Robert Sward — *Kissing the Dancer* (Cornell, 1964) — lines 7,230

1,010 (10)*
all (50) one (30) only some hundred two three black good (20) other old still white (20)

2,060 (21)
air apteryx beak bird breast (20) child day (30) death dog (30) ear eye (20) evening face (20) fire foot flash Ford garbage God hand head hole horse (20) leaf (30) light love mister moon moth mother

980 (10)
appear become breathe come eat fall go kiss like love make man see stand think unite

1,360 (14)

TABLE 4 (continued)

Poet Birth Date	Work and Edition (first 1,000 lines)	Measure	Total Words	Adjectives	Nouns	Verbs	Connectives
					night (20) nothing people question (20) sand sound stone (20) street sun tooth thing (20) time (20) tree (20) uncle voice way wife (20) wind window woman word		
LeRoi Jones 1934	Preface to a 20 Vol: Suicide Note (Totem, 1961)	lines	5,620	800 (8)* all (30) each no one only some black green long little old young wet	1,420 (14) air day eye face finger the green hand hair man moon morning mouth music night (20) room sister shadow sun (20) thing tree way woman wind window word	720 (7) come (30) get go hear know love make (20) see take	920 (9)
Robert Kelly 1935	Weeks (Yale Lit., Apr. 1965) 300 lines Her Body Against Time (Plumed Horn, 1963) 1,350 lines	lines	5,000	710 (7) dark dead long right white	1,590 (16) body (30) sun (30) day (20) flesh (20) lady (20) light (20) time (20) tree (20) air bone dream eye field face grass hand garden love morning	700 (7) come (20) see (20) give hear hold know make stand take touch walk	940 (9)

			510 (5)	1,090 (11)	640 (6)	700 (7)
Jon Anderson 1940	*Looking for Jonathan* (Pitts., 1968)	lines 5,000	each no one alone black blue cold dark high old own red small soft white	angel arm bed dark door dream eye face friend glass hand (20) head (20) heart home house land lawn leaf light love man (20) moon morning mother name night one room sea shadow tree water wing year	come (20) lie give go grow know look love open remember rise see sleep stand take think touch turn	music name place shadow say street word world week water year

			415 (4)*	1,025 (10)	540 (5)	650 (7)
William Matthews 1942	*Ruining the New Road* (Random House, 1970)	lines 4,000	all no dead new thick	air bed blood body (20) bone breath day ear earth every-thing eye fire foot hood hand house knee lake life light love man night one other skin sleep snow tongue water	come die fall feel go hear know leave live love make sleep think wake	

TABLE 4 (continued)

Poet Birth Date	Work and Edition (first 1,000 lines)	Measure	Total Words	Adjectives	Nouns	Verbs	Connectives
James Tate 1943	The Lost Pilot (Yale, 1967)	lines	6,000	600 (6) all no one last going bad fine good (20) little old white	1,300 (13) day eye face finger flower friend glass ground god head home life man night nothing one other people name room sky something thing time tree voice water way well window word year	920 (9) become believe break call come (30) fall feel find get give go (20) hear keep know (20) leave look make see (20) take tell think (30) walk watch	890 (9)
Victor Cruz 1949	Snaps (Vintage, 1969)	lines	5,000	470 (5)* all (30) no one some (20) going looking walking big cool dark dead good last old same stupid strange	1,150 (12) air ass building car corner day eye (20) floor girl (20) hand head (20) lady man (20) night one (20) people poem shit something street thing (20) time (20) train tree wall window	680 (7) come (20) dance deserve fall get (20) go (30) know live look make marry play run see take talk think tell walk want wonder	670 (7)

* 30 percent or over participial adjectives

Poetry

Author	Word	16th	17th	18th	19th	20th	Total in 50	American Total in 10
Ballads	at	10	10	10	10	9	49	10
	by	10	10	10	10	10	50	10
	from	10	10	10	10	10	50	10
	in	10	10	10	10	10	50	10
	of	10	10	10	10	10	50	10
	on	10	10	10	10	10	50	10
	over	1	1	9	6	6	23	8
	through	5	7	10	9	8	39	5
	to	10	10	10	10	10	50	10
	upon	6	4	5	7	6	28	6
	with	10	10	10	10	10	50	9
	that	10	10	10	10	10	50	10
	and	10	10	10	10	10	50	10
	as	10	10	10	10	10	50	10
	but	10	10	10	10	10	50	10
	for	10	10	10	10	10	50	10
	if	8	9	8	10	6	41	7
	nor	10	8	10	9	6	43	8
	or	10	10	10	10	10	50	10
	than	7	6	5	7	4	29	6
	<until	5	5	8	7	6	31	4
	when	10	10	9	10	10	49	9
Dunbar	among	2	1	1	1	1	6	1
	within	3	1	-	1	1	6	1
	who	9	10	10	8	10	47	10
	where	9	10	10	9	10	48	10
	which	8	10	8	7	6	39	3
Coverdale	how	5	9	4	2	5	25	3
	so	8	6	1	3	4	22	2
	therefore	2	1	-	-	-	3	-
	yet	7	8	9	6	9	39	4
Wyatt	into	2	4	3	5	10	24	6
	under	1	1	-	1	2	5	3
	unto	5	5	-	-	-	10	1
	without	5	-	1	1	2	9	3
	after	1	-	1	2	3	6	4

Prose

Author	Word	16th	17th	18th	19th	20th	Total in 50	American Total in 10
Bible	after	5	5	1	3	4	18	3
	against	3	4	2	2	-	11	3
	among(-st)	4	4	2	2	1	13	1
	and	10	10	10	10	10	50	10
	as	10	10	10	10	10	50	10
	at	10	10	10	9	10	49	10
	because	8	6	2	5	6	27	5
	but	10	10	10	10	10	50	10
	by	10	10	10	9	10	49	10
	for	10	10	10	10	10	50	10
	from	10	10	10	9	10	49	10
	how	6	5	1	6	1	19	4
	if	9	10	8	9	9	45	10
	in	10	10	9	10	9	48	10
	into	9	10	6	6	8	39	7
	°neither	6	-	2	-	1	8	1
	nor	6	7	4	1	1	21	3
	now	1	-	-	-	-	1	-
	of	10	10	10	10	10	50	10
	on	4	9	9	9	9	42	10
	or	10	10	10	10	10	49	10
	over	2	1	-	1	1	5	3
	so	9	8	-	1	1	19	3
	that	10	10	10	9	9	48	10
	then	2	1	-	1	1	6	1
	therefore	2	3	1	-	-	8	-
	through	4	1	1	1	1	8	2
	to	10	10	9	10	9	48	10
	under	2	-	3	-	1	9	2
	unto	7	8	7	-	1	27	3
	upon	7	8	6	8	9	38	3
	what	5	10	6	9	9	43	9
	which	10	10	10	10	9	49	10
	who	10	9	8	8	8	43	10
	with	10	10	10	10	9	49	10
	without	9	7	5	5	1	24	3
	yet	10	9	1	1	1	25	3

TABLE 5 (continued)

Poetry

Author	Word	16th	17th	18th	19th	20th	Total in 50	American Total in 10
Surrey	since	6	2	–	3	1	12	–
	though	3	8	7	5	5	28	4
	against	3	3	–	–	3	9	2
	what	5	10	9	9	6	39	8
Gascoigne	like	4	10	8	10	10	42	9
	out	2	–	–	3	3	8	2
	because	2	2	–	1	1	5	1
	while	3	7	10	7	3	30	4
Spenser	about	1	1	–	1	1	4	1
	before	2	2	1	3	2	10	6
	then	2	3	–	1	–	6	5
Sylvester	>whether	1	1	–	–	–	2	–
Herbert	now	–	1	1	–	–	2	–
	<thus	–	3	–	–	–	3	–
Milton	°ere	–	2	–	1	–	3	–
Thomson	<around	–	–	3	2	3	8	1
	°beneath	–	–	2	3	4	9	2
Gray	amidst	–	–	3	–	–	3	–
Blake	°toward	–	–	1	–	1	1	1
Wordsworth	°why	–	–	1	–	–	1	1
Swinburne	>between	–	–	–	1	3	4	1
Hopkins	off	–	–	–	1	–	1	1
Muir	>above	–	–	–	–	3	3	2
	°across	–	–	–	–	1	1	1
Nicholson	°beyond	–	–	–	–	2	2	2
Jennings	up	–	1	–	–	1	1	1

Prose

Author	Word	16th	17th	18th	19th	20th	Total in 50	American Total in 10
More	before	7	8	1	1	–	17	3
	than	8	10	9	7	8	43	10
	though	9	9	4	3	2	27	4
	<whether	4	2	–	1	–	3	1
	where	3	3	–	–	–	6	4
Ascham	°either	5	1	1	1	–	7	1
Holinshed	out	1	3	–	–	–	4	2
	since	2	3	–	1	–	6	1
	within	1	–	–	–	–	1	1
Hooker	<above	1	1	–	–	–	2	–
Lyly	<between	1	1	–	–	1	2	2
	like	2	1	–	–	–	3	5
Dekker	about	1	1	1	–	–	3	4
	>until	1	3	–	–	–	4	1
Browne	while	–	2	1	–	–	3	3
Milton	°unless	–	1	–	–	–	1	1
Clarendon	°however	–	1	3	–	1	5	2
Gibbon	°during	–	–	1	1	–	2	–
Alison	amid(-st)	–	–	1	–	–	1	–
Pater	up	–	–	–	1	–	1	1
Frazer	>around	–	–	–	1	1	2	1
	>thus	–	1	–	1	2	3	1
Joyce	off	–	–	–	1	1	1	–

SYMBOLS: ° not shared   > preceded by about a century or more   < followed and prose the major additions have been locational and directional—*around, above, between, up, off*; the major losses logical, *if, nor, therefore, because, though, yet*; the major mid-period losses temporal, *until* and *while* and *when*; thus a shift from clause to phrase structures and from subordination of causes and consequences to coordination of settings.

Within this matrix of change, which seems a profound one because it is so deeply embedded in shared practice, so correlated with other practices, so common yet original, so variable yet regular, certain basic traits can be seen. The vocabulary, along with the sound and structure, of literature works within clear limits. Free improvisations of major emphases are rare; authors within spans of time tend to agree on major uses, and the resources seem visible in the most-used language. On the other hand, no two writers' repertoires of major use are the same, and within the limited resources different choices are made by individuals and by groups of common interest either in generation or in type of work, usually in both. Individual variation may become group variation and even major usage over the course of time, sometimes gradually, sometimes quickly. Usually the innovators, those who first emphasize terms which later are emphasized by many more, are what we think of as minor poets. They have some axe to grind, and they are better at the grinding than at the poetry as a whole. So-called major poets, on the other hand, tend to use most fully the emphases already accepted and available to them in the poetry of their time.

Progression from era to era, from one group of agreement to another, proceeds with regularity. At any one time, half the major shared terms are traditional, a quarter coming into emphasis, a quarter fading. Though some terms persist through all the centuries, often the old give place to the new with a generation or so. Especially strong innovation made at the end of the century by those born in the middle of the century, usually includes some reversion to older times long out of use, and some specification of old terms in new ones more particular along the same lines.

Metaphors of change, flowing, pendular, triadic, spiral, need to be taken just as metaphors. In a sense, as any situation includes major and minor elements, even in simple quantitative terms, or focus and fringe elements in aesthetic terms, the one-situation, two-part aspects are supplemented by a third, the basis of division into two. Things don't just "fall naturally" into two parts, or if they do, falling naturally is a third aspect. Adding motion to situation gives a further complexity, as situations seem to move through time. In the language of poets at any rate, we can identify the materials of progression, that is, of gaining and discarding; we can note their fairly regular routes in the relation of individual to groups, and we can see, as principles, a one-directional change by slow gains and losses, yet some reversion to older stages, and some steady particularizing of earlier stages.

Change may be thought of as persistences through varying contexts, or as dominances from time to time, or as tendencies visible toward the future. Every poet and period shares in all three kinds, and so may be characterized by what he preserves from the past, or by what he chooses to stress in agreement with the present, or by what he suggests for the future. Donne, for example, most intensively brought a special scholastic vocabulary and structure from his past into his present by using them consciously; while his effect toward the future had dramatic elements of idiosyncracy in it. Milton, on the other hand, drew relatively little from the main Wyatt-Sidney poetic line of his past, and reinvented much earlier inventions by protestants like Sylvester's Du Bartas and Spenser, as well as the medieval aureate Dunbar, establishing a counter-measure and structure not only for his time but also for eighteenth and nineteenth centuries, especially in America and in science. All the while, qualities of less experimental poets like Waller and Dryden have come into the assured classic equilibrium of

Wordsworth, Yeats, and thence, Eliot, Robinson, Lawrence, into the observational responsive equilibriums of the present day, with its speculations toward what?—toward fragmentation, isolation, autonomy, community of juxtaposition rather than of subordination? Or toward new versions truer to the metaphysical or the sublime than they have recently been? In America and the world over the steps turn not only outward, but away from symbols to objects and then from objects natural to objects human, in a new stage we have only begun to realize.

NOTES TO CHAPTER 3

1. Otto Jespersen, *Essentials of English Grammar* (London: Allen & Unwin, 1933), p. 12.
2. Americans of the 1930s and 1940s studied here are: Gary Snyder, 1930; Jerome Rothenberg, 1931; Michael McClure, 1932; Robert Sward, 1933; LeRoi Jones, 1934; Robert Kelly, 1935; Jon Anderson, 1940; William Matthews, 1942; James Tate, 1943; Victor Cruz, 1949. Though Pound and Eliot are influential, their predecessor Yeats is more so, and their British contemporaries Muir, Lawrence, Nicholson.
3. H. G. Barnett, *Innovation: The Basis of Cultural Change* (New York: McGraw-Hill Book Co., 1953).

II. PARTICULARS

≥≤ 4. Ifs, Ands, and Buts for the Reader of Donne

QUESTIONS asked about Donne a generation ago by editors like Grierson and Potter and poets like Eliot, were questions about his effect upon his readers: what does he mean to us? why do we like him so much? what has he got to tell us? Since then, the inquiries have turned more abstract and definitional: what is the essence of Donne? what is his school, his group, his type? Joan Bennett's *Four Metaphysical Poets* steadily stirred skepticism with its assumptions of grouping, and year upon year of students have read and reread the *Songs and Sonnets* trying to trace a pattern of figurative language, or a philosophical bent, or a violent yoking of ideas, which would yield up the very heart of Donne's matter and also provide a clue to his bonds with his contemporaries, in the often disconcerting presence of Cowley and Cleveland.

Under the impression that the hand is sometimes quicker than the eye, I have wondered whether certain patterns of usage in Donne's writing might underlie both ostensible effects and analytical categorizations; that is, whether a discerning of basic materials and structures in the work might help separate what the writer contributes to the transaction from what the reader contributes to it. Our word *characteristic* often means more characteristic of our interest in the author than characteristic of his own emphases; therefore an abstractive process, which subordinates the actualities and complexities of a qualitative reading to the simplicities, even over-simplicities, of a quantitative and structural analysis may do something to show the reader on what firm ground of actuality in the text some of his reactions may rest.

Consider, for example, the simple content and the major vocabulary of the *Songs and Sonnets*. Professor Hanan Selvin and I have tried to see what a factor analysis would do to help the eye in noting the steady recurrence of main terms of reference from poem to Donne poem and from poet to Donnian poet.[1] *Man's heart, love, soul, name* occur and recur and are constant for his time; *man's death, fear, tear* are, along with negative adjectives *bad, false, poor*, more especially limited to Donne and a small group; and concepts of *time* in *new, day, year* are even more definingly limited in their occurrence. So too with basic actions: *love, make, see* are common to almost all, while verbs of *knowing, telling, thinking* are more Donnian, as are the active reciprocal *find, keep, give, take*. Not characteristic of Donne are the early- and late-century Jonsonian classical and moral terms *friend, fate, god, grace, nature*, the *grow* of Herrick or the religio-aesthetic mid-century *fair, bright, high, heaven, earth*, and *night* of Sandys, Crashaw, Marvell, Walter, and Milton. The classical and the biblical traditions were not his, nor were the moral or the aesthetic traditions. His was rather a vocabulary of concept distinguished by its concern with time, cognition, and truth, positive and negative. It links Donne early to Wyatt and Sidney and later to Herbert and Cowley, more than to the religious poets usually placed with him. His strong use of the terms of formal logic—conjunctive *and-but*, alternative *either-or*, consequent *if-therefore, though-yet*—links him also to Wyatt, Sidney, and especially Jonson, while his powerful descriptive relative clauses and active prepositions relate him also to his predecessors.

Factor analysis indicates a very high relevance of grouping by form as well as content, syntactic as well as lexical. In these terms, no poet in the seventeenth century is so participative in its poetic process as Donne. His are the extremes of the century's norms. More than any other poetry, the seventeenth century's was a poetry of predication, of strongly used verbs in sentences both short and long; and more than any other poet, Donne was the poet of verbs and the clausal connectives for verbs.

The growing tendencies in the century toward emphases on substantives and on adjectives were ignored by Donne; he worked not toward compromise or modification or moderation as Shakespeare did, but rather from what could be called the Wyatt-Sidney tradition and that of the Jonsonian sons like Herrick, Carew, Shirley, Suckling, Cowley, who were nearly as propositional as he, toward a dashing and imperious excess of what was central in his time. Where most poets before and after him used about a verb in every line, ten in every ten, Donne like Sidney and Jonson used a couple extra in every ten. Where others used twelve to eighteen connectives in ten lines, Donne used twenty-four, far more than other English poets of any time. This special structural combination of verbs and connectives means a special clausal structure. It both separates Donne from all other poets by its singularity and also affords a scale of approximations for affinities, by which we may see Jonson, Herrick, and later Coleridge as closest to him.

While vocabulary and structure provide two different scales of comparison, they come close to Donne's poetic focal point by indicating how the specialization of his structure in subordinative propositions and the specialization of his reference in cognitive terms makes a bond which relates sixteenth-century poetic substance of Wyatt and Sidney to the seventeenth-century poetic grammar of Jonson and Herrick, Carew and Cowley, and goes beyond it all to an inencompassable realm, where it is no wonder no one follows.

Some of the chief nonpoetic seventeenth-century structures suggest that this realm of subordinate clauses is a realm of prose. The combination of many verbs and connectives is to be found in Donne's prose and in Hooker, Dekker, Jonson, Bunyan, Addison, Hazlitt, Russell, though it occurs most often in Donne's poetry. Characteristic of the thoughtful and familiar style, this combination is more dramatic in its energy than classically balanced. In some ways it is helpful to see the relation of Donne's poetry to such a style; it shows how he was able to enfold into poetry, as no other poet has, the complexities of logical argument inherent in a passionately active prose.

If Donne is a poet of thought and argument as his interpreters tell us, then readers should be able to receive directly the qualities of the "prose" in the poetry itself, the recurring poetic shapes and the sense of his characteristic line of thought, the structure of his argument. I think a reader can easily have such a sense, because Donne is an actively assertive, deeply repetitive poet who makes plain the pattern he works with. Begin the *Songs and Sonnets,* and after the first few you will be hearing underneath the substance the rhythm of a repeated process: *Goe, and catche . . . Get with child . . . Tell me . . . Teach me . . . If . . . If . . . Yet . . . Though . . . Though . . . Yet.* Or again: *Send home . . . Which . . . Yet . . . Send home . . . Which . . . Which. . . Yet send . . .* Or again: *I do not . . . But; . . . Then feare . . . But . . . O how . . . But . . . ; When . . . when . . . If . . . Let not . . . But.* In poem after poem, early and late in his career, in satires, letters, songs, sonnets, divine poems, Donne addresses, exhorts, argues, and then counters his own arguments.

Of the fifty *Songs and Sonnets,* the majority begin with an imperative or a superlative or a question that needs to be supported and then often is controverted in a stable and persistent structure based upon disjunction of thought and doubleness within the form. Imperatives resemble each other: *Goe and catche; Send home; Come live with me; So, so, breake off; Take heed; Marke, let me breathe; Oh doe not die; Let me powre forth; For Godsake hold your tongue; Stand still; do not harme nor question much.* Similarly questions—*Will he not let us love?*—and superlative statements—*If yet I have not all thy love, / Deare, I shall never have it all*—are controverted, as in this last example by the counterstatement—*Yet no more can be due to mee, . . . Or if then thou gav'st mee all . . . But if in thy heart, . . . Yet I would not have all yet. If thou canst give it, then thou never gav'st it: / Loves riddles are, that though thy heart depart, / It stayes at home, and thou with losing sav'st it.* This pattern, and its resultant feeling, the loving support of a strong and even excessive demand by a resolving of all the exigencies, and a saving resolution by a shift into human terms, constitute a metaphysic.

But this metaphysic is not merely a characteristic of genre, of sonnet or meditation. Donne's first Satire, a hundred lines of iambic pentameter couplets, begins, *Away thou fondling motley humorist, / . . . Here . . . ; and here.* Line 48 begins the next section:

> But since thou like a contrite penitent,
> Charitably warn'd of thy sinnes, dost repent
> These vanities, and giddinesses, loe
> I shut my chamber doore, and come, lets goe.

The last section begins, *Now we are in the street;* and the active dialogue proceeds from there: *And so . . . Yet . . . As . . . till . . . him whom . . . why . . . Why . . . At last.*

In *Satire* II, the disjunction is built into the beginning:

> Sir; though (I thanke God for it) I do hate
> Perfectly all this towne, yet there's one state
> In all ill things so excellently best,
> That hate, toward them, breeds pitty towards the rest.

Then at line 25, an extension to a superlative *but: But hee is worst,* and at line 39, the consoling consequence, *But these punish themselves.* So the Satires move, by hyperbole which gives a second thought to another side or another attitude. Donne counters the hyperbolic extremes, believing that "means" are blessings:

> Carthusian fasts, and fulsome Bachanalls
> Equally I hate; meanes blesse . . .
> > But (Oh) we'allow
> Good workes as good, but out of fashion now, . . .

Similarly, "The Progresse of the Soule" begins, *I sing the progresse of a deathlesse soule,* and then in XII, *But snatch mee heavenly Spirit from this vaine / Reckoning their vanities* . . . ; then comes a narrative sequence—*Next* . . . , *next* . . . — and in conclusion *There's nothing simply good or ill alone,* . . .

Of the Verse Letters, "To Mr. T.W." and many others are good examples: the reasons are given first, and then the petition; in "To Mr. R.W." the argument and counterargument come after the petition as they do in but one of the many to the Countesse of Bedford, with its central turn from *Beeing* and *seeming is your equall care* . . . *But as our Soules of growth and Soules of sense / Have birthright of our reasons Soule,* . . . *toward your whole wisdom and religion.*

The *Divine Poems* maintain the basic structure exemplified by the progression in "La Corona": *Deigne at my hands* . . . *But doe not* . . . ; *Salvation to all* . . . *Which cannot sinne, and yet all sinnes must beare,* . . . *Immensitie cloysterd in thy deare wombe* . . . *But Oh, for thee, for him, hath th'Inne no roome?* . . . *With his kinde mother* . . . *But as for one;* . . . *By miracles* . . . *But Oh!* . . . *Moyst with one drop* . . . *But made that there, of which, and for which 'twas;* . . . *Salute the last,* . . . *But first hee,* . . .

Donne's use of connectives is also exemplified in the Holy Sonnets, published in 1633: *As due by many titles* . . . *Why doth the devill then;* . . . *Oh my blacke Soule!* . . . *Yet grace* . . . ; *This* *is my playes last scene . . . But my'ever-waking part . . . ; At the round earths imagine'd corners, blow . . . But let them sleepe . . . ; If poysonous mineralls . . . But who am I . . . ; Death be not proud, though some have called thee . . . nor yet . . . ; Spit in my face . . . But by my death . . . ; Why are wee . . . But wonder . . ;* What if this present . . . No, no; but as in my idolatrie . . . ; Batter of my heart . . . But is captiv'd . . . ; Wilt thou love God . . . But, that God should . . . ; Father, part . . . Yet such are those laws . . . ;* The mediations added in 1635 show the same kind of poetic progression: *Thou has made me, . . . But our old subtle foe . . . ; I am a little world . . . But blacke sinne . . . ; O might those sighes . . . No ease . . . ;-If faithfull soules . . . But if our mindes . . .* And from the Westmoreland MS: *Since she whome I lovd . . . But why should I . . . ; Show me deare Christ . . . or which rob'd . . . ; Oh, to vex me, contraryes meete in one.*

I have extended these quotations of connective links in order to make clear not only the stability and persistence of the structure of thought, and not only its likeness to that of the *Songs and Sonnets,* but also the basic feeling, the play over address and the disjunction of thought, the doubleness of feeling, within the form. In many of the poems, the break comes at the sonnet sestet; sometimes it comes immediately at the beginning, sometimes not until the end, sometimes it is embedded within a sub-argument, and some few times, as in the last example, it is explicit in the substance.

A break in the pattern comes for Donne in the late hymns. In the "Hymn to God my God, in my sicknesse," the introductory *since* and *whilst* lead to *I joy;* and *the thoughs* and questions are overriden by the concluding *so* and *therefore.* In "A Hymn to God the Father," the petitions to forgive have no alternatives. Yet here, even, the implication of alternatives lies in the poem itself—the *yet* latent in *hast done* and *hast not done,* up to the resolving *having done.*

As a norm, for example, we may look at the whole of the famed Holy Sonnet "At the round earths." Not all are so vividly countered as this, but all are figured by it.

> At the round earths imagin'd corners, blow
> Your trempets, Angells, and arise, arise
> From death, you numberlesse infinities
> Of soules, and to your scattred bodies goe,
> All whom the flood did, and fire shall o'erthrow,
> All whom warre, dearth, age, agues, tyrannies,
> Despaire, law, chance, hath slaine, and you whose
>   eyes,
> Shall behold God, and never tast deaths woe.
> But let them sleepe, Lord, and mee mourne a space,
> For, if above all these, my sinnes abound,
> 'Tis late to aske abundance of thy grace,
> When wee are there; here on this lowly ground,
> Teach mee how to repent; for that's as good
> As if thou'hadst seal'd my pardon, with thy blood.

The poem calls upon angels, in Donne's common imperative, to wake infinities of souls, in an octave of examples. Then comes a sestet of a changed mind—*But let them sleepe, Lord*—or it will be too late for me there; *here* teach me to repent. The *But* takes the poem from the accepted glorious to the truly personal. The following sonnet is also a good example of the break in Donne's pattern:

> If poysonous mineralls, and if that tree,
> Whose fruit threw death on else immortall us,
> If lecherous goats, if serpents envious
> Cannot be damn'd; Alas; why should I bee?
> Why should intent or reason, borne in mee,
> Make sinnes, else equall, in mee, more heinous?
> And mercy being easie, and glorious
> To God, in his sterne wrath, why threatens hee?

But who am I, that dare dispute with thee
O God, Oh! of thine onely worthy blood,
And my teares, make a heavenly Lethean flood,
And drowne in it my sinnes blacke memorie.
That thou remembered them, some claime as debt,
I thinke it mercy, if thou wilt forget.

The octave disputes with its *if . . . why;* the sestet self-disputes, and then calls for a heavenly Lethean flood; it moves from personal to vast, as the preceding sonnet moves from vast to personal. As the other substituted repentance for pardon, this substitutes forgetting for remembering, moves away from God as the other moves toward him. The pattern is in the motion, toward or away, the metaphysical sides of *if-then, and-but.*

The many critics of Donne write a good deal about this procedure as metaphysical, yet they seem to me often to talk about parts rather than wholes. They do not seem to refer to the guiding lines, the chief emphases of the poet. To note what a number of critics have to say is to note a number of converging approaches.

Is this poetic structure singular or shared? In his essay on "The Metaphysical Poets," T. S. Eliot restated the inquiry: "The question is to what extreme the so-called metaphysicals formed a school (in our own time we should say a 'movement'), and how far this so-called school of movement is a digression from the main current."[2] He called attention to the yoking of ideas and feelings—"A thought to Donne was an experience."[3] He emphasized fusion in figure and sensory unities quite alien to the consciously labored logic we have been observing.

C. S. Lewis too has stressed Donne's dramatic argument, his dandyism, and astringency as they suit the present day, his constancy to the themes of parting, secrecy, falseness, fickleness, miseries of love—a limited series of passions: "Donne's love poems could not exist unless love poems of a more genial character existed first."[4] He says that Carew's "When thou,

poor Excommunicate" or Lovelace's "To Lucasta, going beyond
the seas" are built up on Donne's favorite plan, but both lack
his energy in favor of beauty: and that nothing could be more
like Donne than Marvell's "Coy Mistress."

Cleanth Brooks illustrates Donne's use of paradox in "The
Canonization"—the gain by losing the world in sainthood.
Helen Gardner explains Loyola's meditative practice by means
of resignation—the place, the petition, the will; the rhetoric
of proposition—consequence—conclusion. Louis Martz, too,
draws attention to religious visualization, theological analysis, and eloquence of will. And Stanley Archer makes a
tripartite sequence of drama, reason, petition, or strophe, antistrophe, epode, and of meaning, understanding, will. Less
programmatically, Joseph Mazzeo has traced all sorts of possibilities for influence, from Ramism, baroque styles, emblem
techniques to Renaissance interest in universal analogy.

Each critic makes a different emphasis: L. I. Bredvold on
Donne's skepticism like Montaigne's—"I study my selfe more
than any other subject. It is my supernaturall metaphysike, it
is my naturall Philosophy . . . I had rather understand my selfe
well in my selfe, then in Cicero."[5] Paradoxically, Donne was pro
nature, anti book, as well as the opposite! So Joseph Duncan
and F. O. Mathiessen help us see Donne as self-conscious rebel,
Hamlet, for the nineteenth century. S. L. Bethel is especially
revealing in his study of metaphysical wit in the traditions of
Gracian and Tesauro—seeing dialectic as connecting terms as
rhetoric adorns them; seeing both dialectic and rhetoric in art
to seek beauty, a harmonic correlation, a symmetry of proportionate correspondence, implying truth through fiction and
fallacy. So too Unger emphasizes complexity, Williamson, negative figures like *ironia* and *catechresis*, Alvarez and Peterson,
the plain, harsh, personal style, very different from the crafts-
manly Sidney circle, based less on conceit and argument than
on a realism of the intelligence. Especially clarifying is Arnold
Stein's full discussion in *John Donne's Lyrics* of the lyricism

of absent things made present by rhetoric and of things that do not exist nevertheless made to seem as though they did by poetry. The stress is on *differences,* the binary and ternary forms of these. "Characteristic movement of his mind is the energetic pursuit of a limited theme"[6] by witty inversion, through tempering, reconciling, exhausting. The drive toward consciousness, gay and grim, compels Donne's negatives with his positives.[7] "Donne uses the old patterns of the mind's experience as other poets use myths, to be built upon, varied, and revealed by art."[8] *Ergo* and *igitur* were subdued, as Fraunce said, to illustrative substance, yet survived to be mocked by Pope's *The Dunciad.*

Closer to Donne's procedure are the guiding suggestions of earlier critics. For example, Grierson says in *Metaphysical Lyrics,* "Donne, moreover is metaphysical not only in virtue of his scholasticism, but by his deep reflective interest in the experience of which his poetry is the expression, the new psychological curiosity with which he writes of love and religion . . . the peculiar blend of passion and thought, feeling and ratiocination."[9] The most famous words are Johnson's in "Cowley":

The most heterogeneous ideas are linked by violence together; nature and art are ransacked for illustrations, comparisons, and allusions; their learning instructs, and their subtlety surprises. . . . As they were wholly employed on something unexpected and surprising, they had no regard to that uniformity of sentiment, which enables us to conceive and to excite the pains and the pleasure of other minds. . . . Nor was the sublime more within their reach than the pathetic . . . sublimity is produced by aggregation, and littleness by dispersion. Great thoughts are always general, and consist in positions not limited by exceptions, and in descriptions not descending to minuteness. . . . To write on their plan it was at least necessary to read and think.[10]

Johnson named Donne, Jonson, Suckling, Waller, Denham, Cowley, Cleveland as those whose minds were exercised less by direct or general impression than by recollection or inquiry.

Best of all in realizing the implications of such definition was Coleridge. Of "The Canonization" he wrote, "One of my favorite poems. As late as ten years ago, I used to seek and find out grand lines and fine stanzas; but my delight has been far greater since it has consisted more in tracing the leading thought thru'out the whole. The former is too much like coveting your neighbor's; in the latter you merge yourself in the author, you *become He*."[11]

Donne's leading thought is embodied in "The Canonization": *For Godsake hold your tongue, and let me love, Or chide . . . flout . . . improve, Take . . . get . . . Observe . . . Contemplate; what you will . . . So you will let me love. Who . . . Who . . . Who is harmed or even influenced by my love? . . . Call us what you will, wee'are made such by love.* Or—if we do not live by love, we can die by it—if not for tomb, or chronicle, for sainthood. Thus he advises us to invoke from such intensity of earthly love a pattern as from heaven. By the use of an imperative, many inspired possibilities, positive and negative, more and more hyperbolic and conditional, he focuses on love in its intensity. These were what Dryden called in his essay on *Satire* the "nice speculations of philosophy": they concerned, as Donne himself told Jonson of "The Anniversarie," the "Idea of a woman and not as she was."

This is the heart of Donne that makes him different from the rest: the *idea*, and not as she was; the positions limited, exactly as Johnson said they should *not* be, by exception. Here are poetic values not of atmosphere and observation, not of actuality, but of possibility. And here the simplest dictionary definitions of *metaphysical* help us: "concerned with abstract thought or subjects, as existence, causality, truth, etc., concerned with first principles and ultimate grounds, as being, time, or substance." Note the way the principles proceed in the beginning of Aristotle's *Metaphysics*: *All men naturally have an impulse to get knowledge, . . . From memory . . . now experience seems . . . Nevertheless, we believe . . . since . . . These then . . . Hence . . . Yet*. And at the end: *One might also raise the question . . . And if all things . . . But how . . . Some also say . . . However . . . These, then . . . But . . .* Whether from this involved old tradition, from the schoolmen, or from novelty, as Johnson thought, Aristotle's principles provided a world of poetry for Donne far more fully and consistently than for the other religious poets of his time.

> *Take heed . . . not that . . . but if . . . take heed*
> *Take heed . . . or . . . not that . . . and if . . . but then*
> *Yet . . . so . . . because . . . or . . . so . . . yet . . . take heed.*

Donne's colleagues are far stronger in atmosphere than in argument. Herrick's *Hesperides* begins "I sing of brooks, of blossoms, birds, and bowers" and goes on with these *ofs* for fourteen lines. In "When he would have his Verses Read," the sequence of *whens* stands out: in "Upon Julia's Rosemary," he uses imperatives with *and* or *or*; in "The Frozen Heart," an *if* against love; in "To Perilla," the *when* and *which* of foretelling; in "No Loathesomeness," subjunctives as substitutes for *ifs*. The imperative *Get up!* of "Corinna" is followed by manners of *how, while, before, so*. His later religious poems in *Noble Numbers* are similar in an exclamatory *Look*, or *Forgive*, with the appropriate modifiers: *My God! look on me . . . with thine eye / Of pittie, not of scrutinie.* Crashaw hails *Sister Springs*, and asks *What bright soft thing is this.* Herbert cries, *Oh, all ye who pass by . . . Oh, King of Grief, how shall I grieve . . . Lord, how I am all ague, when I seek.*

In Marvell, *See how,* and *when,* are very strong. In Vaughan, there is a more narrative structure: *Here I repos'd; we scarce will set; . . . Oft have I seen . . . But mists and shadows . . .* Jonson does seem closest to Donne, an analysis has shown. In *The Forrest* he addresses and argues, *Thou art not, Penhurst, . . . Let us prove . . . But if we lose . . .* The imperative of his famous song, *Drink to me only with thine eyes / And I will pledge with mine,* also shows his closeness to Donne. But just as everybody said in their day, it was Cleveland and Cowley who were the closest to Donne. See, for example, Cowley's "To the Duchess of Buckingham," or "The Grasshopper," or the ode "Of Wit," or all of "The Mistress." See Cleveland's "Upon the King's return from Scotland": *Return'd? . . . But the Crab-Tropick must not now prevail . . .* Or "Upon a Miser"—*Nor 'scapes he so; . . . But are we Tantaliz'd? . . . But stay awhile; . . .* or Smectymnus? *. . . But doe the Brotherhood?* Cleveland, and Cowley in "The Mistress," submit all to the process of thought. Seldom is a setting established for the sake of atmosphere, rather only for intellectual point. So Donne seldom, despite his *bracelet of bright hair*, really relaxes into a tone of description.

More useful in the search for likeness is to look back to early norms. Here is Petrarch's procedure in the first sonnet: *O ye that hear . . . the sighing On which . . . I turned from fears . . . to hopes . . . If ever . . . Pity, and pardon me this crying! / But Well I know how I must walk derided . . .* This octave is a plea for sympathy, and a sestet of self-scorn. In the second sonnet, octave *courage* and sestet *Thrown off guard . . .* In the third, there is more of a parallel between the two: *I fell a captive* and *Love caught me naked.* So also in IV there is a progressive *He who . . . so* construction, while V returns to a seventh line adversative in *But Tacit peace prevents the end.* In the first ten sonnets, half use a more or less disjunctive form, with *buts* or negatives; the others work, rather, cumulatively, catching up contrasts into a resolving whole.

In Wyatt's "Ten Sonnets," there is a similar pattern. In the first, octave and sestet are parallel in *Who so list . . . Who list,* though within the sections Wyatt's personal negative, *But as for me* appears. Most of the rest of the sestets make a turn with *Therefore farewell, And yet, Nother, But as for me, But since, But since.* In one or two, where a bare statement or a contrasting material is negative, the sestet simply adds evidence.

It is not merely sonnet structure that establishes the pattern of thought. A simple epigram is a model, too.

The fruit of all the service that I serve
Despair doth reap, such hapless hap have I.
But though he have no power to make me swerve,
Yet, by the fire, for cold I feel I die. . . .

The three stanzas of *They flee from me . . . Thankt be Fortune, it hath been otherwise . . .* and *It was no dream; I lay broad waking: / But all is turn'd . . .* gives another version of the pattern. The lively variations in subtle disjunction or negative implication seem unending in their surface forms.

Shakespeare's first sonnet establishes the adverse early, and then goes on to positives. *From fairest creatures we desire increase . . . But thou . . .* Sonnet 2, rather, takes a step forward in degree: *How much more praise . . .* Sonnets 3, 4, 5, 6, 8, 9, 10 support and explain, with connectives *for* and *then*, and extension of degree, and imperatives. But sonnet seven works in the Wyatt way, or more closely in the Petrarchan—as in the three stages of the sun's progress, the third is contrasted to the other two. Shakespeare in these early sonnets is persuading to action; often sestet and couplet move toward this positive end, with a tone quite different from the *But yet* dismays of Wyatt and Donne. Of the last sixty sonnets in the sequence, possibly the most argumentative, about a dozen, or one in five, uses the counter-sestet mode, and then with modification. The *But at my mistress' eye* of 153 is the phrasing of a minor conceit, while in the final, 154, the sequence of action goes—*The Love-god laid by . . . but the votary took up,* and *healthful remedy . . . but I not cured,* leading to the final paradox, *Love's fire heats water, water cools not love*—a characteristic sonneteering antithesis, yet not fully stressed by, rather subordinate to, the octave-sestet structure. There is a true "Shakespearean sonnet" quality in the avoidance of the main structural break. The adversatives, if present, are largely disposed of step by step in the three quatrains.

It is Sidney whom a simple list of conjunctions has shown to be most like Donne, and it is Sidney in fact whose sonnets move, though with simpler thought, in the way Donne's move. Almost every sonnet makes its simple shift: I, *I sought fit words . . . But words came halting out . . .* ; IV, *Let dainty wits cry on the Sisters nine, . . . For me, in sooth, no Muse but one I know . . .* ; CVI, *O absent presence! Stella is not here! . . . But here I do store of fair ladies meet . . .* These are actual literal contrasts where Donne grows more conceptual; but they provide his poetic frame for thought.

Sometimes Donne does use the simple literal sensory materials of all of these others, but even then he complicates them. In "The Computation" he explains why it is best to rehearse parting as the sun does: *For the first twenty years, since yesterday, / I scarce beleev'd, thou coulds't be gone away* counters the simple declarative statement with the hyperbole of time. "The Will" shows a rarely simple parallel structure. "Twicknam Garden" begins with unwonted descriptiveness: *Blasted with sighs, and surrounded with tears, / Hither I came to seeke the spring.* "A Nocturnall upon S. Lucies Day" starts with the atmosphere of:

> 'Tis the yeares midnight, and it is the dayes,
> Lucies, who scarce seaven hourse herself unmaskes,
> The Sunne is spent, and now his flasks
> Send forth light squibs, no constant rayes.

But these, like the rest, go on to counterarguments.

Donne's way is not to narrate, not to set scenes and atmosphere in any thorough way; no more by substantive vocabulary than by connectives does he present and expatiate. As his chief connectives are *and, but that, to,* in disjunction, relation, and direction, and the rest of his connectives support mainly

the logic of alternatives or consequences, so his substantive vocabulary also establishes a world of arguable inference. Looking
back to his chief terms of reference, we remember that *good* is
countered by *bad*, *true* by *false* in a way rare in English poetry; seldom are negatives so dominant. Of his nouns, *death*,
fear, *tear* too have their negative force; the only potentially
objective noun is *sun*. Of his chief verbs, most of them abun-
dantly repeated, none are unusual to his time, but again the
presence of opposites is strong in *come-go, give-take-keep*; and,
though deictic *show* is present, stronger are the more verbal
know, tell, think. No *bright, fair, sweet* of Shakespeare or Jonson, no *rose* of Herrick, no *dust* and *stone* of Herbert, nor *cloud*
and *star* of Vaughan, no *bring* or *call* or *grow* or *hear* or *kiss* or
sing or *feel* or *shine* or *sleep* of Herrick, Herbert, Vaughan, no
dark, high, heaven, light, night, star, wind of Milton, are
used by Donne, at least not with their basic recurrences. Nor
are there many, in parallel, of their stronger adverbial constructions of place and manner. So we have in Donne's *Songs and
Sonnets*, and in his art at large, a persistent characterizing
abstract structure. Farthest from the illustrative and substanti-
ating modes of classicism and from the qualifying modes of
Spenserian and Miltonic sublimity, far even from the natural-
izing progressive variations of the colloquial style, and far
even, in its extremes, from its basic contexts in the counter-
structures of Petrarch, Wyatt, Sidney, Jonson, Herbert, and the
men of faith in doubt, Donne was singular both in his extreme
personal concentration upon one plan and form and also in his
sharing of that plan and form with his whole time. The number
.9 in correlation of Donne's usage with that of others comes
to be seen as the figure of the most intense individualism, the
most intense participation.

Why is it hard for readers to see and feel so vivid a
correlation? Why are our reading critics worried more about
complexities of the metaphysical than they are about respond-

ing to its simplicities? I think it is because their own assumptions, their own simplicities from their own times, stand between them and the poems. This is one valid meaning of the process of interpretation—standing between poem and reader, and making connections, relevances, for both. But simple reading and response in the poem's terms is something else again, richer in time. Our own impositions are those of sense impression, or what Donne calls the phantasie, and the fear of reason. Donne is aware of this very contrast and mocks it, as for example in "The Dreame":

> Deare love, for nothing less than thee
> Would I have broke this happy dreame,
> It was a theame
> For reason, much too strong for phantasie,
>   Therefore thou wakds't me wisely; yet
> My dreame thou brok'st not, but continued'st it,
> Thou art so true, that thoughts of thee suffice,
> To make dreames truth; and fables histories;

" 'Tis not all spirit, pure, and brave," says Donne, "Thou com'st to kindle, goest to come." It is this mixture of physical in metaphysical that constantly necessitates the shifting of ground, the involving of negatives, alternatives, and hypotheticals of logic as reason to humanize substance by thought. There's no harm in calling this *felt thought* as Eliot does in effect, but in so doing, the relation gets stood on its head. To ask how Donne feels his thought is to seek unsuccessfully, as we have long been doing, for sustaining patterns of figure, or even imagery, in poem after poem; rather to ask how Donne thinks his feeling is to seek and find the pattern of exuberant superlative questions and imperatives compellingly tempered by conditionals, adversatives, and straight denials; a pattern that emerges as a simple downright statement of the actuality of language and of life.

NOTES TO CHAPTER 4

1. *The Computer and Literary Style,* ed. Jacob Leed (Kentucky, 1966); all quotations of poetry are from *The Poems of John Donne,* ed. H. J. C. Grierson (Oxford, 1912).
2. Eliot, *Selected Essays* (New York, 1950), p. 24.
3. Ibid., p. 247.
4. "Donne and Love Poetry in the Seventeenth Century," in *Seventeenth Century English Poetry,* ed. William R. Keast (New York, 1962), p. 107.
5. "The Naturalism of Donne" in *Discussions of John Donne,* ed. Frank Kermode (Boston, 1962), p. 53.
6. Stein, *John Donne's Lyrics* (Minneapolis, 1962), p. 163.
7. Ibid.
8. Ibid., p. 161.
9. Grierson, *Metaphysical Lyrics* (London, 1921), pp. xiii–xxviii.
10. *Rasselas, Poems and Selected Prose,* ed. Bertrand H. Bronson (New York, 1961), pp. 470–472.
11. *Coleridge's Miscellaneous Criticism,* Lecture X, ed. T. M. Raysor (London, 1936), p. 137.

✖ 5. Words as Themes
in Milton's Lycidas

REPETITION is at the heart of poetry; poetry's beats, its measures, its assonances and alliterations, its rhymes and refrains, its repeated structures, all by their recurrence provide its meaningful pattern. Different poems repeat in different ways. In *Lycidas*, just the reference, in addition to sound and structure, takes at least three forms of repetition. It echoes for emphasis, *For Lycidas is dead, dead ere his prime*. It parallels for guidance to main points of view, as in the addresses, *Begin then, Sisters . . . , Where were ye Nymphs . . . , O Fountain Arethuse . . . , Return Alpheus*. It recurs in less emphatic positions, in new contexts, to establish the variation of the themes: *For Lycidas is dead . . . For Lycidas your sorrow is not dead*. And, *. . . sunk so low that sacred head of thine . . . , Sunk though he be beneath the watry floor . . . , So Lycidas sunk low, but mounted high*. A look at some of these more subtle recurrences will tell us not only of primary substance and shaping structure but of the poem's place in the continuity of poetry.

Most of the repeated terms in *Lycidas* are of common importance for the poets of Milton's day, especially for that certain group which wrote in the line of the "aureate" poets and

Spenser. Such are the terms like *gentle, old, high, sad, come, go, lie, sing, hear, shepherd, flower, muse, power,* in the pastoral tradition, and *eye, tear, dead, weep,* in the elegiac tradition.

Some, on the other hand, were brought into strong use first by Milton, and these particularly help define the singularities of *Lycidas: fresh, new, pure, sacred, green, watry, flood, leaf, morn, hill, shade, shore, stream, star, wind, fame, ask, touch.* What are the particular qualities of these words as a group? They refer primarily to the natural world, in more specific and sensory terms than were usual before Milton's time. They include an unusually large proportion of adjectives, and the adjectives name qualities of intensive value. The verbs are less essential. The nouns establish a physical world of earth and water freshly seen, emphasized in contrast to star and sun in the more spiritual world of the heavens. Like Satan in *Paradise Lost,* the physical bodily force of earth and water dominates the inventive substance, then to be subdued by the triumph of significant structure, the rising from low to high, from sea and land to heaven, in the sun's motion of renewal. Like Adam and Eve in *Paradise Lost,* the shepherd in *Lycidas* finally takes up life on earth again in the light of his vision of heaven, in the light of hope beyond earth, tomorrow, fresh, and new.

This essential motion from low to high, paralleled by that from past to future, takes place through the primary characteristic words of the poem. The opening words *Yet once more I come* become the completing *At last he rose.* The plucked brown leaves of mourning become the twitched blue mantle of hope. The meed of some melodious tear becomes the nectar pure of the blest kingdoms. The singing of Lycidas' own lofty rhymes moves through the lofty meed of fame granted by Jove, to the singing of the nuptial song by the solemn troops and sweet societies of the blest kingdoms in their glory. The memories both pastoral and mythological, of old Damoetas, old

Bards, Bellerus old, become the reviews of Camus and St. Peter, of false pastors and even of false pastures—valleys low, shades and wanton winds, sad embroideries—as our frail thoughts "dally with false surmise," until at last, presaged by "those pure eyes and perfet witnes of all-judging *Jove*," the angel looks homeward from the whelming tide, and Lycidas, sunk though he be, rises like the day-star, "through the dear might of Him that walk'd the waves," to preside from above as the good genius of the shore. Even the shepherd, bound to the pastoral earth, looks up and forward, to sun and hills, to the pastures of tomorrow. *Fresh, high, new, pure, sacred,* are the especial terms of value; *pure* and *sacred* both classical and Christian, *pure* marking the two key passages of height, the classical and Christian heavens. The poem tries twice for what it achieves; first in the words of Phoebus and Jove, that fame is no mortal plant; then after a deeper pitch into despair of waters and of earth, more triumphantly in the natural analogy of the sun and the Christian terms of grace.

Two passages in the poem participate less than the rest in the process of cumulative repetition. One is the procession of guardians, Hippotades, Camus, and the Pilot of the Galilean lake, with their special details of reference, especially those for the false shepherd: lean and flashy songs, scrannel Pipes of wretched straw, foul contagion, grim Wolf with privy paw, two-handed engine. The other immediately follows, in ostensible contrast, the details of flowers, "so to interpose a little ease": honied showers, rathe Primrose, pale Jessamine, Pansy freak'd with jet. These two passages come between the climactic vision of fame in the first mourning section and the final vision of recompense and redemption in the last section. They make up the central portion, less closely patterned than the rest because, as an antistrophe, like a fourth act in a drama, they explore the counterforms of what the poem has been concerned with, the implications of the pastoral tradition in a world of spirit. Unlike Donne's logical negatives these are thematically sensory. Neither false pastors nor surmised flowers redeem the physical pastoral world of the human spirit; only as it looks higher is it redeemed and reconciled.

These amplifying passages lead us to see another strong characteristic of Milton's language, its richness in adjectival quality. All the way through we have noted repeated nouns, adjectives, and verbs, but where there is least repetition and most variation the inventive variation in the adjectives is especially perceptible. If we try to define actual proportions, in order to corroborate this impression, we find that the poem uses about twelve adjectives, sixteen nouns, and nine verbs per ten lines; in other words, more adjectives than verbs, while most poetry in English uses more verbs than adjectives and proportionately more nouns. The quantitative power of adjectives in *Lycidas* supports the qualitative powers we have noted; namely, the use of recurring adjectives to emphasize structure and theme, the focus on a few key adjectives to carry the *fresh high pure* values of the poem, and the use of strong variety in a few passages of amplification.

When we suggest that Milton's use of repetition, especially his strong repetition of the adjective form, is characteristic not only because of its integral function in the poem itself but also because of its unusualness in English poetry, we move into the realm of comparison. As a unit, *Lycidas* is incomparable, as is any individual work of art. But in its selection and arrangement of materials it may follow choices like or unlike those in other poems, and thus provide some basis for comparison, of elements and patterns if not of wholes. Indeed, comparison by contrast may heighten our perception of the individuality of the poem.

By mid-seventeenth century, few poems were so individual in their use of dominant qualitative language as *Lycidas*. Only one poet, Phineas Fletcher, out of some forty or fifty preceding Milton, had emphasized adjectives as Milton did. Of major terms, those most repeated, only about half in

Lycidas were strongly traditional for poetry: the *dead, dear, old, eye, head, shepherd, power, heaven, flower,* and most of the verbs. Of the rest, a few had been stressed before by a special and limited group: *sad, gentle,* and *new* by Spenser and one or two followers; *sacred* and *muse,* by Sidney, Chapman, and a few others; a few echoes from the "aureate" fifteenth century. This emotional language was poetic language not in the more active traditions of Chaucer, Jonson, and Donne but in the more artful and aesthetic tradition of Spenser and Sidney, the poets most fond of pastoral. A few lines from Spenser's *Astrophel,* the earlier pastoral elegy, will suggest Milton's relation to the tradition.

> A gentle shepherd borne in Arcady,
> Of gentlest race that ever shepherd bore:
> About the grassie bancks of Haemony,
> Did keepe his sheep, his little stock and store.
> Full carefully he kept them day and night,
> In fairest fields, and Astrophel he hight.

The repetitions, of words, of line lengths, of rhyme sounds, of alliterations, of phrasal constructions, are tighter than in *Lycidas,* but less related to meaning. The second characteristic term *gentle* has no particular bearing on the first, for example; and the *borne . . . bore* echo is simple word-play; the adjective *grassie* tells us much; but *fair,* little. Note also the later stanza on Astrophel's soul in paradise: like Milton's it relates flowers to immortality, but much more pictorially, less profoundly. Milton's flowers keep their reality and their relative subordination in fancy and on earth, while Spenser's cheerfully bloom in heaven:

> Ah no: it is not dead, ne can it die,
> But lives for aie, in blissful Paradise;
> Where like a new-borne babe it soft doth lie
> In bed of lillies wrapt in tender wise.

And compast all about with roses sweet,
And daintie violets from head to feet.

What Milton makes of these two concepts, physical and
spiritual, by the widening of the physical and the heightening
of the spiritual, is central to the difference between the two
poets who in their love of æsthetic sense belong to the same
school. Spenser's main repeated terms in *Astrophel* are more
frequent, more abundant, and more usual: *dear, fair, gentle
great, good, day, flower, heart, love, shepherd, verse, make,
see, hear, sing.* These are specializations within the main line
of English poetic vocabulary, upon the sensuous, emotional,
and artful. Milton shared more deeply in these specializations
than in any other, but took them further, into individual emphasis and interpretation beyond the structured thought of a
Sidney or a Donne. As may be surmised, he is no poet of *if* or
but or even *and,* or even of prosaic relative terms; only in
prepositions does he come near to agreeing with Donne.

One reason that his individual emphases do not sound
idiosyncratic to us today is that the language of *Lycidas* has
had a powerful effect on English, especially American, poetry.
The poem drew on the concrete references, the verbal harmonies, the interwoven and cumulative structures of classical
sources, especially Virgil, and turned them to the intense purposes of Protestantism with its sense of the natural scope and
magnificence of the universe as God's creation, encompassing
the depth of hell and sea, the height of heaven and sky. Thus
the special vocabulary of *fresh, high, pure, sacred, new, fountain, hill, leaf, morning, shade, stream, shore, star, wind,* while
extremely rare as dominant vocabulary before *Lycidas,* becomes
dominant in the mid-eighteenth century, with poets like James
Thompson, Collins, Dyer, Blake, and Wordsworth. Especially
in America, from Dwight and Trumbull on, the liberal and
natural Protestant spirit continued its poetizing in these terms
of scope and sacred feeling, one of the most characteristic

American poetic adjectives being the *pure* of *Lycidas.* Today, the integration of sense imagery with sound pattern and emotional harmonic structure is natural to poetry. The imagists and symbolists have called for such integration, and we find it in Keats, in Whitman, in Dylan Thomas, in Hart Crane; these are poets in the tradition of *Lycidas.*

To come back from history and tradition to the poem itself: one good way to read it is in its own terms of emphasis, and one of these is its repetition, with variation, of the primary language. Its thematic terms carry the poem's sense of renewal from old past to new future, from deep waters and sad flowers to high heavens, from Jove's fame to Christ's redemption, from westering to rising star. For *Lycidas,* for Milton, for English poetry, this was a fresh beginning.

✖ 6. Blake's Frame of Language

How DOES a poet surprise his faithful readers? By what he faithfully says, what is therefore inescapably present in the concordance of his work? In the Preface of the Blake *Concordance*, 1966,[1] the editor, David Erdman, writes, "We may have expected to find *man, love, eternal,* and *earth* among Blake's most used words, but not *death* so near the top or *night* so far ahead of *day*. And among those used only once we may be struck to see how many were memorably effective in their single impacts." By a single *regale* or a repeated *eternal* may our reading seem confirmed, yet by a host of *deaths* and *nights* called into question? As a matter of fact, it is most-used *eternal* that should be surprising, because there are very few three-syllable words in the major language of English poetry.[2] But that is a metrical story, well treated by Alicia Ostriker in *Vision and Verse in William Blake*. Can we say with surprise after reading Blake, "I had not thought death had undone so many"? Whether the surprise is induced by a planned or unplanned bias of writing or of reading, it may lead deeper to questions about the nature of Blake's work in relation to the cosmologies of Milton and the eighteenth century.

A concordance, in giving line contexts for the substantial half of a poet's vocabulary, the other half being particles of connection or pronominal reference, gives not only the range of

usage of each word but also the range of distribution and frequency, how many times, how widely recurrent, in what specific
texts. For most poets, especially for Blake, there appear to be
a few words, perhaps a half-hundred, so essential to expression
that they make up in number of occurrences nearly a fifth of
the whole text. At the other extreme, the six or seven thousand
words used only one time to ten times apiece amount to another fifth.

It is the tendency of critics to feel that a word used strongly once can be more powerful than a word used over and over
so much that one takes it for granted. But it is also true that
the most-repeated words have their significance in providing
the underlying fabric, the persistent content of the poetry.
My preconcordance study of Blake's major language,[3] based on
the chief content-words in a thousand lines made up from the
first two hundred lines of major poems from *Poetical Sketches*
through *Jerusalem*, established a list much like that which the
Concordance has revealed for the whole twenty thousand
lines, making clear the homogeneity and consistency of Blake's
usage. Some strengths are related to simple beginnings, the
early pastorals, for example; others, to later technical increases,
like *spectre*, and the power of *Jerusalem*. But in the main the
strengths are in continuities.

Because the *Concordance* lists separately the plurals of
nouns, parts of verbs, and comparisons of adjectives, its list of
frequencies for each word needs to be reorganized in order to
gain a picture of major content. Though the differences between plurals and singulars may be formally significant, for a
general sense of reference we need to combine *hill* with *hills*,
for example, or *man* with *men*, or *come* with *came*, or *love* with
loved. So the list of major terms I give here shows more adjectives, more verbs with their sum of parts (except for participles,
which I take as adjectival), and more nouns with strong plurals,
because of the higher totals of combined forms. Further, the
Concordance prints frequencies but not contexts for the pro-

nouns and connectives which bulk the largest, and does not separate poetry from prose for them, so that the reader must pursue his own sense of structure in Blake's rich prepositional quality.

What is this major substance thus structured? It consists of thirty or so nouns, fifteen or so verbs, fifteen or so adjectives, a number of main adjectives unusually large among poets. The nouns are human or superhuman figures: *man, son, daughter, child,* then *God* and *gods,* and *Satan,* then *spectre* and *form,* in a setting of *earth* and *world* and *heaven,* in *rock, mountain, cloud, fire,* and *light,* in a time of *day, night, eternity,* with the bodily *forms* of *eye, tear, hand, foot, voice,* and the concepts and feelings of *death, love, life, joy;* these thirty chief nouns are modified by the dozen or so chief adjectives *all, no, every, one, none, eternal, dark, sweet, human, divine, bright, deep, golden, little,* in their dozen or so chief actions *see, stand, rise, know, come, go, love, let, say, hear, behold.* As a whole, one can generalize from the *Concordance,* much as I did earlier, that Blake's most traditional materials provide words of scene and feeling and perceiving, moving away from such classical generalities as *nature, youth, fate, virtue, thought,* toward the nineteenth century's *little, child, daughter, death, earth, weep,* and Blake's special *eternal, sleep, cloud, form.*

His colors *black, golden, red* are ballad terms, his *eternal* and *divine* eighteenth-century, his *voice* and *cloud* seventeenth-century biblical especially in the Miltonic line from Sylvester's and Spenser's observing *hear, look,* Crashaw's *black, dark, heaven, fire, night,* Vaughan's *cloud, death, sun, weep, sleep.* In combining the low language of satire with the high of prophecy, Blake followed the tradition of many eighteenth-century odes on superstition: scenes, anatomies, feelings, and the many specific spiders, webs, spectres, clouds, like those in the poems of Samuel Wesley as early as 1700.

Far higher than the most frequent referential *all, men, Los, see,* are the thousands of particles, *the,* and *of,* and a dozen others which even in their bulk should not be ignored, as Rostrevor-Hamilton's *Tell-Tale Article* has shown [4] and as any thorough contrast of pronomial or prepositional uses could well show. My study of the connectives, in *Style and Proportion*, 1967,[5] suggests that Blake is a giant user of locational phrases in the tradition of biblical prose, *of, in, to, with, at, on, from, by,* and then, only less than a standard group of relative *whats* and *whichs* and a few logical *ands* and *buts,* of another dominant set of connectives, *around* and *round, upon, over, down, up, through, beneath, forth, out, among, away,* which suit his chief verbs of presence and perception and give him high position in the eighteenth-century poetics of place signified by Thomson's innovative *around* and *beneath* and Gray's *amidst,* in what can be called the Spenserian-Miltonic tradition. For poetry in English, Blake's is an extremist structure, heightening eighteenth-century locational terminology, as Donne heightened seventeenth-century logical terminology, intensifying the spatial as Donne intensified the temporal and Wordsworth the balanced.

Where do the chief terms lead us? The *Poetical Sketches* begin with embodied seasons, their joy of limb and voice, their daughters, blossoms, songs; the scepter and iron car of monster winter, his seat upon the cliffs. Evening's fair-haired star shines on wolf and lamb, morning light rises from the chambers of the east, her feet upon the hills. *Chill death withdraws his hand, the prince of love, His face is fair as heav'n, innocent eyes, make weep the eyes of day, light doth seize my brain, the voice of Heaven I hear, that sweet village, more than mortal fire, on chrystal rocks, children cry for bread, The armies stand, The King is seen raging afar, The earth doth faint, round the circle of the world, have thy soft piteous eyes beheld.* Each of the *Poetical Sketches* sets its major terms in the embodiments of form in feeling and scene. So also the *Songs of Innocence and Experience: On a cloud I saw a child, he wept with joy to hear, the Shepherd's sweet lot, The Sun does arise, Softest clothing, wooly, bright, there God does live.*

Throughout his work Blake establishes the major terms as central. Poem after poem they recur, *death, dark, daughters, children, mountains, man, fire, cloud,* in varying contexts. In *Tiriel, But now his eyes were dark'ned and his wife fading in death.* And in *The Book of Thel, The daughters of the Seraphim led round their sunny flocks . . . / "Why fade these children of the spring, born but to smile and fall?"* And in *The French Revolution, The dead brood over Europe . . . / Sick the mountains, and all their vineyards weep, . . .* In *The Marriage of Heaven and Hell,*

> The just man rages in the wilds . . .
> Rintrah roars and shakes his fires in the burden'd air;
> Hungry clouds swag on the deep.

In *America, The shadowy Daughter of Urthona stood before red Orc, / When fourteen suns had faintly journey'd o'er his dark abode; . . .* In *Europe, Five windows light the cavern'd Man: thro' one he breathes the air; / Thro' one hears music of the spheres; thro' one the eternal vine.* The [First] Book of Urizen, *Of the primeval Priest's assum'd power. . . .* The Book of Ahania, *And his right hand burns red in its cloud. . . .* In the *Song of Los,* the vast geography:

> Adam stood in the garden of Eden
> And Noah on the mountains of Ararat;
> They saw Urizen give his Laws to the Nations
> By the hands of the children of Los.

In *The Four Zoas,* the song of wrath:

> The Song of the Aged Mother which shook the heavens
> with wrath,
> Hearing the march of long resounding, strong heroic Verse
> Marshall'd in order for the day of Intellectual Battle.

In *Milton, To Justify the Ways of God to Men* / ... the question *And did the Countenance Divine* / *Shine forth upon our clouded hills?* And *Daughters of Beulah! Muses who inspire the Poet's Song*, ... And in *Jerusalem*, the joining anatomy, theology, cosmology:

> Again he speaks in thunder and in fire!
> Thunder of Thought, & flames of fierce desire:
> Even from the depths of Hell his voice I hear
> Within the unfathom'd caverns of my Ear. . . .
> "Awake! awake O sleeper of the land of shadows. . . ."

These bardic beginnings, these sweeps of the strings, are not all of Blake; they are not the vital minutiae of Blake; but they establish the scope of his steady reference in his major language. In the light of these beginnings, the siftings of the *Concordance* are understandable, the grains of sand do contain the heavens they reveal. On the cosmic stage—but this is an alien term—in the cosmic landscape, loom the bodily forms of human passions, the druidic identities of earth, anatomy, and belief. All the eternal divine and human, dark, bright, and deep forms of Man, god, Satan, spectre, son, daughter, child, in hand, foot, head, voice, eye, tear, joy, over the earth and heaven, mountain, rock, in cloud and light, shadow and fire, come, go, rise, stand to see, behold, and hear, to know, love, and weep. They move in the *states* of which Blake speaks, of vision rather than of action, in Laokoonish coils caught and beheld.

In this great scene are the smaller shapes we treasure, babe, lamb, worm, flower, the London streets, the middle vocabulary in all its variety, between the uncommon once-words and the essential always-words, ever-forms. General forms have their vitality in particulars, as *Jerusalem* says: yet in Gothic, not Grecian, living forms; forms cannot be annihilated, and divine-humanity is the only general and universal form. The little reside in the bosoms of larger, and time moves by days and nights in the forms of eons.

Within the spatial frame is there a basic structure of contraries—counter, opposed, diametrically different, incompati-
ble? Blake wrote often of contraries. Did he set up a contrarious
structure for his poetry in the opposing of major terms? The
primary *death* and *night* which surprise Erdman at their highest
level of usage equal to that of the major proper names Los,
Albion, and Urizen, and of *man* himself, meet a countering *life*
and *day* not much more than half so frequent. The next strongest *love* has positive support in *joy*, but no major counter
hate, sorrow, tear, fear except at lower levels of frequency.
Man and *God*, *man* and *child*, *God* and *Satan*, *son* and *daughter*, *earth* or *world* and *heaven*, *earth* and *fire*, are contrary in
a different sense, in pairings asymmetrical. *Light* and *shadow*,
time and *eternity* make fairer pairs. *Eye, head, foot* are anatomies not seeming opposed. The other major nouns, some of
these most special to Blake, are *voice, form, cloud, spectre,
power, self*, and in these we may see some contrast of *form* to
spectre, cloud to *rock* and *mountain*. In all, the diameters seem
to suggest places of reference, high and low, substantial and
insubstantial, rather than contrasting feelings or persons, a
vertical rather than a horizontal *agon*.

Action too is not toe-to-toe. *See* is primary, along with
behold; *hearing* and *knowing* are supplementary. Actions of
motion are *come, go*, and *stand*; *let* is important along with
say. Otherwise, *love* and *weep* are major, not necessarily contrary. These are verbs of the paintings—being there, seeing, expressing attitudes.

The chief epithet *all*, Blake's most frequent referential
term, is countered by *no* or by *one* at only minor levels—no
contest in the logic! The chief descriptive *eternal* is supported
by *divine*, perhaps then countered by *human*. *Sweet, cold,
deep, little, golden*, receive little contrast, except for some *great*
and *black*; what happens to Milton's major *high* in its line
from *deep*? *Cold* has little *hot* or *warm*. The one clear pair is
dark-bright, with *dark* consistently the stronger. A lesser *loud*

and *silent* support the noun *voice* and verb *hear*; *good* is lesser also, though important in the prose; it sets up little *bad* in moral opposition.

Blake gives us clearly strong contrast in visible light and audible sound, in conditions of perceiving; otherwise, we must look not to objects and persons but to qualities and forces if we are to find the nature of his conflict at its major scale.

Qualities, adjectives, as in Wallace Stevens's third world of perception, carry the power upward, from Hell and Earth to Beulah and Heaven in a dynamic of spiral motion, not classical and not Hegelian, not Greek but Gothic, as Blake says, forging forms on earth to rise high into eternal forms. For the engraver they must be engravable, to be seen by vegetable eyes; they do not win over or lose to each other, but ascend out of the struggle which is scarcely even a contest.

> All Human Forms identified, even Tree, Metal, Earth & Stone: all
> Human Forms identified, living, going forth & returning wearied
> Into the Planetary lives of Years, Months, Days & Hours; reposing,
> And then Awaking into his Bosom in the Life of Immortality
>
> [*Jerusalem* IV, 99; Keynes, p. 567[6]]

In her helpful dissertation, "Visionary Forms: Blake's Prophetic Art and the Pictorial Tradition,"[7] Margaret Shook clarifies the linear direction of the poetry. Blake's "bounding line" recovered the clear and the universal from hazy blurs of preromanticism. His particularity is not object, but species, or clearly delineated human parts like Vasari's "feet, hands, hair, and beards" (*Lives of the Most Eminent Painters, Sculptors, and Architects*, 1550[8]).

> NATURE & Art in this together Suit:
> What is Most Grand is always most Minute.

Rubens thinks Tables, Chairs & Stools are Grand,
But Rafael thinks A Head, a foot, a hand.

> [*A Pretty Epigram*, Keynes, p. 658]

And this is the manner of the Sons of Albion in their
    strength:
They take the Two Contraries which are call'd Qualities,
    with which
Every Substance is clothed: they name them Good & Evil
From them they make an Abstract, which is a Negation
Not only of the Substance from which it is derived,
A murderer of its own Body, but also a murderer
Of every Divine Member: it is the Reasoning Power,
An Abstract objecting power that Negatives every thing.
This is the Spectre of Man, the Holy Reasoning Power,
And in its Holiness is closed the Abomination of Desola-
    tion.

> [*Jerusalem* I, 10; Keynes, p. 442]

Of the Roman soldiers in his sublime painting "The Ancient Britons," now lost, Blake says in the *Descriptive Catalogue* that each shows "a different character, and a different
expression of fear, or revenge, or envy, or blank horror, or
amazement, or devout wonder and unresisting awe" [Keynes,
p. 612]. Fuseli[9] relates these types of energies in various Greek
heroes to "emanations of energy that re-unite in one splendid
centre fixed in Achilles." These types are thus not generalities;
they are a sort of shared particularity of type, as the eighteenth
century would see it. That is, as human minds would see it.
"Mental Things are alone Real; what is call'd Corporeal, Nobody Knows of its Dwelling Place: it is in Fallacy, & its Existence an Imposture. . . . Error is Created. Truth is Eternal. Error,
or Creation, will be Burned up, & then, & not till Then, Truth
or Eternity will appear" [*A Vision of the Last Judgment*, Keynes
p. 651]. It is here that Blake asserts his vision of the sun not

as "a round disk of fire" but as "an Innumerable company of the Heavenly host" [Keynes, p. 652].

Yet early and late he can think of nature formally if he thinks of every eternal form.

The great and golden rule of art, as well as of life, is this: That the more distinct, sharp, and wirey the bounding line, the more perfect the work of art; . . . What is it that builds a house and plants a garden, but the definite and determinate? What is it that distinguishes honesty from knavery, but the hard and wiry line of rectitude and certainty in the actions and intentions? Leave out this line, and you leave out life itself; all is chaos again, and the line of the almighty must be drawn out upon it before man or beast can exist. [*A Descriptive Catalogue*, Keynes, p. 617]

Idealized type is allegorical image. "Moderns wish to draw figures without lines, and with great and heavy shadows; are not shadows more unmeaning than lines, and more heavy? O who can doubt this!" [*A Descriptive Catalogue*, Keynes, p. 607].

The hard and wiry line is a springing, not a balancing, line, and the dynamics is not so much dramatic or narrative as lyric, as both Fisch and Hartman have recently shown,[10] rising from shadow to substance in form, from earth to heaven, from fire's heat to fire's light as the dualism is burned away. So the perspective of the poems is from death and from night and from son and man, and from earth, these being Blake's major nouns, moving toward less common life, form, heaven, joy, day, light, eternity by way of the body and light of fire and the qualities dark, sweet, human toward qualities bright, eternal, divine.

These are the Sons of Los: These the Visions of Eternity,
But we see only as it were the hem of their garments
When with our vegetable eyes we view these wondrous
    Visions.
                [*Milton* I, 28, 10–12; Keynes, p. 408]

Form is true Nature—

> "Whatever can be Created can be Annihilated: Forms
> Cannot:
> "The Oak is cut down by the Ax, the Lamb falls by the
> Knife,
> "But their Forms Eternal Exist For-ever."
> > [*Milton* II, 35, 36–38; Keynes, p. 418]

The Oak dies as well as the Lettuce, but Its Eternal Image & Individuality never dies, but renews by its seed; just so the Imaginative Image returns by the seed of Contemplative Thought. . . . [*A Vision of the Last Judgment*, Keynes, p. 638]

With Fuseli's thought that "In forms alone the idea of existence can be rendered permanent,"[11] Blake would have fire and forge hammer out forms even of wrongs

> "That he who will not defend Truth may be compell'd to
> defend
> "A Lie: that he may be snared and caught and snared and
> taken:
> "That Enthusiasm and Life may not cease . . ."
> > [*Jerusalem* I, 9, 29–31; Keynes, p. 441]

"Now intreating Tears & Sighs / O when will the Morning rise?" [*The Golden Net*, Keynes, p. 110]. The true vision is a lowly and nighttime vision:

> God Appears & God is Light
> To those poor Souls who dwell in Night,
> But does a Human Form Display
> To those who Dwell in Realms of day.
> > [*Auguries of Innocence*, Keynes, p. 121]

Thus the topography of the poetics of night:

> Far above Time's troubled Fountains,
> On the Great Atlantic Mountains,

In my Golden House on high,
There they Shine Eternally.

[*Fragment*, Keynes, p. 127]

Thus the paradox and asymmetry:

To be in a Passion you Good may do,
But no Good if a Passion is in you.

[*Auguries of Innocence*, Keynes, p. 121]

"I slept in the dark
"In the silent night
"I murmur'd my fears
"And I felt delight.

"In the morning I went
"As rosy as morn
"To seek for new Joy
"But I met with scorn."

[*The Wild Flower's Song*, Keynes, p. 96]

And thus the rising of forms:

There is a place where Contrarieties are equally True:
This place is called Beulah. It is a pleasant lovely Shadow
Where no dispute can come, . . .

[*Milton II, 33, 1–3*; Keynes, p. 415]

"Awake, Awake, Jerusalem! O lovely Emanation of
    Albion,
"Awake and overspread all Nations as in Ancient Time;
"For lo! the Night of Death is past and the Eternal Day
"Appears upon our Hills. Awake, Jerusalem, and come
    away!"

[*Jerusalem IV, 97*; Keynes, p. 564]

When he says in *The Marriage of Heaven and Hell* that "Without Contraries is no progression. Attraction and Repulsion, Reason and Energy, Love and Hate, are necessary to Human existence" [Keynes, p. 181], and says that good passive reason is Heaven, evil active energy is hell, one sees his teasing of progression.

What dialectics there are, are limited by the shifting of the contraries in man, in the circling of day and night. "Active evil is better than passive good," he said; it springs from body, from energy; its relation to good is asymmetrical, it is capable of good, as good is not of it; it can be regenerated into good [*Annotations to Lavater's "Aphorisms on Man,"* Keynes, p. 724]. It can be forgiven, not avenged [*Jerusalem* III]. Its vigor, in experience, leads innocence to wisdom, to states beyond the fluctuating and the changing.

Blake, as he wrote George Cumberland, desires that state of entities beyond dialectic, that state "in which every man is King and Priest in his own house. God send it so on earth, as it is in heaven." He needs physical anatomy, an eye, an arm, a hand; he needs physical geography, rock, cloud, and mountain; he needs cosmology, heaven, time, eternity, divinity; he needs forms with names and feelings and monumental actions providing presence; he needs the earthly energy of bounding lines in order to make his pictures. He needs wrath, forge, and fire to regenerate the generated and vegetable forms into their states beyond time, change, and progression. Contraries are for him not so much dramatic as lyrical, not so much clashing as pushing onward, from innocence, not ignorance, into experience, and from experience to a higher state of innocence related to wisdom.

Even his ballad lines carry paradoxes, so that they will not settle into the sequences of narrative; narratives press heroes onward to transformations—Adam to Satan and on, son to father to son, by jolts of energy. *Form* and *fire*, with all their visual trains, dominate the scene as they move upward from night to day and earth to heaven, the heart of fire regenerating the forms, to the light of states of eternal mental reality; a painter's sublime world springing beyond pathos.

The frequencies of the *Concordance* do not belie or conceal or distort this painter's reality but rather allow its naming. Coming to recognize the persistences in Blake's vocabulary, his chief bodily and sensory terms, his highly adjectival and phrasal structures, his vertical scenes read from below, his firm edges and boundaries springing into states without bonds but strong in identity, we can answer the question why among chief *Concordance* terms *death* is so dominant and *night* so far ahead of *day*, and realize how the guiding terms of substance, of dark, of death, of earth, of experience, of Albion, provide the ground for the feet of human figures, the forge for the lighting and consuming fires, the flame that, over and over and over, around and around, again and again and again, only sometimes, but into eternity, breaks forth to become light.

What about the reader's surprise? If he is able to get beyond surprise and to see in the pattern of major terms revealed by the *Concordance* a pattern revealed also in the text he has read, is he willing to change surprise to wonder at the thoroughgoing forces of the poetry? Many critics today emphasize a kind of discrepancy in the relation of author to reader: either a usage unconscious for the author yet discerned by the reader, or unconsciousness in the reader yet guided to his purposes by the author. In the middle ground of major usage, in the major vocabulary and sound and syntax of the text, is ground for agreement conscious or unconscious. The steadygoing assumptions find expression in major frequencies and find corroboration in repeated recognitions. In poetry especially what counts is not only what the reader is carried toward but what he is brought back to. Blake's reader is brought back to engraved forms, on earth, in night, that he may begin again.

NOTES TO CHAPTER 6

1. Ithaca, New York: Cornell University Press, 1966.
2. See G. K. Zipf, *The Psycho-Biology of Language* (Boston: Houghton Mifflin Co., 1935).
3. *Eras and Modes in English Poetry*, rev. ed. (Berkeley and Los Angeles: University of California Press, 1964).
4. New York: Oxford University Press, 1950.
5. Boston: Little, Brown and Co., 1967.
6. All quotations from Blake are taken from *Poetry and Prose of William Blake*, ed. Geoffrey Keynes (London: Nonesuch Press, 1948).
7. University of California, Berkeley, 1966.
8. *A Documentary History of Art.* ed. Elizabeth Gilmore Holt (Garden City, N.Y.: Doubleday & Co., 1958), vol. 2, p. 27.
9. *Lectures on Painting by the Royal Academicians*, ed. Ralph N. Wornum, (London: Henry G. Bohn, 1848), p. 359.
10. *Essays for S. Foster Damon*, ed. Alvin H. Rosenfeld (Providence, R.I.: Brown University Press, 1969). See also in this volume Robert F. Gleckner, "Blake's Verbal Technique."
11. Quoted by Margaret Shook, "Visionary Forms," p. 170.

🔗 7. Eighteenth-Century
Prose Revelation

DISCUSSION of the concept of change draws upon certain metaphors like the influences and confluences of rivers, or the swing of the clock's pendulum, or the pushing of a balance into disequilibrium, or the waxing and waning of the moon, or the assuming of a mask. For the concept of change in the language of literature in the eighteenth century I'd like to try the metaphor of fabric, a contexture in which the design fades out in some parts as it increases in others, against a background of persistence; a weaving of strands, in which a loss of one makes way for, and is perhaps pushed by, the increase of another. Does a new usage push out an old, or does it rather wait for an empty place to fit? What are the dynamics of a design in motion? There is no era more amazing for the asking of these questions than the beginning of the eighteenth century. Strands other than poetic provide a vivid context. A royal strand broken and rebegun, a theatrical strand broken and rebegun, a scientific strand begun with new enthusiasm, religious strands of new variety, a shift in coloration from French to German, a shift back (for new security?) to classical materials— a reaching out from poems like *Lycidas* and *Paradise Lost*, a searching out for new lines in the weaving of the web.

There are literal disadvantages in all metaphors; but an advantage in this one is that small quantifiable strands can be distinguished minutely and then seen in their relation to larger less isolatable, more blurred and interwoven, materials. The strand I follow here is one of changing sentence structure, the proportioning of adjectival to other materials as it vividly increases first in poetry and then in prose from early eighteenth to early nineteenth century. A pervasive sentence structure may well have both an effect and a purpose, a relation to larger cultural matters, and these we may speculate about after we have observed the details of their functioning. An increase of qualifying structures is not merely a matter of ornamentation, as many eighteenth-century and twentieth-century critics have complained it is, but is also a new sort of statement-making in terms of a new sort of statement needing to be made.

Technically, the relevant details of proportions in English poetry, and in both prose and poetry in more concentrated form, which appear in *Eras and Modes* and *Style and Proportion* can be summarized as follows: in the mid-eighteenth century a dominantly adjectival structure characterized a majority of well-known poetic texts; in the late eighteenth and early nineteenth centuries the same was true for prose. Adjectival usage increased out of all proportion to preceding or following uses. "Well-known texts" I have taken to be a seven- or eight-thousand-word section widely accepted as representative of the best of the time; "dominantly adjectival structure" I have taken to mean the use of adjectives more than verbs by 20 percent or more, with a concomitantly high proportioning of nouns and prepositional connectives. "Adjectives" I have taken to mean descriptive, numerical, and participial adjectives, not articles or demonstrative or pronomial adjectives because of the functional characteristics which set these apart.

Now to the chronology: with the chief exception of Milton, the structures of seventeenth-century poetry and prose were almost all strongly predicative, either in the curt manner of many short statements, or in the periodic manner of coordinate or subordinate clauses. But then in the early eighteenth century, with James Thomson, born in 1700, poetry picked up the cues of earlier poets Spenser, Sylvester, Milton, Blackmore, and developed, expanded, intensified its qualifying, at the expense of its predicating, structures. With Adam Smith and Edward Gibbon prose also picked up earlier cues, from the prose of Thomas Browne, for example, as well as perhaps from contemporary poetry, and expanded qualification as a structure, until by the nineteenth century the majority of prose writers, different as they were from each other, Ruskin from DeQuincey, Darwin from Carlyle, Macaulay from Pater, shared the emphasis on adjectival forms and functions, with some few exceptions like that of the adjectival participle.

We can seriously call the eighteenth century, in relation to all the other names it has been called—the century of neoclassicism, romanticism, reason, prose, enlightenment, gothicism, revolution—the century of the adjective. Is this label a triviality? Rather, I think, it suggests some of the ways in which the other names are related. Edward Surtz in his illuminating small essay on the epithets in Pope's *Messiah* shows how aware of, how worried about, how sensitive to their adjective structures were the writers and critics of the age. R. F. Jones in *The Triumph of the English Language*[1] has recorded lively instances of self-consciousness about the language: the dangers of too many English monosyllables, too many particles, thus too many connectives and connected clauses; the higher beauties of more seamless, less articulated, structures; the beauties of general truths, of qualifiable similitude; the virtues, in fine, of a Virgilian style, and the need somehow to relate these to the non-adjectival but phrasal style of sublime Isaiah or Jeremiah. The worry was that by the biblical criterion of high simplicity in, for example, the phrasing *Let there be light,* special epithets, as distinguished from participles and other descriptive forms, might well be extraneous, too ornamental; on the other hand, the classical "golden line" incorporated just such additive forms, an adjective for each of its two nouns, and treated them as essential. A difficulty was that Hebrew, in contrast to Latin, used phrasal forms rather than adjectives, *in wisdom* for *wise*; the increase of phrasal forms in the eighteenth century shows how strong was this biblical influence and how strong the need to bring the alternatives into play. Furthermore, some contrast between adjective and verb lay in the contrast between the classic *enargia*, vividness, and *energia*, momentum. The latter, advised many critics, needed verbs; the former, as in *spiry fir*, functioned to make more visible.

But the sources of debate were not all linguistic and literary. There was also a moral and social sense, as Ian Gordon shows in his *Movement of English Prose*[2] that there should be a plain economy to a gentleman's style, a spare prose, if not a spare poetry, as in the prescriptions of the Royal Society. Does this mean that prose and poetry were separating after their seventeenth-century agreements? If so, not for long. Cicero, Seneca, Tacitus provided supports to adjectival prose, though not as strong as Virgil's. But the problem for both forms was, What is spare, what is economical, in terms of what wants to be said? If an economy of words is called for, then the adjective is the sparest, unless one does not want to hear what the adjective has to say.

Perhaps here the deliberations of the Cartesian philosophers, as Noam Chomsky has recently revived them, may be reviewed. They analyze the possibilities of alternatives open to grammatical statement. One can make successive statements; or one can subordinate some statements to others; or one can reduce some statements to adjuncts, in which case their truth will be assumed rather than asserted. In the first method, every concept has its predication: *The world is visible. God is invisible. God has created the world.* The economy here is one which spares subordination; all is open, level, parallel, sequential. The second, *God, who is invisible, has created the world, which is visible.* A sparing here of periods; a creating of link-ages. Third, *Invisible God has created the visible world:* a sparing of verbs, and then of connectives also, a minimum of actual words by virtue of the power of adjectives to stand for assumed statements. It was this third economy which the eighteenth century seemed to move toward, first in poetry, then in prose; the use of qualities rather than actions to characterize; the suggestion that old assertions are now presentable as qualities.

For eighteenth-century prose, this great qualifying power was not so quickly moving as for the poetry. True, there had been Browne; but not until Gibbon and Adam Smith was there a sense of a new prose, and then tentative. The main line of prose continued on from the seventeenth century, from Hobbes, Clarendon, Milton, Dryden, and Locke to Addison, Swift, Berkeley, and Johnson—a relatively argumentative, assertive, and on-going style which suggested some sense of the future perhaps in a shift of connectives from clausal to phrasal, with a supporting increase of nouns. Eighteenth-century prose seemed clearly consolidated with seventeenth and clearly on its way to the assertive declarations of Russell, Churchill, Orwell, and others in the twentieth. Then in seemingly belated response to the language of its poetry, or in admiration of Gibbon and Smith, or, should one speculate, in response to the increasing demands of scientific objectivism, the prose of the nineteenth century, of writers as different as Macaulay, Ruskin, as Pater and Carlyle, and DeQuincey and Darwin, burst into various designs of adjectival qualities. Here is how the structure works for Darwin in "The Formation of Vegetable Mould":

> Worms have played a more important part in the history of the world than most persons would at first suppose. In almost all humid countries they are extraordinarily numerous, and for their size possess great muscular power.[3]

Qualities of degree are dominant in Darwin's thought here: *more important . . . than most persons . . . in almost all . . .*

extraordinarily numerous . . . for their size . . . great power.
The scientist's careful qualifications of context are fully evident.
If such a thought were to have been written in its basic verb
form it would proceed by fits and starts of articulation: *Worms
have played a part. The part is important. It is more important
than . . . They are numerous in countries which are humid. They
possess power. The power is muscular.* These are only some of
the root statements necessary to spell out the message in detail,
and they would halt and constrain the thought if so fully
spelled out. The adjective has become a necessary technical
form.

In many parts of England a weight of more than ten tons of dry
earth annually passes through their bodies and is brought to the
surface on each acre of land; so that the whole superficial bed of
vegetable mould passes through their bodies in the course of every
few years.[4]

Muscular, dry, whole, superficial—all central adjectives, and
supported by phrases—*through their bodies, to the surface.*
　　The earlier qualifying structure of Gibbon was not unlike
Darwin's though the tone and substance were, to say the least,
different.

　　The greatness of Rome (such is the language of the historian)
was founded on the rare and almost incredible alliance of virtue
and of fortune. The long period of her infancy was employed in a
laborious struggle against the tribes of Italy, the neighbors and
enemies of the rising city.[5]

　　Such is the language of the commenting observer, historian
or scientist, who will make progress not merely through his
observation, but especially through his comment, and so does
not stop to analyze: *The greatness was founded on the alliance.
The alliance was rare. The alliance was incredible. The period
was long. The struggle was laborious. The city was rising.*
Rather, these vital qualifications are subsumed as adjectives
under the two verbs used as vital to the progression: *was*

founded and *was employed*. So eighteenth-century meditation on the past brought it up to the present, well furnished and ready for new social contexts. "Trade is a very noble subject in itself, more proper than any for an Englishman." So Edward Young's "Imperium Pelagi," written in "Imitation of Pindar's Spirit"—and thus of the adjectival sublime—set the tone of style for Adam Smith's doctrines of trade.[6]

A century before, Thomas Browne had shown the way with a style rare for his time and, though often called poetical, almost as rare in poetry as in prose. He dealt with a soil more elegant than Darwin's yet more earthy than Gibbon's.

> Now since these dead bones have already out-lasted the living ones of Methuselah, and in a yard under ground, and thin walls of clay, outworn all the strong and specious buildings above it, and quietly rested under the drums and tramplings of three conquests: what prince can promise such diuturnity unto his reliques, or might not gladly say, *Sic ego componi versus in ossa velim?*[7]

The qualities *dead, living, thin, strong* play their variations over the new essential time-setting verbs, *have outlasted, worn, rested*. With them, Browne gives substance of actuality, by generous specification of quality, to an observation taken to be factual and informative beneath its interpretings and in its sensitivity to degree.

> Our days become considerable, like petty sums, by minute accumulations; here numerous fractions make up but small round numbers; and our days of a span long, make not one little finger.[8]

These were the discriminations which developed slowly from Browne, to Gibbon and Adam Smith, and then to the detail of nineteenth-century prose perception. They were the discriminations too of characteristic eighteenth-century poetry. But it took a while for them to develop through other stronger forces in eighteenth-century prose, chief of which was the more articulated subordinate clausal structure which Bacon and

Hobbes and Milton and Burke continued to share, different as they were, because of their shared interest in argument.

When at the beginning of the *Areopagitica* Milton explicitly "supposes," then he writes as adjectivally as Browne.

> They, who to states and governors of the Commonwealth direct their speech, High Court of Parliament, or, wanting such access in a private condition, write that which they foresee may advance the public good; I suppose them, as at the beginning of no mean endeavor, not a little altered and moved inwardly in their minds:

But then, in the next paragraph, the action of argument:

> For this is not the liberty which we can hope, that no grievance ever should arise in the Commonwealth—that let no man in this world expect; but when complaints are freely heard, deeply considered and speedily reformed, then is the utmost bound of civil liberty attained that wise men look for.

When it appears, the label *wise* has been prepared for by a whole sequence of negative and positive verbs, a situation established not by qualities but by actions.

> For he who freely magnifies what hath been nobly done, and fears not to declare as freely what might be done better, gives ye the best covenant of his fidelity; and that his loyalist affection and his hope waits on your proceedings.[9]

The adjectives of *best covenant* and *loyalist affection* are guarded in explicit verbs in clauses: *He who freely magnifies . . . and fears not . . . gives.*

The lighter style of Addison, in its mockery of the logic of historical reference keeps this active tone.

> We are told that the Spartans, tho' they punish'd theft in their young men, when it was discovered, looked upon it as honourable if it succeeded. Provided the conveyance was clean and unsuspected, a youth might afterwards boast of it.[10]

Leading to *honorable* is the clausal complexity of *We are told . . . that though they punished yet looked upon . . . when it was discovered . . . if it succeeded.* Quality was the structural outcome of action.

For some seventeenth-century prose writers qualities were even more reliant upon predicative structures—for Bunyan exceptionally, and for Dryden with a certain modernist distinction.

A heroic poem, truly such, is undoubtedly the greatest work which the soul of man is capable to perform. The design of it is to form the mind to heroic virtue by example; 'tis conveyed in verse, that it may delight, while it instructs.[11]

Assertion: precise, direct assertion. As Hazlitt would say at the end of the century, "It is not easy to write a familiar style . . . To write a genuine familiar or truly English style, is to write as anyone would speak in common conversation, who had a thorough command and choice of words, or could discourse with ease, force, and perspicuity, setting aside all pedantical and oratorical flourishes."[12]

This setting aside of a style opposed to his, an objective and unfamiliar style cumulatively developed from the eighteenth-century's poetry and prose, was not wholly fair because not wholly understanding of new purposes. Even the major vocabulary, the terms used most in both poetic and prosaic texts of his time, shows how unoratorical was the new need for the adjectival style. The need was to increase the terminology of observed qualities. As verbs decreased, they changed too, from words like *know* to words like *feel,* from words of construction and interaction to words suitable within scenes like *rise, stand.* Nouns like *scene* itself increased, at the expense of terms of concept like *soul, time, world.* The new *nothing* countered the old *thing.* New nouns of sense for poetry like *land* and *mountain,* for prose *country* and *color,* and in addition the new social concepts of *power, occasion, opinion, association, principle, government.* The adjectives to go with these—*sad* and *soft* and *wild* for poetry, *certain, different, same* for prose.

Above all, a sharing of rejection of conceptual terms like *good* and *true*, along with a continued sharing of the major terms of *man* and *love* and *heart*, *seeing* in *day* and *night*. So subject matters strengthened scene and society in general views, adjectives came to discriminate qualities in likeness and difference: Gibbon's *rising city*, Darwin's *almost all humid countries* and *extraordinarily numerous worms*.

To speculate upon purposes in these patterns leads us to a number of concerns. One of those was, as the vocabulary and structure have suggested, for similarity. About this value, and its newness of import, Wordsworth was very explicit:

And where lies the real difficulty of creating that taste by which a truly original poet is to be relished? Is it in breaking the bonds of custom? . . does it consist in divesting the reader of the pride that induces him to dwell upon those points wherein men differ from each other, to the exclusion of those in which all men are alike, or the same? [13]

For the Preface of 1815, the powers of the Imagination are "the conferring, the abstracting, and the modifying powers." The adjective rests upon the values of shareable and extendable likeness. Again, the adjective fosters response as prior to action. As Wordsworth's Preface proposed in 1800, "Another circumstance must be mentioned which distinguishes these poems from the popular poetry of the day: it is this, that the feeling therein developed gives importance to the action and situation, and not the action and situation to the feeling."[14] This proposal, amplified in 1805, that the values of Aristotle be reversed, had earlier shape in Davenant's theory expressed in his correspondence with Hobbes:[15] ". . . wise Poets think it more worthy to seek out truth in the Passions than to record the truth of Actions . . . it being abler to contemplate the general History of Nature, than a selected Diary of Fortune." In similar tone, Wordsworth in a late letter[16] wrote, "I have endeavored to dwell with truth upon those points of human nature in which all men resemble each other rather than in those accidents of manners and character produced by time and circumstances." Poetically *The Borderers* said it in Act III:[17] Action is transitory —a step—a blow / The motion of a muscle—this way or that— / . . . suffering is permanent . . ."

Such belief, persistent through the eighteenth century, seems a good clue to the grammar of literature in the century. If truths exist most deeply in similarities, because the similar joins and generalizes while a difference separates and isolates, then similes are truer than metaphors, and adjectives of lasting quality are more valuable than the transitory verbs of "a step —a blow." No matter, the loss of Aristotle's meaning, that action is crucial decision, the choice which tests and reveals the quality in character; for the eighteenth century, the concomitant gain was great: the sense of steady, static, pervasive universal generalities which did not need to be asserted, as by verbs, but which were indeed beyond the limits of particular human assertion and thus best accepted or assumed, as by adjectives.

In addition to the changing preference, for assumption from assertion, for general similitude from differences, and for the truths of passion from the truths of action, a fourth eighteenth-century preference which fits with the other three is that for spatial in contrast to temporal values. The eighteenth century was distinctively a spatial century, as we have seen in its changing verbs, the abandoning of temporal actions in favor of actions at least spatial, at most no actions or tenses at all, but a transformation to participles or epithets. The Cartesian commonplace, according to Stephen Toulmin's and June Goodfield's *Discovery of Time*,[18] was "a static and unhistorical system of natural philosophy, in which fixed species of living creatures and solid unbreakable atoms alike conformed to the unchanging laws and specifications appropriate to their various kinds." It was only at the turn of the century,[19] only along with such returning predicates as the *Ancient Mariner's*, that the geologists could register how

the sound which to the ear of the Student of Nature seems continually echoed in every part of her works, is—
Time!—Time!—Time!

There are visible then, even as far away as the *massif central*, signs external to the literary pattern, yet with evident relevance to it. Not only were eighteenth-century poets tired of old dominating logics and over-successful metaphors and verbal turns and subordinations; not only did eighteenth-century prose writers admire and slowly follow their moves toward a newly observational and responsive vocabulary and syntax, but also poets and prosaists seemed to move in accord with forces outside of yet pervasive in literature: beliefs strengthening spatial views, static views, generalizing and similitudinizing views, emotional and sensory views, accepting rather than asserting views, qualities rather than the truths of temporal propositions.

In populous cities, which are the seat of commerce and manufactures, the middle ranks of inhabitants, who derive their subsistence from the dexterity or labor of their hands, are commonly the most prolific, the most useful, and, in that sense, the most respectable part of the community.[20]

So Gibbon on the greatness of Rome.

How cold is all history, how lifeless all imagery, compared to that which the living nation writes, and the uncorrupted marble bears! —how many pages of doubtful record might we not often spare, for a few stones left one upon another![21]

So Ruskin on the lamp of memory. The adjectives of this prose embed in this syntax the slowly achieved and vividly expressed values of a general and accepting humanity in the eighteenth century, and record in one traceable structure of language the consolidation of a structure of belief.

NOTES TO CHAPTER 7

1. Stanford, Calif.: Stanford University Press, 1951.
2. Bloomington, Indiana: Indiana University Press, 1966.
3. Charles Darwin, from *The Formation of Vegetable Mould, Through the Action of Worms, with Observations of Their Habits*, 1881. In *Classic Essays in English*, ed. Josephine Miles. 2d ed. (Boston: Little, Brown and Co., 1965), p. 224.
4. Ibid.
5. Edward Gibbon, from *The Decline and Fall of the Roman Empire*, 1781. In *Classic Essays*, p. 162.
6. See John Holloway, *Widening Horizons in English Verse* (Evanston: Northwestern University Press, 1967).
7. Thomas Browne, "Conclusion," *Hydriotaphia, or Urn-Burial*, 1658. In *Classic Essays*, p. 57.
8. Ibid., p. 58.
9. John Milton, *Areopagitica*, 1644. In *John Milton, Complete Poems and Major Prose*, ed. Merritt Y. Hughes (New York: Odyssey Press, 1957), pp. 717, 718.
10. Joseph Addison, *The Spectator*, Tuesday, February 19, 1712.
11. John Dryden, Dedication of *The Aeneis*, 1697.
12. William Hazlitt, "On Familiar Style," from *Table Talk*, 1821–1822.
13. William Wordsworth, *Essay Supplementary to the Preface of 1815*.
14. William Wordsworth, Preface to the *Lyrical Ballads*, 1800.
15. William Davenant, Preface to *Gondibert*, 1651.
16. William Wordsworth, *Later Years*, p. 27.
17. William Wordsworth, *The Borderers; A Tragedy* written 1795–96, first published 1842.
18. New York: Harper & Row, 1965, p. 101.
19. Ibid., p. 170.
20. Gibbon, in *Classic Essays*, p. 168.
21. John Ruskin, from *Seven Lamps of Architecture*, 1849.

✏ 8. Victorian Reality

WHEN AT the beginning of the twentieth century Ezra Pound in his imagist manifestos declared war on adjectives in poetry and even in prose, he seemed to many, in dim memory, to be challenging the drab general subjective in favor of the bright specific objective; to be rejecting sentiment in favor of sense. We thought this was all to the good and tut-tutted Victorian vagueness and preciosity of feeling, now fortunately left behind for the sake of new accuracies and precisions. I. A. Richards and John Dewey, different as were their philosophical perspectives, agreed that the power of literature was the power to point, denote, evoke the thing in itself.

But it was very hard to tell what was the thing itself. How get at it? By naming? by describing? by relating to responses—then no longer "in itself"? The urgencies of Hemingway, Santayana, Stevens, Williams, different as they now seem to us, all shared at that time the feeling of rediscovery of new values in objectivity, though ways toward it were not always clear.

> A poem should be palpable
> and mute
> As a globed fruit. . . .
> for all the history of grief
> An empty doorway and a maple leaf.

How many times still we hear and accept these lines of MacLeish:

> A poem should not mean,
> But be.

Yet if we look back to the Victorian art against which we seemed to be rebelling, we may find it in some ways almost opposite to what we remember—we who liked T. S. Eliot felt a sense of false poetics in what we thought to be the embroidered overloading of a Swinburne—yet we failed to recognize the same sort of richness functioning in the notebooks of a young scientist like Darwin in the *Voyage of the Beagle*, or in the minutely careful and "objective" observations of a field naturalist like Julian Huxley. These men were striving for the very objectivity we thought they lacked, and they used a style we thought long outmoded in poetry.

Darwin's *Journal* of his voyage on the *Beagle* begins as follows:

> After having been twice driven back by heavy south-western gales, Her Magesty's ship *Beagle*, a ten-gun brig, under the command of Captain Fitz Roy, R.N., sailed from Devonport on the 27th of December 1831. . . .
>
> The neighbourhood of Porto Praya, viewed from the sea, wears a desolate aspect. The volcanic fires of a past age, and the scorching heat of a tropical sun, have in most places rendered the soil unfit for vegetation. The country rises in successive steps of table-land, interspersed with some truncate conical hills, and the horizon is bounded by an irregular chain of more lofty mountains. The scene, as beheld through the hazy atmosphere of this climate, is one of great interest; if, indeed, a person, fresh from the sea, and who has just walked, for the first time in a grove of cocoa-nut trees, can be a judge of anything but his own happiness.

After a few paragraphs:

> . . . When the line has been caught up by the scoriaceous fragments of the lower surface of the stream, it is converted into groups of beautifully radiated fibers resembling arragonite.[1]

On the Origin of Species begins:

When we look to the individuals of the same variety or sub-variety of our older cultivated plants and animals, one of the first points which strikes us, is, that they generally differ much more from each other, than do the individuals of any one species or variety in a state of nature. . . . It seems pretty clear that organic beings must be exposed during several generations to the new conditions of life to cause any appreciable amount of variation; and that when the organization has once begun to vary, it generally continues to vary for many generations.[2]

Of this prose Albert Guérard, Jr., writes: "The scientist Charles Darwin, may be considered a master of forth-right, efficient, wholly unpretentious prose. His *Voyage of the Beagle* is the account of a famous surveying expedition made in 1831–1836. Darwin was a man intensely interested in everything he saw, and one who was not afraid to react to it. Here we detect no screen of words between the man and his experience, no tendency to embellishment or verbal display. This is plain 'unliterary' prose of the highest efficiency."[3]

Yet this is the very adjectival style held to be overpoetic by Pound and his followers. Note the imagery of Huxley's scientific generalizations also:

It is a surprise to find a frog that weighs as much as a fox terrier. It is a still greater surprise to know that there exist fully formed adult insects—a beetle or two, and several parisitoid wasplike creatures—of smaller bulk than the human ovum and yet with compound eyes, a nice nervous system, three pairs of jaws and three pairs of legs, veined wings, striped muscles, and the rest! It is rather unexpected that the smallest adult vertebrate is not a fish, but a frog; and it is most unexpected to find that the largest elephant would have an ample clearance top and bottom inside a large whale's skin, while a full-sized horse outlined on the same whale would look hardly larger than a crest embroidered on the breast pocket of a blazer.[4]

Harry Levin's description of Hemingway's "plain" style is clear about the grammatical contrasts:

If we regard the adjective as a luxury, decorative more often than functional, we can well understand why Hemingway doesn't cultivate it. But, assuming that the sentence derives its energy from the verb, we are in for a shock if we expect his verbs to be numerous or varied or emphatic. His usage supports C. K. Ogden's argument that verb-forms are disappearing from English grammar. Without much self-deprivation, Hemingway could get along on the so-called "operators" of Basic English, the sixteen monosyllabic verbs that stem from movements of the body. The substantive verb *to be* is predominant, characteristically introduced by an expletive. Thus the first story of *In Our Time* begins, and the last one ends, with the story-teller's gambit: "there was," "there were." In the first two pages of *A Farewell to Arms* nearly every other sentence is of this type, and the third page employs the awkward construction "there being." There is—I find the habit contagious—a tendency to immobilize verbs by transposing them into gerunds. Instead of writing *they fought* or *we did not feel*, Hemingway writes "there was fighting" and "there was not the feeling of a storm coming." The subject does little more than point impersonally at its predicate; an object, a situation, an emotion. Yet the idiom, like the French *il y a*, is ambiguous; inversion can turn the gesture of pointing into a physical act; and the indefinite adverb can indicate, if not specify, a definite place. Contrast, with the opening of *A Farewell to Arms*, that of "In Another Country": "In the fall the war was always there, but we did not go to it any more." The negative is even more striking, when Frederic Henry has registered the sensations of his wound, and dares to look at it for the first time, and notes: "My knee wasn't there." The adverb is *there* rather than *here*, the verb is *was* rather than *is*, because we—the readers—are separated from the event in space and time. But the narrator has lived through it, like the Ancient Mariner, and now he chooses his words to grip and transfix us. *Lo!* he says. *Look! I was there.*[5]

Perhaps some clarification of style's relation to subject and purpose will help us understand the shift. Why should Pound be averse specifically to adjectives? Why should there seem to be a direct relation between a value and a part of speech?

After you feel at home with making sentences and changing them around in many basic ways, you can begin to see that all the other words in a larger sentence, longer than subject-verb-object, are extras, or adjuncts, which tell more about the time, place, or manner of what is going on. For example: "In the morning the grey cat climbs the tree and yowls loudly to the neighbors." The first extra information here is *when*: in the morning, in the present tense. The second is the adjective *grey*, the third is *to the neighbors*. The basic sentence is: "The cat climbs the tree and yowls." The extra materials are *phrases*, begun by prepositions; they are word groups acting like words. The single words *grey* and *loudly* are also added; that they are called *ad*jectives and *ad*verbs shows the idea of adding. Even clauses, groups having verbs, can be treated like single added words, as in "The cat, which is grey like smoke, climbs the tree and yowls loudly to the neighbors, who cannot see where he is."

A sentence states a situation, makes a connection, and so is like a little play. You could choose parts and act it out. The *subject* can be surrounded with his or her adjuncts (adjectives and phrases and clauses), and the *object* with his; and then the *verb*, with his, can bring them together into an act or relation within a scene.

A paragraph is like a fuller statement, a larger sentence. When the adjuncts get too many and heavy and important, they become sentences of their own, and then they still cluster around their chief, or topic, sentence. For example:

"It is morning. The cat is as grey as smoke and as quiet. He knows he will not be seen. He climbs the tree; when he has reached a sheltered spot, he crouches down and begins to yowl loudly. At whom is he yowling so loudly? Probably he is looking at the neighbors."

Notice that each new sentence gets some new adjuncts, and that each of these sentences could be expanded to a paragraph too. The kernel of a paragraph is one sentence; the context of a kernel sentence is a paragraph, its adjunctive sentences. In further expansion, certain paragraphs may be adjunctive to kernel paragraphs, chapters to kernel chapters. These adjunctive relations may also be stated in the old terms of case.

As Charles Fillmore says in "The Case for Case":

The sentence in its basic structure consists of a verb and one or more noun phrases each associated with the verb in a particular case relationship. . . . The case notions comprise a set of universal, presumably innate, concepts which identify certain types of judgments human beings are capable of making about the events that are going on around them, judgments about such matters as who did it, who it happened to, and what got changed.[6]

Paragraphs expand some or all of the units of relation. Writing endeavors to provide situations for its statements; it wants to locate its predication in time, place, manner, consequence; it wants to provide a *where, when, how, why*, for its *who does what*. In speaking, much of this work can be done by gesture. In writing, it needs to be spelled out, perhaps as minimally as by an -s-z signal of person in time: *he plays*; or by the demonstrative contrast between *this* and *that*, or by the specific-general contrast of *the-a*, or by the character-manner contrast of *ish-ly*; perhaps, on the other hand, as maximally as by a two-volume novel's contrasting episodes of *boy meets girl*: (1) by accident, in the jungle; (2) on purpose, three years later, in the desert.

Between these extremes of syllable and volume come sentence and paragraph. The name of the latter emphasizes its written nature. As spoken, it seems an anomaly, because of its relative lack of mnemonic device for so great a length; yet it does flourish in oratory as written to be spoken, and its writer may well be cognizant, therefore, of listening ear as well as reading eye. What is its relation to the sentence? A paragraph is a group of sentences; but what sort of group? Any sort of group. How then a group? By reason of, as we have already suggested, such pertinent concerns as the *when, where, how, why* of assertion. Just as qualifiers, phrases, and clauses are outriders upon a sentence-nucleus, so qualifying, phrasal, and clausal paragraphs are outriders upon nucleus-paragraphs.

The sentence may read: "Carefully he drove to town" or, more generally, "These plans need to be followed carefully." The paragraph, as Francis Christenson has shown, may begin with a number of sentences conveying in greater extension the idea of "carefully," and then a number of sentences conveying the action of driving to town or following plans. Even more fully, as the one sentence is derivable from two, so the one paragraph may be derivable from two, the first on care, the second on driving. So there may even be various sorts of care, with a paragraph to each; and various stages of driving, or following, each with its own paragraph.

In other words, paragraphs, like words and like sentences, may try to be portmanteau, carrying the event and the fullness of its situation all in one unit; or may try to work step by step, devoting one or more wholes to each of the concerns of *when* and *where*, *why* and *how*.

The conclusion that "to insist that logic establish every indentation is to ignore several of the prime resources of good prose" perhaps overstresses logic as the art of syllogism. Logic takes into account conjunction, disjunction, alternatives, implication, concession, and all such relating of possibilities; that such a relation as "He was careful; he drove to town" is not in focus for logic does not mean that it is illogical. The qualifying outriders of assertion, in that they are assumed rather than asserted, do not challenge logic, but work within its realm. *Mortal* Socrates has other fish to fry than the assertion of his mortality; therefore a well-turned paragraph or two on his mortal qualities may well precede that paragraph which asserts some other activity of his.

One reason I think it important to recognize the nucleus-plus-adjuncts quality of paragraph, as of sentence, is that the explicit connective terminology of sentences plays across and beyond the mere sentence unit. The "when-when-when-then" structure of a Shakespearean sonnet is equally suited to paragraph or whole essay as to single sentence. The traditional proportion of connectives to verbs in English prose is about two to one, which means either that a predication is supported by two prepositional phrases, "He drives to town with care," or that independent as well as dependent verbs are linked by explicit connectives. That is, even the independent predicate-nucleus can be seen to be introduced by capitalized *Nevertheless, However, But, Then, Or, On the other hand, Therefore.* The indentations of paragraphs may stand for semicolons as well as periods, semistops as well as full stops.

To consider purpose in writing is to remember that not all purpose is to assert-question-exclaim; much is to locate in context, to qualify by assumption, in word, in phrase, in clause, as in sentence, so in paragraph.

The focus of such expanding structure of prose is in the Victorian period: from DeQuincey to Carlyle to Macaulay to Darwin, Ruskin, Arnold, Pater, and then to Julian Huxley, with the support of poets like Keats, Tennyson, Swinburne, Whitman. The great poetic period for descriptive observation had been the eighteenth century of Thomson, Gray, Collins, Cowper, with a mere beginning for prose in the work of Gibbon and Adam Smith. Now in the forty years of mid-century, from 1830 to 1870, powerful new motives for prose in fidelity to quality and to objectivity took over style. Many of the conscious rhetoricians, from Blair to Churchill, Connolly, and Orwell praised a clausic balance between curt and full, but even as they argued for what Orwell called an "aura of plausibility," they were arguing more than they realized for an abundance of observing and assuming of generalizing spatial adjectives. As Ruskin said, don't discuss, describe. The result for these writers was a prose passage with a characteristic introductory setting, an aloofly objective passive voice, a nominalization of verbs and actions into substances.

So Pater praised his early precursor Sir Thomas Browne

partly as a poet but mostly as a scientist: "As with Buffon, his full, ardent, sympathetic vocabulary, the poetry of his language, a poetry inherent in its elementary particles—the word, the epithet—helps to keep his eye, and the eye of the reader, on the subject before it, and conduce directly to the purpose of the naturalist, the observer."[7] Note that in the grammar of Pater not the connective but the epithet is termed the elementary particle.

If we hear a list of Darwin's chief epithets, we may see how he combines tradition with new interests in the contrast and comparison for which discerned qualities are necessary: his *black, certain, common, different, direct, distinct, domestic due, good, great, large, like, little, long, same, slight, such, white, whole, wild* support main nouns of nature and structure like *animal, bird, character, condition, country, degree, effect, feather, form, individual, law, man, nature, plant, sheep, structure, variety, view, wing* and verbs of observing like *appear, become, believe, compare, descend, differ, vary* as well as traditional *find, give, keep, know, see, seem, show, think.* Huxley, two generations later, confirms these interests with *animal, early, great, high, human, large, some, social, such, unique, action, difference, process, period, species, appear, become, develop, evolve, reach.* Both share with most of their contemporaries certain new basic contrasts of human with animal, part with whole, large with small, same with difference, social with individual; and a basic predication of process: *become, believe, develop, differ, change, vary.*

Coming back to the mid-twentieth century, we may wonder where the process will lead from here. To some degree it would seem that knowledge of past developments should give us some sense of future possibilities. Misunderstanding as we have been of our Victorian ancestors, blaming them for a màndarinism, a false poeticism, quite alien to that objective accuracy for which they were striving, we may try to guess from our own usages where our values are now taking us. It seems that we are turning away from comparison and contrast on qualitative bases toward the synapses of juxtaposition, Charles Olson's sparks of energy jumping across chasms of disrelation.

A few years ago a friend in Psychology, Benbow Ritchie, suggested that, inasmuch as the chief words of poetry and prose appear in but do not exhaust the Thorndike-Lange lists of most-used words, we might expect to find latent in the words not yet literary a potential for signs of new and next powers in value. So as I read him the words not yet enlisted in the ranks of major terms in mid-century, he suggested the potent possibilities; such new fields of stress as inquiry in *answer, ask, question, reach, suppose, wonder*; of construction in *build, city, corner, door, floor, glass, ice, iron, road, room, street, window*; of further quantification and discrimination as *add, figure, increase, large, least, low, mean, mile, north, week, morning, rock, roll, cool, warm, measure*, such contrasts as part to *whole*, individual to *public* and *social* and *system*. In other words, a rich extension of the Victorian vocabulary into confirming present values. And these are indeed, we find, some of the chief terms of the very young writers today. The curious mixture of nature with construction, of fields with houses, we see in Hundertwasser's note for a painting: "We should be glad when rust settles on a razor blade, when a wall grows mouldy, or when moss grows over the geometric angles of a corner, because, together with microbes and mushrooms, life thus moves into a house."

Object and subject move upon each other, and sentence structure changes again to fit and form. What we may learn from the grammar of the Victorians is the linguistic resource expressive of faithful scientific observation, fidelity, as Pater says, to what is *true*, and thus assumable; not arguable in the classic rational subordinative way of a Bertrand Russell, not lived on the nerves in the curt style of a D. H. Lawrence, not with the extended sensibility of a Hemingway, but with the

exuberant absorption of a Dickens or a Faulkner, a taking on
of the world in the shape of its modifying qualities.

NOTES TO CHAPTER 8

1. Charles Darwin, *Journal of Researches into the Natural History and
   Geology of the Countries Visited During the Voyage of H.M.S. Beagle
   Round the World*. New ed. (New York: D. Appleton & Co., 1871),
   pp. 1–2, 6.
2. *On the Origin of Species*. A Facsimile of the First Edition (Cambridge:
   Harvard University Press, 1964), p. 7.
3. Albert Guérard, ed., et al. *The Personal Voice* (Philadelphia: Lippin-
   cott, 1964), p. 3.
4. Julian Huxley, *Man in the Modern World* (London: Chatto & Windus, 1950), pp. 74–75.
5. Harry Levin, "Observations on the Style of Ernest Hemingway,"
   in *Contexts of Criticism* (Cambridge: Harvard University Press, 1958),
   pp. 157–158.
6. In *Universals in Linguistic Theory*, ed. Emmon Bock, Robert T. Harris
   (Holt, Rinehart and Winston, 1968), pp. 21, 24.
7. Walter Pater, *Appreciations* (London, 1901), p. 145.

❧ 9. Robinson and the Years Ahead

THE TITLE of Edwin Arlington Robinson's early book, *The Children of the Night*, suggests its place in romantic tradition and its participation in the poetics of the 1890s, the poetics of starlight, dream, and death. The first poem begins:

> "Where are you going to-night, to-night,—
>   Where are you going, John Evereldown?
> There's never the sign of a star in sight,
>   Nor a lamp that's nearer than Tilbury Town.
> Why do you stare as a dead man might?
> Where are you pointing away from the light?
> And where are you going to-night, to-night,—
>   Where are you going, John Evereldown?"[1]

Much of his poetry is in these lines—the strong formal use of repetition, the tone of conversation, the ballad-like mysteries and assumptions, the language of dreary atmosphere. Robinson's contemporaries in British poetry were Swinburne, Hardy, Housman, Wilde, Yeats; after Dickinson, in American, Sill, Lanier, Guiney, Moody, Sterling, Frost. He is clearly of their number in the tradition of major vocabulary of *good, god, man, time, world, make, see,* and in the romanticisms from the earlier world of Coleridge which supply at least a third of his chief substance.

It was Coleridge above all who turned away from the acceptances of the eighteenth century, away from these even in his own poetry, toward a new implicativeness of inner searching. Often when such a turn is made, it is made in terms of a familiar old antique material. As the young Chatterton purportedly experimented in the recovering of old styles and seemed new in his uses, which were actually close to the classical narrations of his predecessor Waller, so Robinson was taken as notably new for his day, while he retold again the Arthurian stories which Tennyson had told before. As Coleridge's monody recalled,

> And we, at sober eve, would round thee throng,
> Hanging, enraptured, on thy stately song;
> And greet with smiles the young-eyed *Poesy*
> All deftly masked, as hoar *Antiquity*.

The young-eyed poesy was the poesy of noble narrative for Chatterton. Whether ballad-like or satiric, it was commonly martial, and it dealt with great virtues and passions.

> O Chryste, it is a grief for me to telle,
> How manie a nobil erle and valrous knyghte
> In fyghtynge for Kynge Harrold noblie fell,
> Al sleyne in Hastyngs feeld in bloudie fyghte,
> O sea! our teeming donore han thy floude,
> Han anie fructous entendement,
> Thou wouldst have rose and sank wyth tydes of bloude,
> Before Duke Wyllam's knyghts han hither went;
> > Whose cowart arrows manie erles sleyne,
> > And brued the feeld wyth bloude as season rayne.

> And of his knyghtes did eke full manie die,
> All passyng hie, of mickle myghte echone,
> Whose poygnant arrowes, typp'd with destynie,

Caus'd manie wydowes to make myckle mone.
Lordynges, avaunt, that chycken-harted are,
From out of hearynge quicklie now departe;
Full well I wote, to synge of bloudie warre
Will greeve your tenderlie and mayden harte.
　　Go, do the weaklie womman inn mann's geare,
　　And scond your mansion if grymm war come there.

This beginning of his "Battle of Hastings," characteristic
of his work as a whole, takes the view of a narrator; he *tells*,
he *sings*, of those heroes who *rise, stand, seek, fly, fall, die*.
The persons are *kings, knights, earls*, classical *friends*, and, as
in the ballads, *fathers* and *sons*; the scene is *ground* and *plain*,
the tools are *spears* and *arrows*, thus antique; the results,
wounds, blood, woe. For all these, the chief value terms are
in keeping, the relatively rare *bloody, brave, dead*, the rarer
mickle, and then the neoclassical *good, great, high, noble,
sweet* of Edmund Waller exactly, and in part of Denham, Joseph
Warton, Creech, Fairfax, that is, of the classical narrative tradition in English.

The Wartons and others who argued the dating of the
Rowley poems recognized "in point of style, composition, and
sentiment" the very traits which this vocabulary represents:
the ideal and abstract terms, compound epithets, smoothness
of meter, "all that elegance, firmness of contexture, strength
and brilliancy, which did not appear in our poetry before the
middle of the present century."[2] True, the central neoclassical
mode; but its early name was Waller; it was held in check,
away from the Gothic sublime extremes of the Wartons, by the
pull of the narrative, even the ballad narrative, tradition.

Percy's *Ballads* were not folk ballads in structure, because
they smoothed the lines to a classical norm, filled in with adjectives and sentiments, and generally did to "Chevy Chase"
what Pope did to Donne, or what her family did to Emily Dickinson: tidied up the implications and made both beat and sentiment regularly explicit. Given the steadiness of frame and

feeling, the eighteenth-century "firmness of contexture," Chatterton was able to work in the opposite direction, to irregularize intermittently, by means of a lively action and a mixed vocabulary, the smooth neoclassic conventions of narrative in his time. In Waller, the pose of this tradition, the first of "Love's Farewell,"

> Treading the path to noble ends,
> A long farewell to love I gave,
> Resolved my country, and my friends,
> All that remain'd of me should have.

Like Waller, Chatterton explored a variety, straight and satiric narrative, pastoral, a kind of ballad tradition; the very curious mixture of conventions which we see in his vocabulary provided a neoclassic basis for romance. "He fell in love," his mother said, "with the illuminated capitals of an old musical manuscript in French."[3] The mickel illuminations of antiquity, of romance, graced Chatterton's text on its surface and in its spirit of Miniver Cheevy with which Robinson sympathized.

Those most conscious of moving ahead are most deeply involved in the past. As Chatterton cast an atmosphere forward, so did Robinson. Robinson shared his atmosphere with a few poetic allies and set his name upon it for the future. His especially are the adjectives of *desolate, human, lonely, lost, sad,* the nouns of *faith, flame, gleam, glory, shame, truth, thought, touch, hell, music, song, woman, wisdom, wall;* the verbs of *call* and *feel,* the chief connectives characteristically few except for the relative *that.* The atmosphere, the yearning, the generalizing of human values in inner hope and shame:

> Go to the western gate, Luke Havergal,
> There where the vines cling crimson on the wall,
> . . . But go, and if you listen she will call.
> No, there is not a dawn in eastern skies
> To rift the fiery night that's in your eyes;
> . . . God slays Himself with every leaf that flies,

And hell is more than half of paradise.
. . . Nor think to riddle the dead words they say,
Nor any more to feel them as they fall; . . .

So the lines of every poem are loaded and reloaded with the
terms of value. From "Three Quatrains," for example, the music, with abstraction: "As long as Fame's imperious music
rings. . . ." From "Dear Friends" too:

> . . . So, friends (dear friends), remember, if you will,
> The shame I win for singing is all mine,
> The gold I miss for dreaming is all yours.

From "The Story of the Ashes and the Flame," the emotional
strains of "The story was as old as human shame, . . ." From
"Zola":

> Because he puts the compromising chart
> Of hell before your eyes, you are afraid; . . .
> Never until we conquer the uncouth
> Connivings of our shamed indifference
> (We call it Christian faith) are we to scan
> The racked and shrieking hideousness of Truth. . . .

From "The Pity of the Leaves": "Loud with ancestral shame
there came the bleak / Sad wind. . . ." From "Cliff Klingen-
hagen": "And when I asked him . . . he only looked at me /
And smiled, . . ." The whole thought of "The Dead Village"
and of "Credo"—the ghost of things—and, from "Verlaine,"
"Song sloughs away the sin to find redress / In art's complete
remembrance: . . ." From "Supremacy," the measures of
"There is a drear and lonely tract of hell." And the full array
of "Octaves":

> We thrill too strangely at the master's touch;
> We shrink too sadly from the larger self . . .
> We dare not feel it yet—the splendid shame
> Of uncreated failure; we forget,

The while we groan, that God's accomplishment
Is always and unfailingly at hand.

And:

With conscious eyes not yet sincere enough
To pierce the glimmered cloud that fluctuates
Between me and the glorifying light
That screens itself with knowledge, I discern
The searching rays of wisdom that reach through
The mist of shame's infirm credulity,
And infinitely wonder if hard words
Like mine have any message for the dead.

And "L'Envoi":

Now in a thought, now in a shadowed word,
Now in a voice that thrills eternity,
Ever there comes an onward phrase to me
Of some transcendent music I have heard;
No piteous thing by soft hands dulcimered,
No trumpet crash of blood-sick victory,
But a glad strain of some vast harmony
That no brief mortal touch has ever stirred.
There is no music in the world like this,
No character wherewith to set it down,
No kind of instrument to make it sing.
No kind of instrument? Ah, yes, there is;
And after time and place are overthrown,
God's touch will keep its one chord quivering.

These are the poems of the nineties, of Robinson's first
work. Thirty years later, in *Avon's Harvest* and other poems,
and in his most famous *Tristram*, in culmination of the Arthur
sequence, the same characteristic phrasings prevail.

Fear, like a living fire that only death
Might one day cool, had now in Avon's eyes
Been witness . . .

> He smiled, but I would rather he had not. . . .
> I was awake for hours,
> Toiling in vain to let myself believe
> That Avon's apparition was a dream, . . .

Steadily the insistence is on the mystery, interiority, often horror, sometimes majesty, of human feelings scarcely formulable —the "old human swamps" of Avon, the phantom sound of Roland's horn for Mr. Flood—the vividly implicative narrative turning inward so characteristic of the English nineteenth century in Coleridge, Browning, Yeats. "Modernities" is a fine and explicitly commentary example in concentration. "Tristram" takes up the same ground in a more leisurely way: *Isolt of the white hands . . . white birds . . . remembered . . . her father . . . smiling in the way she feared . . . Throbbing as if she were a child . . . For making always of a distant wish / A dim belief . . . How many scarred cold things that once had laughed . . . a cold soul-retching wave . . . And body and soul were quick to think of it . . . Smiling as one who suffers to escape / Through silence and familiar misery, . . . Lost in a gulf of time where time was lost—and at the end—He smiled like one with nothing else to do; . . . It was like that / For women sometimes, . . . Alone, with her white face and her gray eyes, / She watched them there till even her thoughts were white, . . . And the white sunlight flashing on the sea.*

The terms in which the later poems differ from the earlier are mostly terms required by the content: for example, the *father, king,* and *queen, forget, remember,* and *wait* of Isolt's life in the Tristram story. Some of the differences are, however, more significant of attitude. Later *sick* takes the place of earlier *dead; sensory cold* and *white,* the place of more commentary *desolate, lonely, sad.* Similarly, objective nouns *bird, fire, moon, shadow* take the place of more commentary *gleam, glory, faith, shame.* The musical references fade. The ironies of *laugh* and *smile* are heightened. In other words, objectivities do more of the work in the later verse; it is the same work, cooled.

We saw that fire at work within his eyes
And had no glimpse of what was burning there. . . .
. . . and there was now
No laughing in that house. . . .
. . . without the sickening weight of added years.
. . . a made smile of acquiescence, . . .
. . . he who sickens . . . over the fire of sacrifice . . .
He smiled, but I would rather he had not.

These lines and many more in their vein from *Avon*; and, from
"Rembrandt," "shadows and obscurities":

"Touching the cold offense of my decline,"
. . . like sick fruit . . . our stricken souls . . .
Your soul may laugh . . . or grinning evil
In a golden shadow . . .
Forget your darkness in the dark, and hear
No longer the cold wash of Holland scorn.
The moon that glimmered cold on Brittany . . .
How many scarred cold things that once had laughed
And loved, and wept, and sung, and had been men, . . .
. . . a cold soul-retching wave
. . . And body and soul were sick to think of it.
. . . White birds . . . Before his eyes were blinded by white
  irons . . .
                        And when slow rain
Fell cold upon him as upon hot fuel,
It might as well have been a rain of oil
On faggots round some creature at a stake
For all the quenching there was in it then
Of a sick sweeping beast consuming him
With anguish of intolerable loss.
. . . The still white fire of her necessity.

With these backward looks of his, Robinson also looked
forward. If not an innovator, he was at least an early participa-
tor in new and future developments. While with Frost he was

one of the last to stress thought and thinking, his feeling, telling, singing, song, and music he shared with his contemporary
William Vaughn Moody, with Chivers and Sterling, and then
with Wallace Stevens. His verb of *touch* he shared with Sill and
Swinburne; his *human*, with Sterling and Stevens; his *face*
and *nothing* with Poe and Stevens. Then, especially with the
young modern poets of mid-twentieth century, his romantic
cold, small, white, bird, fire, flame, dream, shadow, and his
especial *sick*.

Writers on Robinson have agreed with Redman, one of
the earliest, that his first books revealed the method and matter
of his maturity and that his New England childhood, Harvard
education, New York and McDowell work and writing, all kept
him to "the seasons and the sunset as before." He was no ex-
plorer or revolutionary. He saw each man trying to cope with
his own demon, as in "Rembrandt," and each a child "trying
to spell *God* with wrong blocks."[4] So he saw experience and
expectation often at odds, and so his characteristic early vocabulary gives us the heart of his poetry with its blend of sense
and sensibility—*touch, sing, shine, flame, gleam*, with *desolate,
lonely, human, shame, wisdom, truth*, while *Avon* and *Tristram*
add *cold, sick, white, shadow, smile, remember* to *nothing* and
time. This was a world already established by Coleridge and
Poe, and enforced by Robinson's own contemporaries, yet in a
way he was right that he looked forward, because much of his
terminology has been strengthened by the poets of the mid-
twentieth century. Sill's *small, still, touch, watch*, Stirling's
vision and *gleam*, Moody's *low, sick, road*, Stevens's *large, human, music*, Williams's *flame, call, seek*, W. T. Scott's *memory*
and *remember*, Hecht's *cold*, move into Rothenberg's *lost, hell,
grow, leave*, much *white* and *shadow*, the *cold* of Snyder and
others, Ray's *woman*, Kelly's *music* and *song*, and McClure's
sick, dream, flame, memory, nothing, wall, remember, touch—
the connotative, implicative, nostalgic sense of beauty in the

world today. Esther Willard Bates reported, in *Edwin Arlington Robinson and His Manuscripts*,[5] "He told me that he was, perhaps, two hundred years in advance of his time, indicating in brief half-statements, with pauses in between, that his habit of understatement, his absorption in the unconscious and semi conscious feelings and impulses of his characters were the qualities in which he was unlike his contemporaries. . . . He said he wondered if he wasn't too dry, too plain, if he wasn't overdoing the simple, the unpoetic phrase."

Yet this was the poet who "knew his Bible" and who was quoted by his biographer Hagedorn as characteristically writing, "In the great shuffle of transmitted characteristics, traits, abilities, aptitudes, the man who fixes on something definite in life that he must do, at the expense of everything else, if necessary, has presumably got something that, for him, should be recognized as the Inner Fire. For him, that is the Gleam, the Vision, and the Word! He'd better follow it."[6]

What have the Gleam, the Vision, and the Word got to do with understatement dry, plain, and unpoetic? How does Robinson reconcile objects of nature with concepts of desire, Tennyson's atmospheres with Browning's interior psychologizing, rich sense with metaphysical thought so that he seems at once modern and out of date, at once reminiscent and inventive? His major vocabulary provides one suggestion toward an answer: that his chief material is romantic natural beauty, but that his treatment of it is skeptical, unhappy, in a metaphysics of *shame, lonely,* and *sick.* Such a tone preserves him his modernity through a moonlit world. *Desolate, human, shame, truth, wisdom* are the terms of interpretive comment which his critics call literary, and which distinguish him from metaphysicians like Frost, on the one hand, and in their negativity from the American poets of praise like Whitman, on the other hand. He praises with nostalgia and he blames with apprehension; many young poets today share this combination of attitudes and even this vocabulary of values. To see more vividly how little "metaphysical" was his tradition, we may look again at Donne, to see what we have lost and what we have gained.

NOTES TO CHAPTER 9

1. All quotations from Edwin Arlington Robinson are taken from *Collected Poems* (New York: Macmillan, 1937).
2. Thomas Chatterton, *Works* (London, 1803), I cxxxvii.
3. Ibid., iv.
4. Ben Ray Redman, *Edwin Arlington Robinson* (New York: R. M. McBride & Co., 1926).
5. Maine: Colby College, 1944, p. 3.
6. Herman Hagedorn, *Edwin Arlington Robinson, A Biography* (New York: Macmillan Co., 1938), p. 29; epigraph.

III. PRESENT VALUES

✵ 10. Twentieth-Century Donne

WHAT DID Donne give to English poetry in the twentieth century? To my recollection, it was the *bracelet of bright hair about the bone,* so bright that bedazzlement for many years kept me from recognizing what else was in the poetry. Merritt Hughes said we kidnapped Donne for our own purposes; he thought we were drawn to Donne's skepticism; rather, as I remember, we were drawn to his sense, his "direct sensuous apprehension of thought" as Eliot put it, at the same time that we welcomed, over against Whitman, the tensions of that thought. With him, we might have our cake and eat it too. Now as I read Donne I marvel at what I did not read before, the simplicity and extremity of his conceptual construction which few in the twentieth century have been capable of or even aspired to. Our cake is scarcely his. But the "scarcely" is worth exploring.

A characteristic poem by Donne proposes an excess, by superlative or imperative, then negates the excess. It makes an argument with many subordinate clauses and thus many verbs and logical conjunctions like *but, if, though, yet.* Its essential content is conceptual—adjectives of value like *good, bad, false,* nouns of abstractions, *thing* and *nothing,* terms of *fear, time* and *death;* verbs of interaction, not only *telling* and *thinking,* but *giving* and *taking, finding* and *keeping.* Such characteristic structure and substance differ from that of other "meta-physical" poets, seventeenth-century or modern, by extremes of usage: far more verbs and connectives than for anybody else, far less concretion than for most others, a far more persistent pattern of poetic construction. Call him dramatic or dialectic or rhetorical or meditative or psychological and you get nuances of a complex whole which is not after all so complex in its persistent repetition. We see it in short, familiar form in "Song," the imperatives *Goe, and catche* and *Ride* carrying toward the negative of *a woman true, and faire*, and then the conditional *if* and contrastive *yet*:

> If thou findst one, let mee know,
>   Such a Pilgrimage were sweet;
> Yet doe not, I would not goe,
>   Though at next doore wee might meet,
> Though shee were true, when you met her,
> And last, till you write your letter,
>   Yet shee
>   Will bee
> False, ere I come, to two, or three.

The conclusion *Yet doe not* is supported by its set of concessive hyperboles. The concrete terms like *starre, foot, wind, haires* are illustrative, not substantive. The actions are characteristically discursive—*go, tell, teach, find*. The concepts are the central thematic material, in *things invisible, ten thousand days and nights, nowhere, a woman true, and faire*.

From the beginning of *Songs and Sonnets* to the end of *Divine Poems*, and even in the longer, more complex poems, proceeds to explicit countering of concepts in extremes: *Send home my long strayd eyes* (Yet keep them), *Send home my harmlesse heart* (yet keep it), *Yet send me* back my heart and eyes. So it is in "Witchcraft": *My picture drown'd in a transparent teare, / But now I have drunke thy sweet salt teares.* In "The Broken Heart" the intense heart breaks, *Yet nothing can to nothing fall.* And the contrast is central in "A Valediction: Forbidding Mourning": *Dull sublunary lovers love / But we by a love so much refin'd.* In "The Triple Foole," the consciousness is of verse itself:

> Griefe brought to numbers cannot be so fierce,
> For, he tames it, that fetters it in verse.
> But when I have done so,
> Some man, his art and voice to show,
> Doth Set and sing my paine.

The extremes of "Lovers Infinitenesse" are balanced, like the vivid counter in "The Prohibition":

> Take heed of loving mee,
> Take heed of hating mee,
> Yet love and hate mee too.[1]

In "Batter my Heart," the strong imperative verbs, the concept of making new, the sense of truth, all are bound by the recurrent *buts.*

This essential counterstructure with its concomitant vocabulary of concept is missing from much poetry of both Donne's contemporaries and ours. Herbert, Vaughan, and Marvell far less than Donne used exceptive or negative structures, and far fewer verbs, connectives, abstractions. Sometimes, famously, the parallels are great. When, for example, the quatrains of Marvell's "The Definition of Love" are compared with Donne's similarly squared-off "A Feaver," "The Extasie," or "The Undertaking"—*But yet thou canst not die . . . But as all severall soules containe . . .* But he who *loveliness within Hath found . . .* there is a similar strong sequence:

> III—And yet I quickly might arrive
>   Where my extended Soul is fixt,
>   But Fate does Iron wedges drive,
>   And alwaies crouds it self betwixt . . .

VII—As Lines so Loves *oblique* may well
Themselves in every Angle greet:
But ours so truly *Paralel*,
Though infinite can never meet.

These stanzas with their future Donnian vocabulary of *so divine a thing, extended Soul, jealous Eye, two perfect Loves, Loves whole World, some new Convulsion, so truly Paralel*, and so on, make a fine metaphysical poem. Yet it is one as rare for Marvell as many in Cowley's *Mistress* are rare for Cowley. That is, in addition to the Donnian metaphysics in which most seventeenth-century poets to some degree participated, making Donne by their assent their extreme leader, there were other modes which they used though he did not. As we saw earlier, the figure of factor-correlation .91 shows how nearly complete was Donne's sharing of main terms with his contemporaries; so high a correlation makes for negative correlations with other groups—for the varied classical qualities of the Jonson-Dryden tradition, of the Biblical-aesthetic of Milton, Marvell, Waller, Sandys with their highest correlations only in the .70s. Only a few bracelets of bright hair for Donne, then, and only a few like Herrick's "Blossomes, Birds, and Bowers," Vaughan's clouds and wings, Marvell's garden grass. The sensory beginnings of "Twicknam Garden" and "A Nocturnall" are rare for Donne, as are the *bright, fair, sweet, rose, stone, grow, feel, sing, shine* of his confrères—no one of which, however, anywhere near, met his power of inclusive leadership.[2]

Not long in the seventeenth century after Donne did the essential metaphysical vocabulary survive in the poetry of his followers; and not much in the poetry of his twentieth-century followers did it return. As it was a language of conceptual evaluation, it was a poetry of thought and exchange, of anxious weighing, of oppositions and subordinations. The eighteenth century discarded most of this language, even so poetically prosperous a term as *good*, using *sad* for *bad*, and *hope* for *fear*, and *rise* and *fall* for *give* and *take*. The nineteenth century then picked up part of the past, but put it in such a new context that it was often unrecognizable. Note for example Byron's satiric return to *good*, Wordsworth's to *poor*, the pre-Raphaelites' to *time* and *death*, Hopkins's to *keep*. The most strongly metaphysical vocabulary in the nineteenth century in both content and structure was Swinburne's, with his *death, face, sun, tear, year*; how vividly then we may feel the sense of sea change. The more truly metaphysical is supposed to be Browning, but his adaptations are general—as in *good, sun, thing, world*—in psychological process.

Did the Donne of 1912 bring back a richer metaphysical substance for the poets of the new era, the late nineteenth century and later? Their tone was sensuous, the language full of colors and material objects, with only an implication of concept. Of major sensuous terms, Donne offered only *sun*, and this he used more for its relations than for its qualities. Apart from the personified "busie olde foole," the sun was chiefly maker of shadow, maker of time. Donne's contributions would be basically through the shape of thought carrying his chief concepts, his thought of bad and good, false and true, life and death, thing and nothing, give and take, a poetry which would rely upon these forces and counterforces.

Death and its variations persist for Lawrence, Sitwell, Owen, Graves, Auden, Barker, Jennings, Gunn; less for the Americans, Eberhart, Rukeyser, Lowell, Rothenberg. The language of thing and nothing is of Yeats, Auden, Ridler, Jennings, and Graves and strong in America. The language of time lessens for all but a few like Auden, Crane, and Warren. Truth and value are explicit in Lawrence, Muir, Auden, Ridler Robinson, Eliot, Williams, Frost, Cummings, Jeffers, Eberhart, Warren.

As for Donne's logical vocabulary, his terms of connection, there are few moderns to follow him. Connectives as a whole have declined in poetry, and especially the logical ones of disjunction, concession, exception, explanation in which, even in Donne's own time, no other poet was so strong as he. Essentially, the *but*, the *if*, the *though* define his poetry's nature. At best in modern poems this nature works at half his strength: the *but* in Robinson, Sitwell, Auden; *if* in Robinson, Lawrence, Eliot; *because* in Yeats and Eliot; *therefore* in Graves; *though* and *yet* in Crane, Sitwell, Jennings. For locational prepositions, on the other hand, modern poets are far stronger: Dylan Thomas's *in*, twice Donne's; Sitwell's *of* and *on*, three times his.

When in *Primitivism and Decadence* Yvor Winters wrote an analytical survey of structural methods of American poetry, along with the "the method of repetition" and "narrative," "pseudo-reference," "qualitative progression," and others he proposed "the logical method" as "simply, explicitly rational progression from one detail to another: the poem has a clearly evident expository structure."[3] He referred to seventeenth-century metaphysical poets for its use and misuse. But his very description is surprisingly scant: what sorts of logic, what kinds of connections are to be found? For many metaphysical poets, a simple additive sequence is logical enough. For Donne, the pattern is more fixed, clear, characteristic in its conditional and contrastive forms: the *if* or *though* of hyberbole; *but*, *yet* of counterthought. It may be suggested that the sonnet form itself is influential; maybe, but other sonneteers are not so argumentative, and Donne himself argues also in other forms.

To garland the Donne tradition as the chief seventeenth-century tradition, in some important ways distinct from classical and biblical, is to garland a highly special and limited tradition in the twentieth century—that of the poetry of concept countered by concept, the true yet false, good but bad, *thing* though *nothing*, of the metaphysical concept.

Our greatest modern metaphysical poet, if we are to move from this center, is W. B. Yeats. Yeats and Donne agree in more than half their chief terms, and steadily in adversative structures. Chiefly they differ in values and actions of persons,

Donne's negatives not matched by Yeats's *ancient, old, young, child, mother, dream, call, cry, sing. The Tower's* first poem begins with a negative, moves to a *therefore* for its positive. So also in the three sections of *The Tower* itself. In *Meditations,* subordinate *buts* yet support cumulative conclusions; *give, place, turn away* do the work of logical disjunctives: "But O! ambitious heart . . . It had but made us pine the more." Nineteen Hundred and Nineteen" begins with its negative "Many ingenious lovely things are gone" and continues "Now days are dragon-ridden," working by contrasts, not disjunctions. Then, finally, "But is there any comfort to be found?" or again, "A sudden blast of dusty wind . . . But now wind drops . . ." The contrast, one sees, is between two views of time, *then, but now,* a shift in motion, a pressure in the cycle of vision rather than an alternative.

> Much did I rage when young,
> Being by the world oppressed,
> But now with flattering tongue
> It speeds the parting guest.[4]

Often, as in "A Man Young and Old," the connective *and* can work for its opposite, because the added materials themselves make the contrast.

The flickering perspectives of Eliot's Prufrock, on the other hand, are joined by *ands*, not argued; he is trying to convince nobody. The crucial negative is an exclamatory No! The ending verb is *drown.* Other phrases—"My self-possession gutters . . . with smell of steaks in passageways . . . submarine and profound . . . his dry and passionate talk"—combine or fuse disjunctions. In "Gerontion" the old man's "thoughts of a dry brain in a dry season" are given more semblance of argument than Prufrock's, but sardonically: "I have lost my passion? why should I need to help it / Since what is kept must be adulterated?"

The phrase *But Doris* in "Sweeney Erect" satirizes the *buts* of the metaphysical quatrain poem. In "A Cooking Egg" the "But where is the penny world I bought?" come closer, and closer yet the mock logic of "The Hippopotamus" and the triumph in "Whispers of Immortality" of

> And even the Abstract Entities
> Circumambulate her charm;
> But our lot crawls between dry ribs
> To keep our metaphysics warm.[5]

That's not Donne's story, that "No contact possible to flesh / Allayed the fever of the bone"!

In *The Waste Land*, "*respondebat illa: ἀποθανεῖν θέλω*" / I want to die. In this land, wish is no argument. "I will show you fear in a handful of dust. Fear death by water . . . But / O O O O that Shakespeherian Rag—. . . But if Albert makes off, it won't be for lack of telling . . . But at my back from time to time." And elsewhere: "—For Thine is the Kingdom—Because I do not hope . . . Pray for us . . . Although I do not hope . . . Let my cry come unto Thee. But to what purpose / I do not know. Words, after speech, reach / Into the silence." The detail of the pattern is movement.

The 1934 *Poems* of Auden vigorously return to us the metaphysician: the concepts, the fear, the exceptive central turn in the poem.

I. "Yet wear o ruffian badge . . ." II. "But waking sees . . ." III. "Nor even is despair your own . . ." IV. "But poised between . . ." V. "But now . . ." VI. "But not . . ." VII. "But should the walk . . ." VIII. "But of no use . . ." IX. "But what does it mean . . ." XI. "But seldom this . . ." XIV. "But in between . . ." XVI. "But thinking so . . ." XVII. "But this was never . . ." XVIII. "But here . . ." XX. "Yet there's no peace . . ." XXIII. "But we in legend not . . ." XXIV. "Yet glory is not new . . ." XXV. "There is no change of place . . ." XXVI. "But happy now . . ." XXVII. "But the answer . . ." XXVIII. "But their ancestral curse . . ."

Throughout XX, for example, the tensions of concept, the archetypal face, fear, these tears, and years all round upon the turn "Yet there's no peace."

> Fear, taking me aside, would give advice
> "To conquer her, the visible enemy,
> It is enough to turn away the eyes."

> Yet there's no peace in this assaulted city
> But speeches at the corners, hope for news,
> Outside the watchfires of a stronger army.[6]

The turns of concept in Auden, for which see also the sonnets "In Time of War," are less of argument, more of atmosphere than in Donne; the whole step toward modernity is taken in the assortment of sensuous imagery, which we then tend to read back, far too richly, into Donne. But the skeleton of unease, which says to the poet over and over, this way it is, yet not fully, not wholly, not really, not metaphysically, persists and provides the bond between centuries.

In the *Collected Poems* of 1945 the first and simplest of ballads runs:

> As I walked out one evening . . .
> I heard a lover sing . . .
> "Love has no ending" . . .
> But all the clocks in the city
> Began to whirr and chime:
> "Oh let not Time deceive you,
> You cannot conquer Time."

And the epigraph to the volume is:

> Whether conditioned by God, or their neural structure, still
> All men have this common creed, account for it as you will:—
> The Truth is one and incapable of contradiction;
> All knowledge that conflicts with itself is Poetic Fiction.

This is the fiction-making of the metaphysician. Cummings recognizes it too:

> if you can't sing you got to
> die and we aint got
>
> Nothing to die,come on kid
>
> let's go to sleep[7]

This is the metaphysical language if not the structure of Cummings's *50 Poems* (1939). And this is even the structure in "anyone lived," and "i say no world," and "these people so-called"and many more.

> We're
> alive and shall be:
>   . . . but we've
> such freedom such intense digestion so
> much greenness only dying makes us grow.

In "proud of his scientific attitude" the logical connectives are present and sardonic. *Which but*) is a turning point in "mrs." And then again the beautiful

> until out of merely not nothing comes
> only one snowflake(and we speak our names

Robinson Jeffers had not seemed to me metaphysical, Donnian, except as he shared the Random House bindings of the 1930s; yet he makes the basic turn of thought, in *Such Counsels* and earlier.

> Men suffer want and become
> Curiously ignoble; as prosperity
> Made them curiously vile.

> But look how noble the world is,
> The lonely-flowing waters, the secret-
> Keeping stones, the flowing sky.
>
>   ["Life from the Lifeless"]

For the Greeks the love of beauty, for Rome of ruling; for
    the present age the passionate love of discovery;
But in one noble passion we are one.

                 ["Shine, Republic"]

But the innocent and credulous are soon corrupted.
                   ["The Coast Road"]

                  But for each man
There is real solution, let him turn from himself and man
    to love God

             ["Going to Horse Flats"]

                  Because only
    tormented persons want truth . . .
Not a man sinning, but the pure holiness and power of
    God.

             ["Theory of Truth"] [8]

More usually considered, accepted or rejected, as metaphysical have been the poems of Wallace Stevens. In *Transport
to Summer* (1942):

It is here, in this bad, that we reach
The last purity of the knowledge of good.

The crow looks rusty as he rises up
Bright is the malice in his eye . . .

One joins him there for company,
But at a distance, in another tree.

*. . . But this book . . . And not yet to have written
a book . . . These are real only if I make them
so . . .*

One might have thought of sight, but who could think
Of what it sees, for all the ill it sees?
Speech found the ear, for all the evil sound,
But the dark italics it could not propound.

> And out of what one sees and hears and out
> Of what one feels, who could have thought to make
> So many selves, so many sensous worlds,
> As if the air, the mid-day air, was swarming
> With the metaphysical changes that occur,
> Merely in living as and where we live.
>
> But see him for yourself. / The fictive man . . .
>
> There is one dove, one bass, one fisherman.
> Yet coo becomes rou-coo, rou-coo. How close
> To the unstated theme . . .

Fully concerned with the power of imagination and the creat-ing of the fictive man, Stevens is less concerned with the meta-physical counter. But when as conscious artist he seriously turns to the metaphysical mode, he uses it so carefully that he defines it for us: the paradoxes, the conditional, and then the turn, *But suppose,* and the return to language and concept, as in "Connoisseur of Chaos"—"If all the green of spring was blue, and it is"—

IV

> A. Well, an old order is a violent one.
> This proves nothing. Just one more truth, one more
> Element in the immense disorder of truths.
> B. It is April as I write. The wind
> Is blowing after days of constant rain.
> All this, of course, will come to summer soon.
> But suppose the disorder of truths should ever come
> To an order, most Plantagenet, most fixed . . .[9]

The metaphysical order admired and praised by the poets and critics of the next generation reached less poetic expression than one might expect. Robert Penn Warren is by far the strongest because he can face and make use of negatives; he

can except and deny as well as add. His early version has now
a familiar literary ring, as in "Kentucky Mountain Farm."

> Now on you is the hungry equinox,
> O little stubborn people of the hill,
> The season of the obscene moon whose pull
> Disturbs the sod, the rabbit, the lank fox,
> Moving the waters, the boar's dull blood,
> And the acrid sap of the ironwood.
>
> But breed no tender thing among the rocks.
> Rocks are too old under the mad moon,
> Renouncing passion by the strength that locks
> The eternal agony of fire in stone.
>
> Then quit yourselves as stone and cease
> To break the weary stubble-field for seed;
> Let not the naked cattle bear increase,
> Let barley wither and the bright milkweed.
> Instruct the heart, lean men, of a rocky place
> That even the little flesh and fevered bone
> May keep the sweet sterility of stone.

More vividly new is "Insomnia," from "Tale of Time":

> Come,
> Crack crust, striker
> From darkness, and let seize—let what
> Hand seize, oh!—my heart, and compress
> The heart till, after pain, joy from it
> Spurt like a grape, and I will grind
> Teeth on flint tongue till
> The flint screams. Truth
> Is all. But
>
> I must learn to speak it
> Slowly, in a whisper.
> Truth, in the end, can never be spoken aloud,

For the future is always unpredictable.
But so is the past, therefore

At wood's edge I stand, and,
Over the black horizon, heat lightning
Ripples the black sky. After
The lightning, as the eye
Adjusts to the new dark,
The stars are, again, born.

They are born one by one.[10]

A long view back over five centuries of English poetic usage shows certain main strands in the pattern. These can be given traditional names: certain temporal groupings can be seen to have great power, so that "eighteenth-century poetry" can be a meaningful phrase; certain groupings across time can be given conceptual titles like "classical" and "romantic." The term "metaphysical" has a clear seventeenth-century focus—an extension from, say, Wyatt through Sidney and Donne to Cowley—and then also a modern application, strong after 1912 and 1921. Especially, through the words of T. S. Eliot, attention fell upon Donne. What seventeenth-century metaphysical, what Donnian traits could be useful to the present? A true metaphysical complex, aside from small tokens, would need to include the following: a concern with the range of concepts, of truth and falsity, good and bad, what is and what is not. Thus a concern with death as with life, thus things and nothings as well as people, thus time in relation to space, thus human give and take, thus fear as well as love. Thus also an exceptive and limiting structure, not merely *and* but *but*, and *yet*, with implicative *ifs* and concessive *thoughs*—not a balanced but a subordinating structure, not a weighing of alternatives and *either-or*, but an ebullient setting forth and then a check, a back and forth relation between heaven and earth, *ought* and *is*. The propositional structure asserts life *but* the actuality of death, the power of spirit *but* the power of body, the absurdities *but* the moderations of human existence.

By such criteria, the twentieth-century metaphysicals are not just the ones we might guess; not the Fugitives so much as the cosmic metaphysicians like Cummings and Jeffers and the younger Rukeyser, Wilbur, Rothenberg. While Eliot, and many in the south, cared about a sort of fusing figure as an extension of symbolic mind, the modern metaphysicals, rather, maintain the subordinating view.

It might be asked how one so involved in the special thought processes of his time as Stein, Tuve, Leishman, Potter, and many others have shown Donne to be can have a strong effect in another century. Should it not be the classicists, the seekers of steady norms, who must recur, as indeed they seem to do, from one cultural context to another? How can a scholastic serve the twentieth century? By touching, I think the new need of the poets to think about their new cosmology, their new learning. Classicism and romanticism accepted, elevated, subjectivized the natural world; what the twentieth century needed was to grasp a whole new natural world brought in by the new learning, a new outer and beyond and other and double. The central focus on sense-impression made by imagism and symbolism did not much allow for discursive exploration; one needed to think about, know about, as well as observe, the new phenomena. So *new* itself is an important word for metaphysical time, and the *something-nothing* of speculation, and the *life-love-death, giving-taking* of human response.

The modern critics stressed less what they found new in Donne than what they found familiarly their own, the "imagery" and feeling. In his authoritative edition of 1912, Grierson countered Courthope's old-fashioned emphasis on quaintness and ingenuity with his own on depth of wit.

Alike in his poetry and in his soberest prose, treatise or sermon, Donne's mind seems to want the high seriousness which comes from a conviction that truth is and is to be found. A spirit of

scepticism and paradox plays through and disturbs almost everything he wrote, except at moments when an intense mood of feeling,
whether love or devotion, begets faith, and silences the sceptical and
destructive wit by the power of vision rather than of intellectual
conviction.

This is a romanticizing of Donne, even though Grierson wisely
observes that "not much of Donne's poetry is given to description";[11] Yeats, too, romanticizes in response to Grierson, "the
more precise and learned the thought, the greater the beauty,
the passion." What is wise is the attention to the guidance of
thought. Over against "direct sensuous apprehension of
thought" and "sensibility which could devour any kind of experience" one needs to remember the seventeenth-century
emphasis on concept as in Sir Aston Cokayne's guidance of
1658:

> Be metaphysical, disdaining to
> Fix upon anything that is below.[12]

Donne's own, "To the Countess of Bedford,"

> *Beeing* and *seeming* is your equall care,
> And *vertues* whole *summe* is but *know* and *dare.*

And, as Grierson quotes "The Anniversarie," (*Poems of
Donne*, p. xxix):

> In this low forme, poore soule, what wilt thou doe?
> When wilt thou shake off this Pedantery,
> Of being taught by sense, and Fantasie?

To be, to know, to dare are the merits—and they are verbs—
not the false forms of sense and the illusionary impressions of
appearance. The power of sense for Donne worked as loving
apprehension susceptible of thought.

Some other modern critics, Cleanth Brooks, for example,
have emphasized Donne's power of thought as power of dialectic and paradox. A paradox seems contrary to normal categories

yet conveys a hidden truth, an acceptable reversal such as that it is better to be poor than rich, or foolish than wise; that an extreme, foolish act is the same as its opposite extreme; that order can be reversed, as by Jonson's *Silent Woman*. A paradox takes many forms. For nineteenth century Browning, as W. D. Shaw says, it meant multiple points of view; conflicts and internal contradictions meant inner growth,[13] union by reverting to and releasing the world. Donne's negatives were different—in his sense of the wrong of overcommitment, whether Ovidian or scholastic. I do not think it is so much the complexity of Donne's arguments that is important for us to note as it is their basic recurrent structure, their simple balancing upon a counterpoint. He was no stylistic systematist, as he said himself: "I ever thought the study of [law] my best entertainment and pastime, but I have no ambition nor design upon the style." Rather, his own character and feeling in relation to the pressures of his day, the sense of building up and excess, and then the sense of counterbalancing truth gave him his steady style in poetry and prose as well: "I leave a scattered flock of wretched children, and I carry an infirm and valetudinary body, and I go into the mouth of such adversaries as I cannot blame for hating me, the Jesuits, and yet I go."[14] Grierson is right when he says (*Poems of Donne*, II, i), "Effort is the note which predominates." Donne's is the poetry of effortful articulation of thought; it is spelling out of problems, analyzing of motives and situations, a learned exploring of extremes of the planes of existence now and hereafter, of the cosmos below and above.

Rupert Brooke, Walter de la Mare, Elinor Wylie, Dylan Thomas, the Fugitives, many more have been interested in Donne in the twentieth century and found in him some clue to poetic value. But few I think have tried for or achieved that combination of values which makes for a whole likeness rather than a scattering of likenesses. The favorable reviews of the 1912 edition and of the Hayward 1929 edition in *Athenaeum*,

Spectator, Nation, and elsewhere made little sense of what sense Donne might make for a new time. The power was Eliot's, George Williamson's, Theodore Spencer's suddenly to verify the vogue. But much of the glamour of what we felt to be Donnian belonged rather to Herbert or Marvell or Vaughan, to the more aesthetic mode which shared affinities with symbolism. So students during a half century of "close criticism" have puzzled over the true nature of the metaphysical mode they were seeing essentialized in Donne, alien in most ways to their own. Poets like Robinson and Ransom, with strong metaphysical vocabularies and structures, nevertheless so often combined them with nineteenth-century terms and narrative sequences that the effect was special. Intellectual Tate and Kunitz, like Eliot, thought in progressions more than counterforces. Pound, Williams, Moore, Crane, Roethke, Lowell even less could be looked to; they were of a different tradition.

For the young poets writing in the second half of this century, Donne's direct whole effect is minimal. Thom Gunn and Elizabeth Jennings make some strong connections; in America after Warren and Rukeyser, there are a few like Rothenberg with their sense of *death* and *sun, telling* and *thinking,* Snyder and a few with *time,* McClure, Mezey, and a few with *thing* and *nothing.* Their combining into structures of effortfully articulated argument is rare. I'd like to see, but do not expect to, a new poetry of metaphysics come into being in which, as in Donne, the process of thought is the shaping force of the poem, not a fusion but an articulation of thought giving shape to feeling: thought-feeling rather than felt-thought.

But meantime, in single contemporary poems, curious ghosts emerge. The long lyric "Fear" by W. S. Merwin[15] is a twentieth-century metaphysical poem for us; it keeps the essentials of language and attitude and moves them up through nineteenth-century romanticism via Eliot and Cummings into the present day. Fear as a metaphysical emotion in making its connection with the unknown suggests two worlds. Merwin addresses it much as Donne addressed fear or death, as an inner presence, even in name.

> Fear
> there is
> fear in fear the name the blue and green walls
> falling of and numbers fear the veins that
> when they were opened fear flowed from and
> these forms it took a ring a ring a ring

The blue and green walls are by now I hope recognizable, like the bracelet of bright hair, as appurtenances of the modern. They develop in this poem through clusters of specifics that are characteristically twentieth-century poetic, in the *rain falling,* the *grass-green alley, glass giants, shoes, shadows, song, silence, parents, house, stone, forgetting, remembering, mouth, loves, small door, the bird feather by feather, hair, edge, building, the long crying, cold lights, star, from the beginning.* At the same time, across the loosely constructed sentences in their loosely four-beat lines moves a metaphysical structure and reference, a proceeding by concept and even argument, in

> fear into fear and the hatred and something
> in everything and it is my death's
> disciple leg and fear no he would not
> have back those lives again and their fear as
> he fared he would say but he feared more he
> did not fear more he did fear more
> in everything it is there a long time.

Key terms, *thing, death, life, time*; key conflicting formulations. Then also

> fear etcetera water fire earth air
> etcetera in everything made of

human agency or divine fear is
in the answer also

And, more ritually,

                                          but fear

says logic follows . . .
hearts smoke in the gusts on earth as it is
in heaven with the sentence beginning
before the heavens were or the earth
had out of fear been called and any began . . .
and shall I couple heaven when the fear
shall fear and those who walked in fear shall see
fear their very form and being for
their eyes shall be opened it was going
on in everything and I forgot but if you
stand here you can see . . .
I'm telling you I'm asking you I'm dying . . .
the next I said fear come on you it's you / I'm
    addressing . . .
mean there is you fear me fear but you
must not imagine fear through which the present
moves like a star that I or that
you either clearly and from the beginning
could never again because from the beginning
there is fear in everything and it is
me and always was in everything it
is me

Carrying Eliot and Cummings—even Olson, as in the
shift in the final line breaks—farther than they might wish to
be taken into a blur of past and present, Merwin makes a portmanteau journey with his fear. It is almost as if the metaphysical structure began faintly but then, under the influence
of its crucial abstractions, strengthened its adversary tone of
logic; the modern abolishment of punctuation called up an

older need for connections, and to the early *and*s accrue more *if*s and *but*s than one might have expected at the onset of "fear in fear the name the blue and green walls." Be the bracelet of bright hair as it may, the survival of the skeleton of exceptive and adversative concept in a poem such as this seems a wonder worth remark, a suggestion of the surviving power of Donne's thought in the twentieth century.

NOTES TO CHAPTER 10

1. For the structure, see Thomas O. Sloan, *QJS*, 48 (1962): 38–45. Other good examples are numbers 53, 63, 64, 65, 69; and among the Holy Sonnets 171, 173, 174, 175, 178, 180, 190, 193.
2. See my *Eras and Modes*, rev. ed. (Berkeley and Los Angeles: University of California Press, 1964); *Style and Proportion* (Boston: Little, Brown, 1967); and essay in *Computer and Literary Style*, ed. Jacob Leed (Kent, Ohio: Kent State University Press, 1966).
3. Arrow ed. (New York, 1937).
4. "Youth and Age," by W. B. Yeats, in *The Collected Poems of W. B. Yeats*, copyright 1928 by the Macmillan Company, renewed 1956 by Georgie Yeats; by permission of the Macmillan Company.
5. From "Whispers of Immortality," by T. S. Eliot, in *The Complete Poems and Plays*, 1952; by permission of Harcourt Brace Jovanovich, Inc.
6. This quotation (from poem XX in *Poems*, 1934) and the next (from "As I walked out one evening") are in *Collected Shorter Poems 1927–1957*, 1966, by W. H. Auden; by permission of Random House, Inc.
7. This quotation and the next two are from poems 3, 5, and 16, by E. E. Cummings, in *Poems 1923–1954*; by permission of Harcourt Brace Jovanovich, Inc.
8. From "Life from the Lifeless," by Robinson Jeffers, in *The Selected Poetry of Robinson Jeffers*, 1937; by permission of Random House, Inc.
9. These quotations are from "No Possum" and "Connoisseur of Chaos," by Wallace Stevens, in *The Collected Poems of Wallace Stevens*, and the last stanza of "Esthetique du Mal," by Wallace Stevens, in *Transport to Summer*, 1947; by permission of Alfred A. Knopf, Inc.
10. Quotations from "Kentucky Mountain Farm" and "Insomnia" in "Tale of Time," by Robert Penn Warren, in *Selected Poems New and*

Old 1923–1966 (New York: copyright Random House, Inc., 1966); reprinted by permission of the publisher.

11. *The Poems of John Donne*, 2 vols. (London: Oxford University Press, 1912), II, x, xiii, xxix, li.

12. Edward LeComte, *Grace to a Witty Sinner* (London: Victor Gollancz, Ltd., 1965), p. 228.

13. *The Dialectical Temper* (Ithaca, N.Y.: Cornell University Press, 1968).

14. Quoted by Mary Clive in *Jack and the Doctor* (London: Macmillan & Co., 1966), pp. 95, 44.

15. Originally in *The New Yorker*; from *The Carrier of Ladders* (New York: Atheneum, 1970), © W. S. Merwin.

🙠 11. Mid-Century

THE POETRY of those born in mid-twentieth century delineates in black and white. Its poet, whether man, woman, or child, gives us shots of intensely focused-upon objects significant to mood. The season is specific, often winter, snow on the ground, or rain or water, trees black in the air, an edge on things, an assumption of likeness to body, with a phrasal progression from item to item, and a sense of meaning beyond statement. Jim Harrison's "Park at Night" is a simple example:

Unwearied
the coo and choke
of doves
the march of stone
an hour before dawn.

Trees caged to the waist
wet statues
the trickling of water—
in the fountain
floating across the lamp
a leaf
some cellophane.[1]

Not merely observed, but interpreted in such words as *march* and *caged* and even in the punctuation, the *water, bird, stone, tree, light,* and *leaf,* all reflect Mr. Harrison's cool sense of them. I do not say his view of them, because this is scarcely a scene, so much is it caught by other senses.

Robert Wallace makes two extensions in "Above the River Country": he interprets not only by metaphor and punctuation but by a formal linear pattern and by an abstraction, a culminating commentary, *beautiful:*

> Incredible
> > as the tall moon is,
> > > lighting the fields above the river country,
>
> its fencerows,
> > and the shadowy woods
> > > through which the road
>
> curves
> > down to the sliding river,
> > > the silvered bridge under
>
> which the river goes,
> > light
> > > among the dark trees and rocks,
>
> light in the dark leaves,
> > beautiful
> > > as you are.[2]

Other poets of such intense exactitude are Robin Blaser, Tram Combs, Dan Allen, Isabella Gardner, Carolyn Kizer, Paul Petrie, Raymond Roseliep. Formally effective as is phrasal arrangement, others draw more strongly upon syllabics or stress patterns, as do John Knoepfle, Irving Feldman, Theodore Holmes, Roger Shattuck; or they draw upon the close metrical foot patterns of Davie, Mueller, Humphries, Moss, MacIntyre, of Gilman, Squires, Swift. Often along with the firmest metrical patterns go the most generalizing tones, the *thes* which remind us that the seasons recur. Robert Francis's "Nothing is Far" is an epitome:

> Though I have never caught the word
> Of God from any calling bird,
> I hear all that the ancients heard.
>
> Though I have seen no deity
> Enter or leave a twilit tree,
> I see all that the seers see.
>
> A common stone can still reveal
> Something not stone, not seen, yet real.
> What may a common stone conceal?
>
> Nothing is far that once was near.
> Nothing is hid that once was clear.
> Nothing was God that is not here.
>
> Here is the bird, the tree, the stone.
> Here in the sun I sit alone
> Between the known and the unknown.[3]

In contrast to such metric and metaphysical certainty, the stress patterns of the younger more improvisatory poets seem very free, though in comparison to free-verse wheeling they seem solidly and literally blocked. Michael Goldman's "First Good Day" is an example.

> This room in shadow,
> a forest of misplaced things; the air outside
> raked by a spare light, breezy, a brace of leaves
> rustling the pane.
>
> Thrust the window up
> with that small tenseness of the body, and return
> here in our hearts of clutter, this dear room,
> to heed the visits of the air.

We took it quickly—it was there—
debating in its dust a month;
and darkness hardened in its breath;
there was no end to dust.

Here is the unmade bed, the chair
with waterglass and socks;
we read and dropped our bread in crumbs,
and stony silence for a month
handled the dust.

Come sit upon the bed with me and gloat.
We have outlived one winter and will run,
as much in love as air redeems the sun,
hand in hand into the street to be
with the light leaves, the town's bright stone.[4]

This bluff stress suggests more of participation than either
the fixity of meter or the transitoriness of cadence. Another
poem of its kind providing a good contrast to both other sorts,
to Dijkstra, McGaugh, Meltzer, to Davidson, Fowler, Pick,
Spicer, to Harrison's fragmented park quoted earlier, is David
Slavitt's "Central Park: April":

A season of tops and radios; the sun,
sponged by the fitful breeze at the tingling point
of perspiration, while loud children run
the park into the eyelid's blood-red streaming
(the shouts, the music, growing ever more faint),
sets the sprawled women, strolling young men dreaming.

This first voluptuary day in the park,
this Sunday soaking of light and warmth on benches,
and into prams and onto blankets where dark
glasses are put aside, skirts hiked up, wrenches
the year around in a suddenly glimpsed moment:
her, for example, running rather to fat,

asleep in the sun and showing a small extent
of winter-white thigh, sharp as the crack of a bat.[5]

The white thigh cracks with the insistence of body, of
flesh, in this world of poetry, part of the force that carries it
away from sighted or envisioned scenes to sensed dreams. So
Ray's "Midnight."

The linoleum has archipelagoes of socks
You would have picked up.
My need for your love
Is like an intense, high-pitched
Coded scream that floats out over valleys.
No one sleeping in the farms between us
Can hear this cry for help.
I wonder if you do.
Do you think it is the scream of an animal?[6]

The man as animal is often vitally sensuous but bewil-
dered, often tortured, a bird or monkey in the tree, a fish in the
sea, a token, in Zukovsky's guiding lines, from *All*, #14.

The sand: For the cigarette finished
on the beach the universal ash-tray:

or where the bacon grease is spilt:
Knowledge: smell is taken up

and off by the seas'
winds:

             a ship's
funnel is seen from this house
and rain drenches a witness of departure:

love as the relaxation among breakers
a dog-carcass—its wet—a reminder:[7]

Jean Valentine's playful "Fish-belly, glue-eyed prince ... /
How deep we met, how dark / How wet! before the world be-

gan"[8] shares in the seriousness of implication of the salmon in
Thomas Parkinson's *Thanatos*, or of David Wevill's "The Birth
of a Shark"—"strength of a man's thigh / wrapped in emery,
his mouth a watery / Ash of brambles,"[9] and Howard Mc-
Cord's "Purification": "Yes, I bear children / dark as ti-
gers."[10] So Lew Welch asks in *On Out #4*, "Did it mean nothing to you / Animal that turns this / Planet to a smokey
rock?"[11]

The shot in black and white therefore moves, not only in
leaves upon the water, not only in such storms of weather as
Harris's, Gilman's, Oppen's, Oliver's, Lowenfel's, Wallace's,
but in passionate bodily motion, with fear in it. W. R. Moses
exactly reports the development in "Contemporary Romantic":

Man may be cold, alone, and melancholy;
The rain of an empty place may fall on his heart.
Wanderer on purpose, for the crosswise pleasure of it,
He may walk on the bleakest shore, all day apart.
He knows what to do with mottled sandpipers flying
Through the cold, grey air and the cold, impersonal rain.
Like the tide that threshes and weaves through the mussel
	rocks,
They have a catalogue number filed in his brain.

The day I saw, by the drowning end of the jetty,
A big grey fin for a moment out of the sea,
I was startled. Consulting the catalogue of romantic
Fittings, I could not place it with certainty.
It was truly unknown, and, easy in ocean violence,
Suggested the vicious strength to compel true death.
I watched it hard till it sank in the roughening water,
And remember it well, though a long time has passed.[12]

Belonging to the generation of partial metaphysics, as do
many, like John Holmes, Kenneth Hopkins, Marya Zaturenska,
Roger Shattuck, and most of the poets published by Alan

Swallow, Moses meditates and remembers, even begins to make explicit, as a more awkward but similarly protentous poem, Shaw's "Arena," does not:

> Wrestlers wild,
> black and white,
> plunge and pitch
> and exchange whips
> through factious night!
>
> After howling prowling
> whirlpool throes:
> brilliant hills
> and buried walls,
> deep snows
>
> and the stillness that follows
> victory or great truce,
> and a twig of spruce
> shakes down to remind
> of tension Time. [13]

The season is winter; the time childhood, or the childhood or animalhood of hate and love; the weather, stormy; the action, wrestling; the metaphors, intensities, distortions, fragmentations, of dreams; the colors, black and white. Tree and snow, rock and water, hair and flesh, blood and bone, night and day, season and season, life and death, death and life. The contrasts do not provide fixed allegory; white is sometimes death-dealing, sometimes life-dealing, for example; but the contrasts do provide a theme of contrast, a relation of opposition, not polar though sometimes called so, but antipathetic or complementary. The focus has narrowed down from nineteenth-century romantic inheritances: from the sea to the fin, as W. R. Moses tells us.

The older world had more color in it, more golden, green, blue, red; more explicit feeling, pleasure, weeping, sorrow;

more mediating degrees of pale, grey, dim, shade, shadow. Further, the words which themselves had narrowed from earlier poetry: *morning* from *day, child* from *man, mother* from *woman, wave* from *sea, tree* from *woods, wing* from *bird, moon* and *star* from *sky, rose* from *flower, hill* and *stone* from *earth, hair* from *head* and from *body, silence* from *sound, wall* and *bed* from *house, turn* and *watch* from *go* and *see*:—now focus further: from *great* to *little* and *full,* from *body* to *flesh, skin, blood, finger, lip, mouth, teeth, tongue,* from *sound* to *music,* from *feeling* to *pain,* from *house* to *room, door, window,* from *stone* to *sand,* from *way* to *road* and *street,* from *come* and *go* to *run, walk, wait, touch,* from *light* and *dark* to *white* and *black.* Clearly, too, the terms of flesh, sound, touch will foster new sensory adjectives, not only the *cold* and *warm* of the nineteenth century, but Eliot's *dry,* and the wet of *water, mouth, rain.* A romantic fading and blurring of the visual scene becomes, in these terms, an intensification of kinetic and tactile sense, and therewith a bodily identification both with animal and with the human construction of roads, rooms, windows.

I have been making these generalizations about present poetic materials upon two bases: upon the books of poems published in America and received by the *Massachusetts Review* in 1965 and 1970, and upon an analysis of the chief words, measures, and structures in books of poems published in the 1960s and 1970s by ten poets born since 1930 and so now in their twenties, thirties or forties: Jones, Kelly, McClure, Rothenberg, Snyder, Sward, Anderson, Mathews, Tate, Cruz. My emphasis is, therefore, within the matrix of present-day poetic tradition, upon the choices characteristic of the younger writers. An important phenomenon is that writers do agree from era to era, and that major agreements grow from minor agreements and individual innovations. So our poets—the terms and structures they agree upon—partly continue the major emphases of English poetry from its beginning: on man, his eye, face, hand, love, his hearing, knowing, making, seeing of air, light, sun, time. Partly they confirm certain specific tendencies of the nineteenth century, as I have shown in *Eras and Modes in English Poetry*: the naming of the natural world and especially the tendencies begun after Swinburne and Whitman: Hopkins's and Lawrence's *flesh*, Henley's *still* and *street*, Muir's whole vocabulary, Raine's *dust, leaf, pain*, Thomas's *mouth* and *tongue*, Nicholson's *street* and *window*; and in America, Moody's *road, street, tree*, Eliot's *garden* and *shadow*, Stevens's *music*, W. T. Scott's *memory, hold, remember*, Rukeyser's *animal, pain, darkness, lover*, Hecht's *flesh*, Lowell's *glass, break, cry*.

Partly, beside continuing and confirming, and concomitantly dropping, a number of words of value as they go, the contemporary poets establish their own center, as I have exemplified it by their poems: an increased specification in the realms of nature and body; and new emphasis on new realms, the animal and the constructional. The sequence of change is not simple. There is backing and filling in inheritance. For a time, the free involvement and bodily intensity of Whitman was suspended in favor of the formal conceptual structures of the metaphysical poets, and the stress measures of the narrators. Zukovsky represents one sort of ancestor, Francis, Humphries, Zaturenska another; in the youth the variations are similar.

Each tradition allows for a rich range of competences, and tastes may differ drastically between the choices. In a poem about trees and water, as it is about himself, a reader wants to hate or love the open lines, admire or abhor the strong recurrences or closures, with their physical and metaphysical tones of feeling. For any one reader, probably only a third or a half of the hundred or more volumes of poems published in 1965 will seem susceptible of fair value-judgment, because only this part will seem poetry at all. But I think that apart from choice of ways and means and taste, the whole hundred is good, worth reading, hearing, thinking about. No single book seems

174 ~ Poetry and Change

174 ~ *Poetry and Change*

to me wholly discardable. All participate in the community of
the whole; none is singular either in kind or in merit.

What distinguishes the better from the worse, beside the
suiting of a taste and a belief? The daring with which the suiting is done. The scope in which the suiting is manifest. With a
leap, the dreamer comes into the scene, involving it, himself,
and the reader, in inexplicable further sensations and experiences. Among the many storms of the year, consider Elizabeth
Bishop's "Electrical Storm":

> Dawn an unsympathetic yellow.
> *Cra-aack!*—dry and light.
> The house was really struck.
> *Crack!* A tinny sound, like a dropped tumbler.
> Tobias jumped in the window, got in bed—
> silent, his eyes bleached white, his fur on end.
> Personal and spiteful as a neighbor's child,
> thunder began to bang and bump the roof.
> One pink flash;
> then hail, the biggest size of artificial pearls.
> Dead-white, wax-white, cold—
> diplomats' wives' favors
> from an old moon party—
> they lay in melting windrows
> on the red ground until well after sunrise.
> We got up to find the wiring fused,
> no lights, a smell of saltpetre,
> and the telephone dead.
>
> The cat stayed in the warm sheets.
> The Lent trees had shed all their petals:
> wet, stuck, purple, among the dead-eye pearls.[14]

Among waters, Julia Randall's "Stygian":

> I had heard in my youth
> Of the water that bound the earth

Like a supple, fatal beast
With his tail in his mouth,
Immense and circular.
I never stopped to fear
The little bending creeks,
Susquehanna's arcs,
Or the turns of Delaware,
Till last night when I came
To the ford at Coldstone Gap.
I saw a serpent's eye
Glint in the running light,
And held one foot in air
And one on the crossing rock.
Something was dead on the shore.
I did not stop to look
But took Catawba's wall
And shouted coming over
To Craig and Newcastle,
"I have crossed the world's river!"[15]

About the dark, John W. Corrington's "Lucifer Means Light":

believing temperature
obeying nerve
succumbing to starch and blood
rejecting a spectrum
of little mercies

cost him darkness

falling was creation
to be is judgment
to be is humdrum sky
dependable fierce stars
a way of unearthly seasons
mad and same

bloating to miniature
fading to monument
the old man never knew him
till he fell

hunched on a dying comet
wrapped in a banner of pronouns
he does not burn
but freezes

not demon but drag
not damned or even dented

only sick vicious and bored
tired of the light in his eyes[16]

Along with this poem, Corrington's grim "Algerien Re-
veur," James Dickey's great fish, Louis Simpson's "Stumpfoot
on 42nd Street," and some of the poems of Eberhart, Jarrell,
and Jones. For the tension of line and body, A. R. Ammons'
"Moment" from *Corson's Inlet:*

He turned and
stood

in the moment's
height,

exhilaration
sucking him up,

shuddering and
lifting

him
jaw and bone

and he said
what

destruction am I
blessed by?[17]

And from tension beyond relaxation of line and body, the end of Gary Snyder's *Mountains and Rivers Without End:*

> We were following a long river into the mountains.
> Finally we rounded a bridge and could see deeper in—
> the farther peaks stony and barren, a few alpine
> trees.
> Ko-san and I stood on a point by a cliff, over a
> rock-walled canyon. Ko said, "Now we have come to
> where we die." I asked him, what's that up there,
> then—meaning the further mountains.
> "That's the world after death." I thought it looked
> just like the land we'd been travelling, and couldn't
> see why we should have to die.
> Ko grabbed me and pulled me over the cliff—
> both of us falling. I hit and I was dead. I saw
> my body for a while, then it was gone. Ko was
> there too. We were at the bottom of the gorge.
> We started drifting up the canyon, "This is the
> way to the back country."[18]

Each of these poems participates in the concerns and the poetics of its contemporaries, yet works with an individual exactitude and assurance.

What is missing from the whole? Above all, people. There are many *I*'s, some *we*'s, some *you*'s, especially as loved, a few grandfathers and other remembered relatives; but not a great variety of complicated live characters. Louis Coxe and Richard Hugo came closest to giving us the narrative event, along with Jones, Gilley, Conner, and Corrington. Again, satire is scant; though in a way many of the lyrics are satiric, antilyric. Again, consequently, the sublime is missing, any heartfelt, soulswept elevation of spirit. And finally, as we have noted, romantic vagueness is missing. The year's poems are, and value what is, clearcut, hard-edged, objective with degrees of homely particularity and participation, disaffected yet eager to be affected, centered in a perceiver whose perception distorts and implicitly interprets the natural world in its analogy to the human.

So the chief qualifying black and white by implication relate dark and light to presence and absence, good and evil, color of skin, color of photographically abstracted impression, aesthetically suggestive of concerns sexual and racial and philosophical, the "power of blackness," the whiteness of the whale, in a curious stripping away of degrees into contrasts. One way in which, increasingly, sound pattern is developing to suit this same contrast, is to abjure the filled line or even the irregularly spoken line, and to build contrasts of silence into the sound, by means of dropped phrases and, in visual terms, the use of white-space to contrast with black print. Many of the more elegant and conservative printers, not recognizing this development, still use wide margins at side and bottom as conspicuous waste, and therefore often seem to impose large insignificant silences at insignificant places, such as before a stanza beginning a new page. Typography, like reading aloud, makes new demands upon structures of contrast between spoken and unspoken, as the lines are sharply drawn, more barely than in the older colorations of rhyme and assonance.

The motion from scene to obscene in its beginning focuses upon bodily senses other than sight, takes poetry not only to the mixed senses of dream, but also to the silences which deepen sense. It is hard to speculate about the new generation in mid-twentieth century, but in part its poetry has been written in the poems here before us; this poetry marks for us the way we have come, and where we are.

In the 1970s we may hear a turn in the poetic process. First, in an early "song" of Wheelock, a kind of objective symbolism like that of MacLeish's "Ars Poetica." Hear the bird in Wheelock's "All Love Songs," an old-fashioned bird:

All love-songs, and the inner sense
Of every song and singing word,

Are consummated in the cry
Of any woodland bird.

Alas, for the blind pain of speech,
And all the strife to comprehend:
The cry of any woodland bird
Has said it all, in the end.[19]

But then the special involvement of his new title poem, Part II:

Resigned? Why now he finds contentment almost
In the contemplation—yes, even a longing,
After the loud day's labor, after the fury,
The turmoil and the torment, to terminate them
Once and for all, that fury and that torment,
That endless labor; give up, go back, turn homeward
Forever, into the darkness of non-being,
One with the universe, not separate now,
Separate no longer—blessèd oblivion.
He enters the bedroom, turning on the light,
And prepares himself for sleep. Opening the window,
The cry of a whip-poor-will out of the darkness
Seems to him now the sound of his own voice crying
Back to him out of the darkness. For a few moments,
He stands there, listening. He turns off the light,
Letting the darkness in.[20]

For Theodore Weiss, too, the poetry is in the living of the life, the thought about it, wherein metaphors make bodily identification, as in "Pleasure, Pleasure."

And watching Hoppy curled up
in my lap, the way he goes
purring under my hand into sleep,
this watching is a pleasure.

A pleasure too Renée
in the next room practicing

the violin, going over the same
tracks again and again, trying

the notes like doors
to stores more and more open
for business, like stars lighting
up some Persian night asleep

under the skin of day.
Is a pleasure and a pleasure
this friend and that, a light
of one color and another,

not only to read
by as the world takes shape,
the sea rolled over like Hoppy
in a rapture of churning,[21]

As for the wounded mattress of Torregian, see "Like
Quilts Crying in an Ecstasy," where the room's windows are
less familiarly located; in most poems now, love is oblique:

Like quilts crying in an ecstasy
Of rock gardens Do you love all the same
To an amnesiac hand succumbing under
Enchanted rivets?

To invent a new diction (like lost cities), forever
Having come from
Cactus tempests like a crash of windows.
Looking for the impossible I tried to rest from
My journies each time

Yet a votary I stood before you
My arms outstretched as if lifted for flight
Never knowing in what direction I should be
Merged. What vestige was
The wind that came a cooing through eyesockets, undis-
    solved

Making all of your heads low in the same finesse!
My branching loves
A white mountain chain a sorrowing Andes
Beneath which I falter[22]

When, counter to this counterimagination, the photographic mode persists, as in Tuohy's "Seasons of Love," it is presented not by words but by actual photographs of rooms and bodies. But in the livest language, in almost every lively poet of the year, a sampler can range with relish: the contrasts in Ammons's "Cascadilla Falls," Birnbaum's mirrors, Blazek's technology, the vigor of Bly, Carver's *Winter Insomnia*, Harper's *Dear John, Dear Coltrane*, Strand's *Darker*, Finkel's "Brume," Howe's variety in *Eggs*, the *roads* of McGrath and Van Duyn, Merwin's and Swenson's many variations, Mezey's *The Door Standing Open*, Jim Morrison's lyrics beyond "The Doors," Thomas Parkinson's and Ishmael Reed's and James Tate's; and Snyder's domesticated "The Bed in the Sky" set over against his epigraph "Wild Nature is the ultimate ground of human affairs."

Most of the major nineteenth-century language of this wild nature is gone now. *Day, light, night,* persist, and specifically *water,* but not *star, moon,* and *leaf.* In major usage action of *moving* and *thinking* persist, especially in specific forms of *touching* and *walking,* and bodily forms of *eye* and *hand* reduced to *shit* as a major poetic term for a number of poets. Less *black* and *white* now, more *blue;* and the fittings for *home* and *house: room, door, window, glass,* and the outside *street;* the strengthened connectives *out of, under, toward, through.* So widely and clearly are these new clusters of terms apparent together that the reader seems guided toward an apprehension of new theme and attitude, new concern in focus, away from more technical considerations of stylistic variety.

Cadences have settled into a free sequential fragmentation, playing some variations over the forceful synaptic verbs of Olson's "projective verse." Some graphic experiments like May

Swenson's, some Saxon lines like McGrath's and Van Duyn's are interesting but not dominant. Sustained narratives or arguments or pleas are infrequent; the poems are rooms, parts of houses. The sequence of *Buffalo Poem* provides an example; Nathan Whiting is one of the youngest poets:

> Today I begin
> being alone. Windows,
> the snow strikes them
> and they have brown curtains.
>
> With a stone from this hand
> I've broken my daily bottle,
> waiting for the bus.
> Seagram's gin.
> Not mine,
> it came from those buildings.
>
> Each room has a specific kind of electric light.
> You can't look into the windows
> from the street
> as you could look through a person's glasses.
> A window today
> is the air I wait in.
> It's filled by the snow, yes,
> and a few leaves.
> Look at me,
> down at me.[23]
>
> What is this
> to be afraid of the dark?
>
> No darker
> than to be alone in bed,
> no lights, but one window
> open to the radios and arguments
> of fifty people,
> can exist.

The seasonal croaking
of those million frogs is nothing
as good.
      The best random noise
has sections as pure
and predictable
as an entire one minute ad
with music.
      and when that is turned off
one more window darkens,
and I feel that more strongly
than a rumor that was true,
not false.[24]

These literal words have a tenuous basis in tradition. For Keats and Poe, *door* and *dream*; for Poe also, *home* and *sea* made a kind of romantic beginning. For Swinburne, the poetic *bed* of "The Complaint of Love" was *strait, small, bridal, underground*, rhyming with *dead*. For Wilde, the city was Rome, *urbs sacra*, and home England; and the room *eterna*; theatrical: From "Fabian Dei Franchi":

The silent room, the heavy creeping shade
The dead that travel past, the opening door,
The murdered brother rising through the floor,
The ghost's white fingers on thy shoulder laid . . .

So a kind of melodrama of realism also in Henley's *In Hospital* and *London Voluntaries*, in William Vaughn Moody's and Edwin Muir's subjectivity (as in his "Mythical Journey") and in the younger Nicholson, Lowell, Rukeyser, Jennings, and Gunn. From a few uses by Eliot, Lawrence, their strange generality of *people*, and Cummings's *everything* and *something* out of older *nothings*, emphasis grew stronger in the next generation with Nicholson and Gunn's *bed* and *street*, Jenning's *room* and Lowell's *glass*, Rukeyser's many terms, to increased agreement by Rothenberg, McClure, Mezey, Sward, and Snyder,

and then by those born in the 1940s, Jon Anderson, Tom
Clarke, William Matthews, James Tate, and Victor Cruz. Considering the youthful environment of the two youngest, Tate's
Middle West, Cruz's East Side New York, and the absence of
any bond of school or friendship between them, one may marvel at their joined assumptions, their terms of value held in
common with the books of 1970.

The younger and newer, the stronger; so that books of
poems published in 1970 seem to have taken a whole long step
from those of 1965, into the world of this new language, into
the language of this new world, yet both of the middle generation. Open, for example, Rosellen Brown's award-winning
Some Deaths in the Delta: the first poem, "Landing in Jackson
(1964)," begins:

> I wear my fear like wool against the skin,
> walking from corner to corner of this graceless city,
> squinting down doorways, warily at faces.
> For a familiar token I take the sky,
> stretched taut between the tent-poles of my sight—
> that northern blue that bore me up for hours,
> then set me gently down in this ungentle place.[25]

See the identification of inner and outer, see the city ecology,
and the color blue. More fully, see "In Rooms":

> I have been alone in rooms,
> in houses, even—their doors barricaded
> with snow, a month from the news.
> Nothing is like it:
> Talk and you wonder if that could be a voice.
> And you lie lightly, skimming the cream
> of sleep off the top of an endless night.
>
> I have been alone in rooms
> with cats dozing—their bodies like snakes
> coiled around air.

Nothing is like it:
Talk and they hear you and don't hear you.
And you sleep tacitly guarded by their claws,
at the side of their breathing that flows and flows like a
    river.

I have been alone in rooms
seething with strangers—their presence demanding
my captured presence.
Nothing is like it:
Talk and they blink and answer and do not hear you.
And you see through a film like sleep how you are drifting
into a whirlpool, down, down to yourself.[26]

This: one motif for rooms, as at the end of the preceding poem,

One day I will wake
knowing
I dream in the language of this house.

Her dustjacket quotes Rosellen Brown as saying that poems
are not action but dreams before and after action, a bill of
damages, an exile from what home has become. Perhaps her
idea is a clue to this new poetic focus. It may suit McLuhan's
idea that we concern ourselves with what we have lost.

Another Browne, Michael Dennis, born in 1940, begins
his book with a somewhat mechanistically spare poem on the
same theme; often both of these poets seem to me to say too
much, spell out too much, but in "Peter" the lyric works:

Peter sleep-walks
And is my brother.

Not knows why. But does.
Not knows why. But is.

Because my father and my mother.

And this night in pajamas
Barefoot

Left the house and walked
Five hundred yards to my sister's house
And knocked
To be let in.

Let me in. I knock.
Let me in.

And walked back,
Saying he did not remember.

I knock. Let me in.
I am asleep.

He was.

O let us in.
We are all asleep.
We are asleep, let us in.[27]

The very titles of Arthur Gregor reveal the relation of
these terms with spirit—his book *A Bed by the Sea*, his earlier
Figure in the Door, his "Sleep Took Me Far," "At-Homeness
in the Self," "Water," "The Walk." The traveler *has thrown
open his being like windows / to the sky and doors to the
street*. . . . For Christopher Hottel, the cities are forests; bodies,
trees; walls, made of broken bread; that is, the surreal metaphor extends the central imagery. Brewster Ghiselin, too,
and many others, make such relation—scarcely now surreal
because it is so acceptable to assumption. An extreme of simplicity is Denise Levertov's "Waiting," Mary Norbert Korte's
"Apres-midi," *as glass fills with sun*, or Sandra Hochman's
Earthworks—"Maps for the Skin," "Leaving False Houses"
—*I'm leaving my house*— / *Going on to another house. I'm
leaving* / *This living room*—or this childhood—or this love—
or this life—lyrically and personally. As Joyce Carol Oates
does also, and Sandra MacPherson in "Selling the House"—
Nothing of ours there now. Nothing to comfort, nothing to

break. More surreal again then in his lucid associational way,
W. S. Merwin, as in "The Old Room":

> I am in the old room across from the synagogue
> a dead chief hands in the wallpaper
> he is shrinking into the patch of sunlight
> with its waves and nests and in the silence that follows
> his death
> the parade is forming again
> with the street car for its band
> it is forming I hear the shuffling the whispers
> the choking then the grinding starts off
> slowly as ice melting
> they will pass by the house
>
> I am in the old room across from the stone star
> the moon is climbing in gauze
> the street is empty
> except for the dark liquid running
> in the tracks of ice
> trying to call
> *Wait*
> but the wires are taken up with the election
> there is a poll at the corner I am not to go in
> but I can look in the drugstore window
> where the numbers of the dead change all night on the
>   wall
> what if I vote *It is not me* will they revive
> I go in my father has voted for me
> I say no I will vote in my own name
> I vote and the number leaps again on the wall
>
> I am in the old room across from the night
> the long scream is about to blossom
> that is rooted in flames
> if I called *It is not me* would it reach
> through the bells[28]

Carruth's initial "Asylum" gives us mauve walls, wind as a stealth of memory, "And here we came to search the self at last." His long line and full expositions, whatever the graphics of print, make an almost essayist exploration. Some poets are philosophical in a more abstract way, as Julia Vinograd is in *Revolution*. Some move quite literally, as Glover Davis does in his unliteral "Fun House" in *Bandaging Bread:*

> And I have made the circuit of all the rooms
> to see what I could see. I slam the bar
> across the door and bolt it into place.
> And then the mirrors on the dressers
> and on the walls begin to distort my face.
> My greatest fear is that the green surf pounding
> at my door will take me in my sleep
> and wash me back through all the rooms.[29]

Regarding walls, Ann Stanford most powerfully makes the psychological extension in the conserving measures of "The Escape":

> The walls were close enough to reach between
> They were of brick and they were slanting in.
> I held them up—one foot, two arms, my head.
>
> I held for hours. When I stirred, they leaned.
> They trembled with my breath but did not fall.
> I shifted feet, my arms were numb.
>
> My head ached with the flatness of the wall.
> I saw my foot set on the concrete ground.
> A spider crawled from one wall to the other.
>
> Nothing else moved. / I could hold no longer.
> I took my foot down. Carefully one hand
> And then the other, I drew gently down
>
> And lifted up my head and saw a door
> And I went out and breathed under the trees.
> I looked back at the walls. They stood alone

A cubicle of dryness on the lawn.
I watched the slow dust as they toppled one by one.[30]

Regarding mirrors, John Hollander writes of William Matthews's *Ruining the New Road*, "These narrowed poems, almost epigrammatic, but ultimately meditative, reflect the sorts of confrontation, such as with mirrors, that will matter in the end." And see Matthews's "Holding the Fort":

At first I feel my arms
go off to rest.
They loop off the bed's end
and crawl away, loud
with relief. The legs
go next
and always hunt in pairs.

Only the brain
is left, tiny
in the vast bed.

Outside, the elms lean
into clumps, gossiping
of violence.
Somewhere blood leaks out
from its shocked skin.

Now there's no hope of sleep.
Under the sheets
my absent body tingles
like an amputated toe.[31]

Lewis Turco makes, with his illustrator Thomas Seawell, a whole book from the figure. *The Inhabitant* carries room prints on its cover, and its contents move from "The Door" to "The Hallway," to "The Livingroom," to "The Bedroom" to "The Mirror" to "The Porch," "The Looking-Glass," "The Dwelling-House"; the beginning of the book: *There is a door* / *made of faces* / *faces snakes and green moss* and the end:

VII. On the morning of the seventh day he woke and
arose. In at the window the dawn blew as he stood
and looked.

On his legs each hair stood in its chill; he felt the morning
moving on his flesh.

In the mirror he saw a man. Upon the surface of the glass
there shimmered the image of someone strange and
real, bearded, the bone hung with blood's fabric.

He went to the door, naked; opened it; moved into the daylight where the world walked. With his eyes he met
other eyes beyond the portal—men, women, and
children who knew his nakedness as he knew theirs.

It was a true flesh the Inhabitant made to walk through
the city: in each eye he saw the image folk saw in
his.[32]

Do not these seem to you good, absorbing, believable
poems? It does not seem to me that questions of value any
more than questions of technique rise to the surface of thought.
These hundred poets are deeply involved in thoughts of self
and involved expertly, deeply. Consistency of form and cadence, and ease of motion from literal to figurative to fantastic,
carry easily because the world of concern is so shared and
sharable. We all live in this house now. The bird cries at a
distance. Our own cries are nearer yet not understood. A few
poets, as ever, may be noted as taking wider risks, making
bigger reaches to qualities of the world both inner and outer,
foreign, wild, urban. Yet their poems function in the whole
context. Robert Bly, for example, flies to domestic sources of
doubt as he begins "The Teeth-Mother":

now we sit beside the dying, and hold their hands, there
is hardly time for goodbye,
the staff sergeant from North Carolina is dying—you
hold his hand,

he knows the mansions of the dead are empty, he has
    an empty place
inside him, created one night when his parents came
    home drunk,
he uses half his skin to cover it,
as you try to protect a balloon from sharp objects . . . .

Artillery shells explode. Napalm canisters roll end over
    end.
800 steel pellets fly through the vegetable walls.
The six-hour infant puts his fists instinctively to his
    eyes to keep out the light.
But the room explodes,
the children explode.
Blood leaps on the vegetable walls.

Yes, I know, blood leaps on the walls—
No need to cry at that—
Do you cry at the wind pouring out of Canada?
Do you cry at the reeds shaken at the edges of the
    sloughs?
The Marine battalion enters.
This happens when the seasons change,
This happens when the leaves begin to drop from the
    trees too early
"Kill them: I don't want to see anything moving."
That happens when the ice begins to show its teeth in
    the ponds
that happens when the heavy layers of lake water press
and ends

    And return to earth crouched inside the drop of sweat
        that falls again and again
    from the chin of the Protestant tied in the fire.[33]

James Dickey's "Knock," "The Eye-Beaters," and especially
"Living There," the first of "Two Poems of Going Home,"
savagely re-place the dilemma in the local scene and heart.

The Keeper
Is silent   is living in the air not
Breathable, of time. It is gray
Winter in the woods where he lives.
They've been cut down; you can see through
What he is keeping   what used to be a room
In a house with one side turned
To trees. There are no woods, now, only other
Houses. Old Self like a younger brother, like a son, we'd
    come rambling
Out of the house in wagons, turn off the back
Driveway and bump at full bump-speed down
Through the woods, the branches flickering
With us, with the whole thing of home
A blur, gone rolling in leaves. But people are always
    coming

To know woods   to know rooms in houses
That've been torn down. Where we live, you and I,
My youth and my middle
Age   where we live with our family, miles away
From home, from my old home,
I have rooms
I keep, but these old ones, the ones where I grew
Up, are in the air
Of winter they are over
Other houses like ghosts. The house lives only
In my head while I look and the sun sinks
Through the floors that were here: the floors
Of time. Brother, it is a long way to the real

House I keep. Those rooms are growing
Intolerable in minds I made

Up, though all seems calm when I walk
Into them as though I belonged there. Sleepers are
    stirring   an arm lies

Over a face, and the lights are burning
In the fish tank. It is not like this,
But it will be. One day those forms will rise
And leave   and age
And come back   and that house will flame like this
In the Keeper's head
With the last sun; it will be gone
And someone will not be able
To believe there is only nothing
Where his room was, next to his father's
Blue-eyed   blue-eyed   the fixer   the wagon-master
Blazing in death
With life: will not be able to look
Into windows of the room where he saw,
For the first time, his own blood.
That room fills only with dying
Solar flame   with only the backyard wind
Only the lack
Of trees, of the screech-owl my mother always thought
Was a hurt dog. And tell me for the Lord God
's sake, where are all our old
Dogs?
Home?
Which way is that?
Is it this vacant lot? These woven fences?
Or is it hundreds

Of miles away, where I am the Keeper
Of rooms turning night and day
Into memory?[34]

In a fine small paperback, Adam David Miller edits "black voices of the seventies," and in these voices these same words are seriously and centrally spoken. Al Young's "Poetry":

It is possible to rest here.
It is possible to arrive home

headed this way
thru the wind & rain of this night
alone
to a place where starlight
isnt the point.
It is true that we are orphans
under the skin
where fluids combine
& organisms function intelligently
where vision or sound
in image or vibration
need only be true
to spark the way there.
There is here & always was.
You sniff & clear your throat
in this unintentional night
borrowed from eternity
or let yourself be saddened by nothing.

I sit in a white kitchen
next to the young walls
yellow paper spread on yellow tablecloth
& scratch helplessly
wanting to take new leave
of the present
which was a gift,
longing to have known everything
& to have been everywhere
before the world dissolves
a tangle of journeys
& messages
unrecorded
undeciphered
wrinkled down into me.[35]

In this collection also see Harrison's "Room" and "Dream," Lucille Clifton's "Good Times," William Anderson's "February Rain," Ishmael Reed's "Beware: Do Not Read this Poem."

Familiarity of association makes it possible now for the rich and complex externals of David Henderson's "Mayor of Harlem" to make inner sense.

I
enter harlem
to walk from the howling cave
called the "A" train /
from columbus circle
                         (find america discovered)
all along a 66 block artillery blitz
                                        to the quarter /
            nonstop
       existential TWA nightcoach
rome to auschwitz express
where multitudes vomit   pass out
witness death by many stabbings
upon pompeii /
                    please close the doors please
before the madness of washington heights
            disembark   / silent moot   of black vectors
to sunder this quarter
                                thru

black mass
black land

-of rhythm n
            blues & fish of jesus frying across the boardwalk
snake dancers walk mojo along wide boulevards
sight for those
                who live away

a new land!
no dream stuff
   in dem black neon clouds of de full moon
            to illume by sun-ra
streets just like you
          no thinking you crazy
vertigo
     under skyscrapers　/[36]

Another extension is into the closed room of the universe. Robert Vas Dias's *Inside Outer Space* anthologizes so many poems of metaphoric connection that the concept of closed spatial environment comes to dominate the mind. The first poem in the collection, by Sam Abrams, moves into the lines

we erect
these these
rooms the
phone rings
     the real
all around us

David Antin's very moving "the roads":

suppose a man travelling in a right line any distance
turning through any angle whatsoever travelling the same
distance likewise in a right line and repeating this process
any number of times encounters a wall　he must step back

Stephen Berg, William Bronk, Robert Creeley, Edward Field, Allen Ginsberg, Daniel Hoffman, Harry Lewis, Clarence Major, Jerome Rothenberg are others, and Michael Heller's "Pressure":

Didn't you say you loved me?

under what conditions

under what
under what
under what

---

under the air
@ 15 lbs per square inch on the roof
on the safety-factored I-beams
                slipping down thru curtainwalls
to the ground
to gravitational bedrock
                accidental center: home[37]

In his *Sky*, Michael Benedikt, author of *The Body*, writes, beyond "The Bed Beyond the Bed," "The Esthetic Fallacy": "We have lingered too long in the house of many means, and now our ends are desperately overdue for condemnation and/or urban renewal." I am not sure that this is the thought which generalizes the poetry of 1970, but it is one worth speculating upon. Poets seem to me now to be assenting to the proposal; to be restless in the house, not retreating to it; to be relatively uninterested and uninteresting in many means; to look out, seek out, reach out, walk out for ends; to use, many times, the block busters of destruction before renewal. Not just urban, though; country as well as city people watch restlessly at door and window as at mirror. I think they are attempting to recreate in poetry what they have made, to value and reshape it; a good attempt, carrying us now way beyond photography and image, beyond allusive symbol, to a world both constructed by and questioned by man's capabilities.[38]

NOTES TO CHAPTER 11

1. James Harrison, *Plain Song* (W. W. Norton & Co., 1965).
2. Robert Wallace, *Views from a Ferris Wheel* (New York: E. P. Dutton & Co., 1965).

3. Robert Francis, *Come Out Into the Sun* (Amherst: University of Massachusetts Press, 1965).
4. Michael Goldman, *First Poems* (New York: Macmillan Co., 1965).
5. David R. Slavitt, *The Carnivore* (Chapel Hill: University of North Carolina Press, 1965).
6. Ray, David, *X-Rays* (Ithaca: Cornell University Press, 1965).
7. Louis Zukovsky, *All* (New York: W. W. Norton & Co., 1965).
8. Jean Valentine, *Dream Baker* (New Haven: Yale University Press, 1965).
9. David Wevill, *Birth of a Shark* (New York: St. Martin's Press, 1965).
10. Howard McCord, *The Spanish Dark* (Seattle: Washington State University, 1965).
11. Lew Welch, *On Out* (Berkeley: Oyez, 1965).
12. W. R. Moses, *Identities* (Middletown, Conn.: Wesleyan University Press, 1965.
13. Carleton F. Shaw, *Desperado* (Barre, Mass.: Barre Publishers, 1965).
14. Elizabeth Bishop. *Poems of Travel* (New York: Farrar, Straus, Giroux, 1965).
15. Julia Randall, *The Puritan Carpenter* (Chapel Hill: University of North Carolina Press, 1965).
16. John W. Corrington, *Lines to the South and Other Poems* (Baton Rouge: Louisiana State University Press, 1965).
17. A. R. Ammons, *Corson's Inlet* (Ithaca: Cornell University Press, 1965).
18. Gary Snyder, *Mountains and Rivers Without End* (San Francisco: Four Seasons Foundation, 1965).
19. John Hall Wheelock, *By Daylight and in Dream* (New York: Charles Scribner's Sons, 1970).
20. Ibid.
21. Theodore Weiss, *The World Before Us* (New York: The Macmillan Company, 1970).
22. Sotère Torregian, *The Wounded Mattress* (Berkeley: Oyez, 1970).
23. Nathan Whiting, *Buffalo Poem* (N.Y., 1970).
24. Ibid.
25. Rosellen Brown, *Some Deaths in the Delta* (Amherst, Mass.: University of Massachusetts Press, 1970).
26. Ibid.
27. Michael Dennis Browne, *The Wife of Winter* (New York: Charles Scribner's Sons, 1970).
28. W. S. Merwin, *The Carrier of Ladders* (New York: Atheneum, 1970).
29. Glover Davis, *Bandaging Bread* (West Branch, Iowa: Cummington, 1970).
30. Ann Stanford, *The Descent* (New York: Viking Press, 1970).

31. William Matthews, *Ruining the New Road* (New York: Random House Inc., 1970).

32 Lewis Turco (Prints: Thomas Seawell), *The Inhabitant* (Northampton, Mass.: Despa Press, 1970).

33. Robert Bly, *The Teeth-Mother Naked at Last* (San Francisco: City Lights, 1970).

34. James Dickey, *The Eye-Beaters, Blood, Victory, Madness, Buckhead and Mercy* (Garden City, N.Y.: Doubleday & Co., 1970).

35. Al Young, in *Dices on Black Bones*, ed. Adam D. Miller (Boston, Mass.: Houghton Mifflin Co., 1970).

36. David Henderson, De Mayor of Harlem (New York: Dutton, 1970).

37. Robert Vas Dias, ed., *Inside Outer Space* (Garden City, N.Y.: Doubleday & Co., 1970).

38. For parallels see Gaston Bachelard, *The Poetics of Space*, translated by M. Jolos (New York: Orion Press, 1964).

ᴥ 12. *World Values and the Poetry of Change*

Iᴛ ɪs at least a reasonable hypothesis that poetry talks about matters important to its authors and its time. For one reason, poetry goes to a lot of trouble, measuring, stressing, rhyming, accentuating, grouping, patterning, to achieve an effect of containment and presentation of value. For another, we find in the poetry of one year or of one generation in one country such agreement of emphasis on certain terms and contexts that an effect of assured insistence is inevitable. What may we expect then from the world's poetry in one generation? Do we have a sort of worldwide consensus? Do we have as many varieties of sets of values as there are countries? Do we have more or less recent stages of interest, different temporal characteristics in different countries?

By use of recent translations of poetry in bilingual texts, comparisons of selective vocabulary can be based on the terms of the translations into English. This focus is not so self-serving as it may seem. True, translation may use the value terms of its own tongue in its own time; but it cannot force these on a truly alien text. It will not present the value of *swords* as the value of *ploughshares*. Further, while sound may suffer, the characteristic usage of structure in a poem's language may best of all convey it, a context to support the relations of the major terms.

Here are all these poets around the world, writing, being read and comprehended to some degree, by means of bilingual texts and some degree of world sympathy. Is it partly that poets have come to certain agreements about values and ways of expressing them, that poems seem to emerge in common understanding?

In English we have seen the change from concept to scene to symbol to human action, as certain well-known poems can briefly exemplify: in the seventeenth century, Lovelace's conceptual "To Lucasta, On Going to the Wars":

> Tell me not, sweet, I am unkind,
>> That from the nunnery
> Of thy chaste breast and quiet mind
>> To war and arms I fly.
>
> True, a new mistress now I chase,
>> The first foe in the field;
> And with a stronger faith embrace
>> A sword, a horse, a shield.
>
> Yet this inconstancy is such
>> As thou too shalt adore:
> I could not love thee, dear, so much,
>> Loved I not honor more.

In the eighteenth, the scenic and moral beginning of Oliver Goldsmith's "The Deserted Village":

> Sweet Auburn! loveliest village of the plain;
> Where health and plenty cheered the labouring swain,
> Where smiling spring its earliest visit paid,
> And parting summer's lingering blooms delayed:
> Dear lovely bowers of innocence and ease,
> Seats of my youth, when every sport could please,
> How often have I loitered o'er thy green,

Where humble happiness endeared each scene!
How often have I paused on every charm,
The sheltered cot, the cultivated farm,
The never-failing brook, the busy mill,
The decent church that topped the neighbouring hill.
The hawthorn bush, with seats beneath the shade,
For talking age and whispering lovers made!
How often have I blest the coming day,
When toil remitting lent its turn to play,
And all the village train, from labour free,
Led up their sports beneath the spreading tree,

H. D.'s imaged "Evening," still descriptive in the twentieth-century way, but implicative, full of suggestion of more than is said:

The light passes
from ridge to ridge,
from flower to flower—
the hypaticas, wide-spread
under the light
grow faint—
the petals reach inward,
the blue tips bend
toward the bluer heart
and the flowers are lost.

The cornel-buds are still white,
but shadows dart
from the cornel-roots—
black creeps from root to root,
each leaf
cuts another leaf on the grass,
shadow seeks shadow,
then both leaf
and leaf-shadow are lost.

Then Charles Olson's more charged symbolic and fragmented
"La Torre":

> The tower is broken, the house
> where the head was used to lift,
> where awe was
> And the hands
>
>> (It is broken!
>> And the sounds
>> are sweet, the air
>> acrid, in the night fear
>> is fragrant
>>
>>> The end of something has a satisfaction.
>>> When the structures go, light
>>> comes through
>
> To begin again. Lightning
> is an axe, transfer
> of force subject to object is
> order: destroy!
>
>> To destroy
>> is to start again, is a factor of
>> sun, fire is
>> when the sun is out, dowsed
>>
>>> (To cause the paws to grind
>>> before the nostrils flare
>>> to let breath in
>
> Stand clear! Here
> it comes down and with it the heart has
> what was, what was
> we do lament
>
>> Let him who knows not how to pray
>> go to sea

> Where there are no walls
> there are no laws, forms, sounds, odors
> to grab hold of

Let the tower fall!
Where space is born
man has a beach to ground on

> We have taken too little note of this:
> the sound of a hammer on a nail can be as clear as
> the blood a knife can make spurt from a round taut belly

2

In the laden air
we are no longer cold.
Birds spring up, and on the fragrant sea
rafts come toward us lashed of wreckage and young tree.
They bring the quarried stuff we need to try this new-
    found strength.
It will take new stone, new tufa, to finish off this rising
    tower.

Al Young's bodily "Dancing All Alone" from his *Dancing*:

We move thru rooms & down the middle of freeways,
myself & I.
A feeling lumps up in the throat
that says I wont be living forever.
The middle of the month signifies
the end of some beginning
the beginning of some end.
Once I thought the heart could be ripped out
like doll filling
& naked essence examined
but I'm a man
not a mannikin.
I would transfer to the world
my idea of what it's like beneath flesh & fur.

I cannot do this without making fools of myself.
Cold winds whoosh down on me under winter stars
& the way ahead is long but not uncertain.
I am neither prince nor citizen
but I do know what is noble in me
& what is usefully vulgar.
It is from this point that the real radiates.
I move & am moved,
do & am done for.
My prison is the room of myself
& my rejection of both is my salvation,
the way out being the way in,
the freeway that expands to my true touch,
a laughter in the blood that dances.

Present chief adjectives show similar progression. Colors
have moved as other value words have moved, from concept
toward percept. In Renaissance England, for example, black
was terrifying, a matter of sin and sorrow for Spenser:

And over all a blacke stole she did throw,
As one that inly mourned; so was she sad.

In the seventeenth century the religious Richard Crashaw
faced the color as a problem, referring to Acts 8: "On the bap-
tized Aethiopian":

Let it no longer be a forlorne hope
        To wash an Aethiope;
Hee's washt, his glossy skin a peacefull shade
        For his white soul is made;
And now, I doubt not, the Eternall Dove
        A black-faced house will love.

His contemporary but more cavalier Lovelace was rich in
blackness; as for example: *With what delight we run / To
some black cave or Grot* (from *A Paradox*). And *I must search
the black and faire* (from "The Scrutinie").

Blake's is the same concern—not only a sensory black
water and coffin, but, "The Little Black Boy":

> And I am black, but O! my soul is white;
> White as an angel is the English child,
> But I am black, as if bereav'd of light.
> . . . And these black bodies and this sunburnt face
> [are] but a cloud, and like a shady grove.

For Coleridge, the process of understanding was more dynamic. From "Religious Musings":

> from the Elect, regenerate through faith,
> Pass the dark Passions.

From "Lime Tree Bower":

> and a deep radiance lay
> Full on the ancient ivy, which usurps
> Those fronting elms, and now, with blackest mass
> Makes their dark branches gleam a brighter hue . . .

And then, from "The Ancient Mariner," concerning the glossy
green and velvet black water-snakes,

> O happy living things! no tongue
> Their beauty might declare:
> A spring of love gushed from my heart,
> And I blessed them unaware:

A pied beauty, too, for Hopkins; though he saw *a pool so
pitchblack, fell-frowning,* and *what black hours we have spent,*
yet he praised the wet freshness of dappled things in mortal
beauty. Most of Browning's speakers had an artistic eye and
spoke of black because they discerned black. Black lyre, black
stone, black bird, black eddy, Dolores' tresses *Blue-black, lus-
trous, thick like horsehairs, glance of that eye so bright and
black, the long black land.* In contrast too, for Browning, both
white and *grey* are unpleasant; poison snakes white; white an-

ger; white sweet faces; *A common greyness silvers everything;
. . . all is silver-grey / Placid and perfect with my art—the
worse!* Perfection is not Browning's admiration; the complexity
of black can be.

In Pound's famous image, black is complex: *In a Station
of the Metro:*

> The apparition of these faces in the crowd;
> Petals on a wet, black bough.

Robert Lowell's heart bleeds black blood. And for Williams,
simple observation turns to richness: *Perpetuum Mobile*—

> . . . At night
>   it wakes
> on the black
>   sky
> a dream
>   toward which
> we love—

The same implicative quality, in the very same terms, is to
be recognized in the poetry of countries of the world. Whether
or not the histories have been similar, and in some ways we
have seen them to be, as in the ballad tradition, the present
stages seem similar. At least half of the two hundred chief
adjectives, nouns, verbs, connectives, of poets writing in
twentieth-century China, India, Israel, Italy, Germany, France,
Poland, Russia, Spain, Sweden, are agreed on by two or more
poets, and the roster of terms is the roster of modernity as we
know it. A sentence of the chief shared terms: *Sun, tree, water,
wind, are black to the eye and hand which come, see, know,
in the time of night.* The dominant adjective is *black* along
with the strong *dark* and *little,* the lesser *good, great, beautiful,
red, white*—a stock of extreme sensory emphasis. The nouns
are correspondingly sensory both in bodily and natural worlds:
blood, eye, face, hand, heart, and *day, earth, light, moon, night,*

sea, shadow, sky, sun, tree, wind, water; only a few traditional abstracts: *death, life, love, man, soul, time,* the new *silence,* and the more humanly constructed *house* and *window.* The verbs are dominantly traditional: *come* and *go,* with *fall, know, live, make, see,* and the new *return.* In sum, man living, moving, dying in nature. Rilke's early "Eingang" or "Prelude" is a fine example of human responsiveness in the human world to the simplest of natural and dark objects—and at the same time the creation of the world and objects.

> Whoever you are: at evening step forth
> out of your room, where all is known to you;
> last thing before the distance lies your house:
> whoever you are.
> With your eyes, which wearily
> scarce from the much-worn threshold free themselves,
> you lift quite slowly a black tree
> and place it against the sky: slender, alone.
> And you have made the world. And it is large
> and like a word that yet in silence ripens.
> And as your will takes in the sense of it,
> tenderly your eyes let it go . . .

The white city is here, in "Lament":

> O how are all things far
> and long gone by!
> I believe the star
> from which I get radiance
> has been dead for thousands of years.
> I believe, in the boat
> that passed over,
> I heard something fearful said.
> In the house a clock
> struck . . .
> In what house? . . .

I would like to step forth out of my heart
under the great sky.
I would like to pray.
And one of all the stars
must really still be.
I believe I would know
which one alone
has endured,
which one like a white city
stands at the end of the beam in the heavens . . .

Across the world in China, too, the contrast of light and dark
in Hsü-Chih-mo's "In Search of a Bright Star":

On the back of a limping blind horse I ride,
    Heading toward the dark night;
    Heading toward the dark night,
I ride on the back of a limping blind horse.

I dart into the dark long night,
    To search for a brilliant star—
    And in order to search for a brilliant star,
I dart into the wilderness without a light.

Worn out, worn out is the horse I ride,
    Yet the star remains nowhere to be seen;
    The star remains nowhere to be seen,
While the rider is already tired, dead tired.

Now as a crystalline brilliance appears in the sky,
    A horse has fallen in the wilderness,
    And in the dark night lies a body cold—
Now as a crystalline brilliance appears in the sky.

A simpler way in Ai Ch'ing's "Autumn Morning":

Fresh and cool morning,
With the sun just rising,
A dawning over a pitiful village.

A little bird with white rings around its eyes
Stands on the black tile of a roof
Pensively
Gazing at the high sky full of colored clouds.

It's autumn
And I've been in the South for a year.
There is no tropical breath here,
No towering coconut trees to be seen.
An inexplicable sorrow has already claimed my heart.

Yet, today when I am about to go away
My heart is curiously troubled
—The villages of China
With their poverty, filth, and shadowy gray, everywhere
Still never fail to make me linger.

In these poems we see how the poet makes man a part of, yet strange to, the natural world, separating yet relating the terms. Special to the Chinese as different from the rest are such adjectives, traditional in English, as *long, old, sad,* such specifications as *soldier, uniform, village, step, street, pain, laughter, wine.* Some of these may be special to their authors, but some, as a study of earlier vocabulary by Lee Winters[1] has shown us, are highly characteristic of the Chinese themes of meeting and traveling and enduring.

Special to Hindi poets, on the other hand, are *new* and *soft* and *melody,* instances of a gentle kind in *evening, river, soul, voice,* the terms they most share. In these they are much like the Hebrew *beautiful, foot, house, morning, silence, water, window, stand,* a poetic of delight in adaption of man to nature. See for example Shlonsky's "Jezrael":

The earth of Spring grew hairy—a great body.
And my flesh sprouted in its Spring.
So shall I stand naked and covet this hairy body of mine.
Here also the dawn grew hairy—and its hair blond.

Good for you that your grassy body stretches out here,
Man!

And goat and sheep will come to crop this tender hair
And bless you: *Meh—Meh—Meh—*
And God too will come down then like a tender kid
To graze here in your flesh, grassy in its Spring.

No single poet presents a strong idiosyncracy of vocabulary. (The abstract *loneliness* of Ekelöf, *darkness* of Neruda, may be translational.) Valéry's adjectives *calm, eternal, profound, tender,* may well be the most symbolizing terms. The *forest* of Russian, German, French, and Italian may be a two-syllabled translation for English romantic *woods.* So also other chief terms afford parallels: Russian *girl, woman, lips,* Polish *flower, hair, sea, stone, town, wall,* and Italian *ancient, dry, night,* with verbs *remain, seem, vanish, watch, weep.* No one set of landscapes or actions seems to isolate one country from another; the likenesses are far stronger than the differences; and they weave from one to another rather than providing strong blocks of contrast. Not only are half the chief terms shared; the other half are similar rather than contrastive.

To compare ten world poets of the twentieth century with our ten most recent American poets born between 1930 and 1970, is to see a vivid correspondence.[2] Breadth of geographic and cultural variety squares with local intensity. As the world poets share half their chief terms with each other, they share also with America, by agreement often of a majority, from terms so traditional as *day, man, time, love, night,* to ones so characteristically modern as *black* and *tree.* They participate strongly in what can be remembered as a Coleridgean complex in *body, dream, moon, star, water, grass, shadow, stone—* now international symbols of physical location. Some American terms, like *long* and *blue,* the world has not heartily adopted. America, in the present at least, shuns the world's still strong *soul.*

For both, it is the substance of waters which characterizes the present; in the new variations of *rain, river, sea, snow, ocean, steam, flood, wet, fill,* along with the new *re-* words, *remain, return, remember,* and the terms of work and buildings, the new frontiers are shared. It is interesting to note that this world of water, now such a dominant element, was once a world of *fire,* for Wyatt and the sixteenth century. After Sylvester's Du Bartas, *air, earth,* (and a lesser *sea*) dominated the scene, especially in the eighteenth and nineteenth centuries; after Coleridge the fourth element *water* developed strongly. *Earth* is less referred to now, but *fire* is returning, and the verb *make* has returned in power also, as if there were a relation between burning and making, as in the metaphysics of Merwin's *fire.* Meanwhile, *water* is our fourth and pervading element.

See Ungaretti's "You Were Shattered":

1

Those many giant, grey and scattered stones
Still shaking from the secret slings
Of primal flames now quenched
Or from the fears that virgin rivers brought
Crashing down in their implacable embrace
—Rigid in the glitter of the sand
On a blank horizon, you remember?

And leaning, opening toward the only
Mass of shadow in the valley,
Yearning, magnified, the Araucaria pine,
Curling into the hard flint with lonely veins
More stubborn than those other accursed,
Its mouth fresh with butterflies and grass
Where severed from its roots,
—Do you remember it, incoherent, dumb,
On a few feet of rounded rock

In perfect balance,
Magically there?

From branch to branch light kinglet,
Your eager eyes drunk with wonder,
You conquered its dappled peak,
Rash, melodious child,
Just to see once more in the lucid depths
Of a profound and tranquil ocean abyss
Fabulous tortoises
Roused from sleep among the seaweed.

Tension of nature in extremes
And underwater pageants,
Funereal admonitions.

2
You raised your arms like wings
And rendered birth to the wind,
Running in the weight of the motionless air.
No one ever saw linger
Your light and dancing feet.

3
Fortunate grace,
You could not help but shatter
In a blindness so hardened—
And you simple breath and glass,

Too human a flash for the pagan,
Sylvan, relentless, droning
Roar of a naked sun.

And Montale's "Under the Rain":

A murmur; and your house grows dim
as in the winter solstice of remembrance
and so the palm weeps, for relentless

presses the decay that holds
within the sultriness of the greenhouse
even bare hopes and remorseful thoughts.

"Per amor de la fiebre" . . . I am carried
into a whirlpool with you. A bright red awning
gleams, a window is closed.
On the maternal slope go walking,
like an eggshell lost in the mire,
bits of life betwixt shade and light.

From the courtyard *Adiós muchachos*
compañeros de mi vida screeched your record:
and dear to me still is the mask
if beyond the whirlwind of fate I am left
with the jolt that leads me back
upon your path.
I follow bright downpours, and beyond, drifting
puffs of smoke from a ship.
A gash of light appears . . .
                                    Because of you
I understand the daring stork
when rising into flight from foggy peaks
he wings his way toward Capetown.

How Neruda then draws up this language in "The
Heights of Macchu Picchu: IV":

Death, overmastering all, has beckoned me often:
eye has not seen it, like brine in the wave,
but invisible savors are shed on the waters,
height, or the ruin of height, a plenitude halved,
enormous constructions of ice and the wind.

I had come to the limits of iron, a narrowing
air, to the graveclothes of gardens and stones,
vacancy starred with the tread of the ultimate,
and the dizzying whorl of the highway:

but not with a billow's successions you come to us, Death!
though the sea of our dying is ample, you strike at a
    gallop,
explicit in darkness, and the numbers of midnight are
    reckoned.

No pickpocket rifler, you come to us; lacking
that scarlet investiture, no advent is possible:
you tread on the weft of the morning, enclosing a quiet-
    ness,
a heritage weeping above us, tears underground.

That tree of our being,
with its nondescript autumns (a thousand leaves dying),
that fardel of fraudulent deaths, resurrections
out of nowhere—neither earth, nor abysses of earth:
I never could cherish it.
I prayed to the drench of life's amplitude, a swimmer,
unencumbered, at the place of the sources;
until, little by little, denied by the others—those
who would seal up their doors and their footfalls and
    withhold
their wounded non-being from the gush of my fingers—
I came by another way, river by river, street after street, . . .

River by river, street after street, black tree by black wall,
the major terms of natural value begin to blend again with
terms of human value in the world's poetry. It is as if human-
ness were being looked into through darkness, with a search
for new insights, in every country and language.

Even in one small city, the worldwide changes have been
particularly visible in this past decade. From the romantically
implicative work of images in Jeffers, Bynner, Taggard, Flan-
ner, Welch, the Lymans, the Erskine Woods, from the experiments of Leite's *Circle*, Russell's *Ark*, Waldport's *Interim*, the
activists under Lawrence Hart, poets in Berkeley moved to the

more open expressiveness of Rexroth, McClure, Ferlinghetti, Everson, Duncan, Spicer, Snyder, Parkinson, which could welcome that of Ginsberg's *Howl* and the tutelage of Olson and Creeley. Devotion to Auden in the 1930s shifted to Thomas and Stevens in the 1940s, Williams since, and Lawrence.

Openness in every way guided the poetry of the 1960s—openness of sound in line and cadence, and in a very vaudeville of delivery; openness of meaning and vocabulary and opinion and action; openness of structures, the relation to proper forms occidental or oriental, of shaggy-dog narratives and ego trips; openness of heart and mind to new experiences and feelings. Meanwhile, through Dylan, Cohen, the Beatles, was preserved the poetry of song in new ways in another force, hard to relate, yet bringing guitar accompaniment, like lyre, and poem together in many variations. Curious mixtures of ballad and cadence, A. R. Ammons, Diane Wakoski, Thom Gunn, Doug Palmer, and the Peace and Gladness poets following Gary Snyder, the openness of spontaneity and a receptive scene. Poetry readings for justice, friends in need, the land. Quieter tones in William Stafford, G. P. Elliott, Ron Loewinsohn, George Starbuck, Leonard Nathan, James Tate, more satiric for Ishmael Reed, George Barlow. For one city as for the world, the turn from "objectivity," toward questions. What is true? Who knows? Who cares? Such feeling does not reinvolve romantic dimness; rather, it intensifies truth and falsity equally, with deliberate accuracy of line.

The positive consequence of our antiobjectivity may involve some fine complexities. For one, a sense of immediate, physical directness. For another, a sense of responsibility in human construction, in objects made rather than found. For a third, a sense of the fuller potentialities of *memory* as a human faculty, as it takes the place of earlier *faith* and *thought*. What we do not get a glimmer of or a clue to is how our systems-civilization will make its way into value; how laws, plans, committees, bureaucracies, machines, will find some human validation. Perhaps as memory systems, perhaps as tools for construction, as extensions of bodily powers, perhaps as a part of community? At the moment, we are so far from a poetic vocabulary of concept and abstraction that the guesses must be nearly groundless. But the further step need not be forced; the present step is the naturally next and informative one, from values of objectivity to values of immediacy and impact.

Most specifically I hope this book has shown the steadiness of change from poet to poet and thus from time to time within the art. Minor usages become major for a few poets, then may become major for most. Sentence structure, sound structure, sense structure move together in their involvement of the reader in their world of values. A Donne makes tremendous exaggerations of the ways of his time, often to counter them and call them into question; a Milton begins a leadership in new thematic ways; a Blake inverts the theme; a Coleridge recalls old structures to new visions; a Wordsworth declares them; a Robinson in his nostalgic way forsees some of the future; a young generation begins constructing new anatomies and architectures of being.

The fact that the major terms and structures of poets in any one time are so alike suggests a profession of poetry, within a profession of literature, an ongoing art in which individuals share to various degrees, forming, shaping, and guiding to their own individual purposes, but never far from center, as if the art were a culture of its own, moving in expression of the culture. The fact that in any one time, half the chief usages persist, a quarter decline, and a quarter newly appear, for individuals as well as the poetry as a whole, suggests some measure of predictability, at least of recognizable pattern, in art and its part in culture. The fact visible in negative reactions of eighteenth century to seventeenth century, of Blake to Milton, of Pound to Wordsworth, and in the dislike and loss of old materials along with the adoption of new, suggests a process of development we may well observe further in its principle of satiety, innovation, and renewal.

As Philip Sidney has said, poetry is both history and philosophy, because it not only declares what it values but shapes and preserves what it values, both in its depths and at its surfaces, in local intensities and world reaches.

NOTES TO CHAPTER 12

1. Lee Winters, "The Relationship of Chinese Poetry to British and American Poetry of the Twentieth Century" (unpublished dissertation, University of California, Berkeley, 1956).
2. Texts used, with proportions listed for about 6,000 words, 1,000 lines each:
   Twentieth Century Chinese Poetry, translated and edited by Kai-Yan Hsu (New York: Doubleday, 1963. Hsu Chi Mo, b.1895; Ai Ch'ing, b.1910), pp. 77–96, 295–313. 870 adjectives; 1,830 nouns; 1,000 verbs; 1,350 connectives. *Modern Hebrew Poetry*, edited by Ruth Mintz (Berkeley and Los Angeles: University of California Press, 1966. Shlovsky through Goldberg), pp. 166–248. 510 adjectives; 1,540 nouns; 750 verbs; 1,090 connectives. *Modern Hindi Poetry*, edited by Vidya Misra (Bloomington: University of Indiana Press, 1965), pp. 41–90. 763 adjectives; 1,860 nouns; 797 verbs; 1,209 connectives. Scandinavian: Gunnar Ekelöf, *Om Hösten, Dikter* (Stockholm: Bonnier, 1951). 570 adjectives; 1,450 nouns; 860 verbs; 1,030 connectives. French: Paul Valéry, *Selected Writings*. Translated by Denis Devlin, et al. (New York: New Directions, 1950). 900 adjectives; 1,700 nouns; 900 verbs, connectives not counted. German: Rainer Maria Rilke, *Das Buch der Bilder* (Wiesbaden: Insel-Verlag, 1954). 480 adjectives; 910 nouns; 840 verbs; connectives not counted. *Contemporary Italian Poetry*, edited by Carlo L. Galino (Berkeley and Los Angeles: University of California Press, 1962), pp. 110–191. 930 adjectives; 1,600 nouns; 700 verbs; 1,230 connectives. *Postwar Polish Poetry*, selected and translated by Czeslaw Milosz (New York: Doubleday, 1965), pp. 90–149. 540 adjectives; 1,570 nouns; 750 verbs; 1,100 connectives. Russian: Andrey Voznesensky, *Antiworlds*. Edited by Patricia Blake and Max Hayward (New York: Basic Books, 1966), pp. 3–46. 500 adjectives; 1,340 nouns; 650 verbs; 850 connectives. Spanish: *Selected Poems of Pablo Neruda*. Edited and translated by Ben Belitt (New York: Grove Press, 1961), pp. 19–189. 590 adjectives; 1,700 nouns; 400 verbs; 1,110 connectives.

✖ Selected Readings

WITH emphasis on theory, classical and contemporary. More complete lists in earlier volumes emphasize work on individual authors.

Abrams, M. H. *The Mirror and the Lamp: Romantic Theory and the Critical Tradition.* New York: Oxford University Press, 1953.

Ackerman, James S. "A Theory of Style." *Journal of Aesthetics and Art Criticism*, 20, no. 3 (spring 1962): 227–237.

Akhmanova, Olga S. *The Principles and Methods of Linguostylistics: A Course of Lectures.* Moscow: Moscow State University, 1970.

Alison, Archibald. *Essays on the Nature and Principles of Taste*, 6th ed. 2 vols. London, 1825.

Alpers, Paul. *Spenser.* Princeton, N.J.: Princeton University Press, 1967.

Alvarez, Alfred. *The School of Donne.* London: Chatto & Windus, 1961.

Arnauld, Antoine, and Pierre Nicole. *The Port-Royal Logic.* Trans. Thomas Spencer Baynes. Edinburgh: William Blackwood & Sons, 1890. Trans. James Dickoff and Patricia James. Indianapolis, Ind., 1964.

Arthos, John. *The Language of Natural Description in Eighteenth Century Poetry.* Ann Arbor: University of Michigan Press, 1949.

Auerbach, Erich. *Mimesis: The Representation of Reality in Western Literature.* Princeton, N.J.: Princeton University Press, 1953.

Bailey, Richard W., et al. "Annual Bibliography for 1968." *Style,* 3 (fall 1969).

———. "Annual Bibliography for 1969." *Style,* 4 (1970): 252–294.

———. "Annual Bibliography for 1970." *Style,* 6 (winter 1972): 90–112.

———. "Annual Bibliography for 1971." *Style,* 7 (winter 1973): 74–118.

Bailey, Richard W., and Sister Dolores Marie Burton. *English Stylistics: A Bibliography.* Boston: Emmanuel College, 1965.

Baker, William E. *Syntax in English Poetry, 1870–1930.* Berkeley and Los Angeles: University of California Press, 1967.

Bally, Charles. *Le Langage et la Vie,* 3rd ed. Zurich: M. Niehans, 1935.

Barber, C. L. "Some Measurable Characteristics of Modern Scientific Prose," *Contributions to English Syntax and Philology,* by C. L. Barber et al. "Gothenburg Studies in English," ed. Frank Behre, vol. 14, Göteborg, 1962.

Barfield, Owen. *Poetic Diction: A Study in Meaning,* 2nd ed. Faber & Groyer, 1952.

Barish, Jonas. *Ben Jonson and the Language of Prose Comedy.* Cambridge: Harvard University Press, 1960.

Barnett, H. G. *Innovation: The Basis of Cultural Change.* New York: McGraw-Hill Book Co., 1953.

Barthes, Roland. *Elements of Semiology.* Trans. Annette Lavers and Colin Smith. London: Cape, 1967.

———. "Style and Its Image." In *Literary Style: A Symposium,* ed. Seymour Chatman. New York: Oxford University Press, 1971. Pp. 3–10.

Bateson, F. W. *English Poetry and the English Language: An Experiment in Literary History.* Oxford: Clarendon Press, 1934.

Baugh, Hansell, ed. *General Semantics.* "Papers from the First American Congress," 1935. New York: Arrow Editions, 1940.

Belknap, George N. *A Guide to the Reading in Aesthetics and Theory of Poetry.* "University of Oregon Publications," vol. 4, no. 9 (July 1934).

Bennett, James R. "Annotated Bibliography of Selected Writings on English Prose Style." *College Composition and Communication,* 16 (December 1965).

Berek, Peter. " 'Plain' and 'Ornate' Styles and the Structure of *Paradise Lost.*" *PMLA*, 85 (1970): 237–246.

Berlin, Isaiah. *Historical Inevitability.* London: Oxford University Press, 1954.

Berry, Francis. *Poet's Grammar.* London: Routledge & Kegan Paul, 1958.

Blair, Hugh. *Lectures on Rhetoric and Belles Lettres, 1762 et seqq.* London, 1813.

Bock, Emmon, and Robert T. Harris, eds. *Universals in Linguistic Theory.* New York: Holt, Rinehart & Winston, 1968.

Boon, James A. *From Symbol to Structuralism.* New York: Harper & Row, 1972.

Booth, Stephen. *An Essay on Shakespeare's Sonnets.* New Haven: Yale University Press, 1969.

Brooke-Rose, Christine. *A Grammar of Metaphor.* London: Secker & Warburg, 1958.

Brower, Reuben. *The Fields of Light.* London: Oxford University Press, 1951.

Brown, Huntington. *Prose Styles.* Minneapolis: University of Minnesota Press, 1966.

Bruneau, Charles. "La Stylistique." *Romance Philology*, 5 (1951): 1–15.

Buffon, George. *Discours sur le Style.* Paris: Librairie Hachette, 1921.

Burke, Kenneth. *The Philosophy of Literary Form: Studies in Symbolic Action.* Baton Rouge: Louisiana State University Press, 1941.

Bysshe, Edward. *The Art of English Poetry*, 9th ed. London, 1762.

Carritt, E. F. *A Calendar of British Taste, 1600–1800.* London: Routledge & Kegan Paul, 1949.

Carroll, John B. *Language and Thought.* Englewood Cliffs, N.J.: Prentice-Hall, 1964.

Cassirer, Ernst. *Philosophy of Symbolic Forms.* Trans. Ralph Mannheim. 3 vols. New Haven: Yale University Press, 1953–1957.

Chafe, Wallace. *Meaning and the Structure of Language.* Chicago: University of Chicago Press, 1970.

Chambers, R. W. *On the Continuity of English Prose from Alfred to More and His School.* London: Oxford University Press, 1957.

Chandler, Zilpha. *An Analysis of the Stylistic Technique of Addison, Johnson, Hazlitt, and Pater.* "University of Iowa Humanistic Studies," 4, no. 3. Iowa City: University of Iowa Press, 1928.

Chatman, Seymour, ed. *Literary Style: A Symposium.* New York: Oxford University Press, 1971.

Chomsky, Noam. *Aspects of the Theory of Syntax.* Cambridge: M.I.T. Press, 1965.

————. *Cartesian Linguistics: A Chapter in the History of Rationalist Thought.* New York: Harper & Row, 1966.

————. *Current Issues in Linguistic Theory.* The Hague: Mouton & Co., 1965.

Christensen, Francis. "A Generative Rhetoric of the Sentence." *College Composition and Communication,* 14, no. 3 (October 1963).

————. "John Wilkins and the Royal Society's Reform of Prose Style." *Modern Language Quarterly,* 7 (1946): 178–188, 279–291.

Cohen, Ralph, ed. *New Literary History,* IV, x (autumn 1972).

Cook, Albert S. *The Bible and English Prose Style.* Boston: D. C. Heath & Co., 1892.

Crane, Ronald S., ed. *Critics and Criticism, Ancient and Modern.* Chicago: University of Chicago Press, 1952.

————. *The Languages of Criticism and the Structure of Poetry.* Toronto: University of Toronto Press, 1953.

Croce, Benedetto. *Logic as the Science of the Prose Concept.* Trans. Douglas Ainslie. New York: Macmillan Co., 1917.

Croll, Morris. "Baroque Style in Prose." *Studies in English Philology.* Ed. K. Malone. Minneapolis: University of Minnesota, 1929.

————. "Attic Prose in the Seventeenth Century." *Studies in Philology,* 18 (April 1921): 79–128.

————. "Muret and the History of Attic Prose." *PMLA,* 39, no. 2: 254–309.

————. *Style, Rhetoric, and Rhythm.* Ed. J. M. Patrick, et al. Princeton, N.J.: Princeton University Press, 1965.

Crystal, David, and Derek Davy. *Investigating English Style.* Bloomington: Indiana University Press, 1969.

Culler, A. Dwight. "Edward Bysshe and the Poet's Handbook." *PMLA*, 63, no. 3 (September 1948): 858–886.

Cummings, D. W., John Herum, and E. K. Lybbert. "Semantic Recurrence and Rhetorical Form." *Language and Style*, 4 (1971): 195–207.

Cunningham, J. V. *Woe and Wonder*. Denver: University of Denver, 1951.

Curtius, Ernst Robert. *European Literature and the Latin Middle Ages*. Trans. Willard Trask. Bollingen Series, vol. 36. New York: Pantheon, 1953.

Danielson, Wayne A. "Computer Analysis of News Prose." *Computer Studies in the Humanities and Verbal Behavior*, 1 (1968): 55–60.

Danto, Arthur C. *Analytical Philosophy of History*. Cambridge: At the University Press, 1965.

Davie, Donald. *Articulate Energy: An Inquiry into the Syntax of English Poetry*. London: Routledge & Kegan Paul, 1955.

————. *The Language of Science and the Language of Literature*. London: Sheed & Ward, 1963.

Davies, Hugh Sykes. "Milton and the Vocabulary of Verse and Prose." In *Literary English Since Shakespeare*, ed. George Watson. London: Oxford University Press, 1970. Pp. 175–193.

Deese, James. *The Structure of Associations in Language and Thought*. Baltimore: Johns Hopkins Press, 1965.

Denniston, J. D. *Greek Prose Style*. Oxford: Clarendon Press, 1952.

Dewey, Edward R., and Edwin F. Dakin. *Cycles: The Science of Prediction*. New York: Henry Holt and Co., 1947.

Dewey, Godfrey. *Relative Frequency of English Speech Sounds*. Cambridge: Harvard University Press, 1943.

Dijk, Teun A. van. "Some Problems of Generative Poetics." *Poetics*, 2 (1971): 5–35.

Dockhorn, Klaus. "Wordsworth und die rhetorische Tradition in England." *Nachrichten der Akademie der Wissenschaften in Göttingen*. "Philologisch-Historische Klasse," vol. 11. Göttingen: Vanderhoeck & Ruprecht, 1944.

Ducretet, Pierre R. "Quantitative Stylistics: An Essay in Methodology." *Computers and the Humanities*, 4 (1970): 187–191.

Eaton, Helen. *Semantic Frequency List for English, French, German, Spanish*. Chicago: University of Chicago Press, 1940.

Eliot, T. S. *The Use of Poetry and the Use of Criticism: Studies in the Relation of Criticism to Poetry in England.* "Norton Lectures," 1932–1933. Cambridge: Harvard University Press, 1933.

Empson, William. *Seven Types of Ambiguity.* London: Chatto & Windus, 1930.

Enkvist, N. E. "On Defining Style." In *Linguistics in Style,* ed. John Spencer. London: Oxford University Press, 1964.

Entwhistle, William J. *Aspects of Language.* London: Faber & Faber, 1953.

Eskey, David Ellsworth. "A Preface to the Study of Literary Style," *Dissertation Abstracts,* 31, 376A–377A.

Faral, Edmond. *Les arts poétiques du XIIᵉ et du XIIIᵉ siècle.* Paris: É. Champion, 1924.

Fénelon, François. *Dialogues on Eloquences, 1718.* Trans. W. S. Howell. Princeton, N.J.: Princeton University Press, 1951.

Fillmore, Charles. "The Case for Case." In *Universals in Linguistic Theory,* ed. Emmon Bock and Robert T. Harris. New York: Holt, Rinehart and Winston, 1968.

——————, and D. Terrence Langendoen, eds. *Linguistic Semantics.* New York: Holt, Rinehart and Winston, 1971.

Firth, J. R. *Papers in Linguistics, 1934–1951.* London: Oxford University Press, 1957 [1961].

Fish, Stanley. *John Skelton's Poetry.* New Haven: Yale University Press, 1965.

——————. *Self-Consuming Artifacts: The Experience of Seventeenth-Century Literature.* Berkeley and Los Angeles: University of California Press, 1972.

——————. *Surprised by Sin: The Reader in Paradise Lost.* New York: St. Martin's Press, 1967.

Fodor, J. A., and J. J. Katz, eds. *The Structure of Language: Readings in the Philosophy of Language.* Englewood Cliffs, N.J.: Prentice-Hall, 1964.

Fowler, Roger. "Style and the Concept of Deep Structure." *Journal of Literary Semantics,* 1 (1972): 5–24.

Frank, Joseph. *The Widening Gyre: Crisis and Mastery in Modern Literature.* New Brunswick, N.J.: Rutgers University Press, 1963.

Freeman, Donald C. *Linguistics and Literary Style.* New York: Holt, Rinehart and Winston, 1970.

Freimark, Vincent. "The Bible and Neo-Classical Views of Style." *Journal of English and Germanic Philology*, 51 (1952): 517–526.

Fries, C. C. *The Structure of English*. New York: Harcourt, Brace & Co., 1952.

Fuchs, Wilhelm. "On Mathematical Analyses of Style." *Diometriku*, 39, nos. 1, 2 (May 1952): 122–129.

Fuchs, Wilhelm. "Possibilities of Exact Style Analysis." In *Patterns of Literary Style*, ed. Joseph Strelka. University Park: Pennsylvania State University Press, 1971. Pp. 51–76.

Fussell, Paul, Jr. *Poetic Meter and Poetic Form*. New York: Random House, 1965.

———. *Theory of Prosody in Eighteenth Century England*. New London: Connecticut College, 1954.

Garwin, Paul, et al. "Predication." Suppl. to *Language*, vol. 43, no. 2, pt. II (June 1967).

Gildon, Charles. *The Complete Art of Poetry*. 2 vols. London, 1718.

Gilson, Étienne. *The Arts of the Beautiful*. New York: Charles Scribner's Sons, 1965.

Gleason, H. A. *Introduction to Descriptive Linguistics*, rev. ed. New York: Henry Holt and Co., 1961.

Gordon, Ian A. *The Movement of English Prose*. Bloomington: Indiana University Press, 1966.

Graubard, Stephen R., ed. "Language as a Human Problem." *Daedalus*, 102 (summer 1973).

Greimas, A. J., et al. *Sign, Language and Culture*. The Hague: Mouton, 1970.

Groom, Bernard. *The Diction of Poetry from Spenser to Bridges*. Toronto: University of Toronto Press, 1955.

Guillen, Claudio. "Poetics as System." *Comparative Literature*, 22 (1970): 193–222.

Guiraud, Pierre. *Essais de Stylistique*. Paris: Klincksieck, 1969.

———. *Les Caractères Statistiques du Vocabulaire*. Paris: Presses Universitaires de France, 1954.

———. "Modern Linguistics Look at Rhetoric: Free Indirect Style." In *Patterns of Literary Style*, ed. Joseph Strelka. University Park: Pennsylvania State University, 1971. Pp. 77–89.

Halpern, Martin. "The Two Chief Metrical Modes in English." *PMLA* (June 1962).

Hamilton, G. Rostrevor. *The Tell-Tale Article: A Critical Approach to Modern Poetry*. New York: Oxford University Press, 1950.

Hamilton, Kenneth. *The Two Harmonies: Poetry and Prose in the 19th Century*. New York: Oxford University Press, 1963.

Harris, Zellig S. *Methods in Structural Linguistics*. Chicago: University of Chicago Press, 1947–1951.

Hartman, Geoffrey H. *Wordsworth's Poetry*. New Haven: Yale University Press, 1964.

Hathaway, Baxter. *The Age of Criticism*. Ithaca, N.Y.: Cornell University Press, 1962.

Hatzfeld, Helmut. *A Critical Bibliography of the New Stylistics Applied to the Romance Literatures, 1900–1952*. Chapel Hill: University of North Carolina Press, 1953.

Henn, T. R. *Longinus and English Criticism*. Cambridge: At the University Press, 1934.

Herdan, Gustav. *Language as Choice and Chance*. Groningen: P. Noordhoff, 1956.

Heron, Patrick. *The Changing Forms of Art*. New York: Macmillan Co., 1950.

Hill, Archibald A. *Introduction to Linguistic Structure: From Sound to Sentence in English*. New York: Harcourt, Brace and Co., 1958.

Hirsch, E. D. *Validity in Interpretation*. New Haven: Yale University Press, 1967.

Hoenigswald, Henry. *Language, Change, and Linguistic Reconstruction*. Chicago: University of Chicago Press, 1960.

Hollander, John. *The Untuning of the Sky: Ideas of Music in English Poetry, 1500–1700*. Princeton, N.J.: Princeton University Press, 1961.

Holloway, John. *The Victorian Sage: Studies in Argument*. London: Macmillan & Co., 1953.

Home, Henry, Lord Kames. *Elements of Criticism*. New York: 1830.

Housman, A. E. *The Name and Nature of Poetry*. New York: Macmillan Co., 1933.

Howell, A. C. "Res et Verba." *Journal of English History* (1946), pp. 131–142.

Howell, Wilbur Samuel. *Logic and Rhetoric in England, 1500–1700*. Princeton, N.J.: Princeton University Press, 1956.

Hymes, Dell. *Language in Culture and Society: A Reader in Linguistics and Anthropology.* New York: Harper & Brothers, 1964.

Ingarden, Roman. *Das Literarische Kunstwerk.* Halle, Germany: Niemeyer, 1931.

Jakobson, Roman. "Linguistics and Poetics." In *Style in Language,* ed. Thomas Sebeok. Cambridge: M.I.T. Press, 1960. Pp. 350–377.

————. "The Metaphoric and Metonymic Poles." In *Fundamentals of Language.* The Hague: Mouton & Co., 1956. Pp. 76–82.

————. "On the Verbal Art of William Blake and Other Poet-Painters." *Linguistic Inquiry,* 1 (1970): 3–23.

————, and Morris Halle. *Fundamentals of Language.* The Hague: Mouton & Co., 1956.

————, et al. *Preliminaries to Speech Analysis: The Distinctive Features and Their Correlates.* Report No. 13. Cambridge: M.I.T. Press, 1952.

Johnson, James William. *The Formation of English Neo-Classical Thought.* Princeton, N.J.: Princeton University Press, 1967.

Johnson, Samuel. *The Lives of the English Poets.* Ed. George Birback Hill. Oxford: Clarendon Press, 1905.

Johnson, W. R. *Luxuriance and Economy.* Berkeley and Los Angeles: University of California Press, 1971.

Jones, Ebenezer. *Studies of Sensation and Event.* London, 1879.

Jones, Richard Foster. *The Seventeenth Century: Studies in the History of Thought and Literature from Bacon to Pope.* Stanford, Calif.: Stanford University Press, 1951.

————. *The Triumph of the English Language.* Stanford, Calif.: Stanford University Press, 1951.

Jonson, Ben. *Timber,* with an Introduction by Ralph S. Walker. Syracuse, N. Y.: Syracuse University Press, 1953.

————. *The English Grammar: Made by Ben Jonson for the Benefit of All Strangers, Out of His Observations of the English Language Now Spoken and in Use.* London: Lanston Monotype Corp., 1928.

Joos, Martin. *The English Verb: Form and Meaning.* Madison: University of Wisconsin Press, 1964.

Joseph, Sister Miriam. *Shakespeare's Use of the Arts of Language.* New York: Columbia University Press, 1947.

Karlsen, Rolf. *Studies in the Connectives of Clauses.* Bergen, 1959.
Katz, J. J., and P. M. Postal. *An Integrated Theory of Linguistic Descriptions.* Research Monograph no. 26. Cambridge: M.I.T. Press, 1964.
Keesing, Felix. *Cultural Change: An Analysis and Bibliography of Anthropological Sources to 1952.* Stanford, Calif.: Stanford University Press, 1953.
Kermode, Frank. *John Donne.* London: Longmans, Green, 1961.
———. *The Romantic Image.* London: Kegan Paul, 1957.
———. *The Living Milton: Essays by Various Hands.* London: Routledge & Kegan Paul, 1960.
Kliger, Samuel. *The Goths in England: A Study of Seventeenth and Eighteenth Century Thought.* Cambridge: Harvard University Press, 1952.
Knights, L. C. "Elizabethan Prose." *Scrutiny*, II (1934).
Kroeber, A. L. *Configurations of Culture Growth.* Berkeley and Los Angeles: University of California Press, 1944.
———. *Style and Civilizations.* Ithaca, N.Y.: Cornell University Press, 1957.
———. "Parts of Speech in Periods of Poetry." *PMLA*, 63, no. 4 (September 1958): 309–314.
Kubler, George. *The Shape of Time: Remarks on the History of Things.* New Haven and London: Yale University Press, 1962.
Kuhn, Thomas. *The Structure of Scientific Revolutions.* 2nd ed., enl. Chicago: University of Chicago Press, 1970.
Kurth, Burton O. *Milton and the English Traditions of Biblical Heroic Narrative.* Berkeley and Los Angeles: University of California Press, 1955.
Lakoff, Robin. "Language in Context." *Language*, 48 (1972): 907–927.
Lamprecht, Sterling P. *Nature and History.* New York: Columbia University Press, 1950.
Landar, Herbert. *Language and Culture.* New York: Oxford University Press, 1965.
Langer, Suzanne. *Feeling and Form: A Theory of Art Developed from "Philosophy in a New Key."* New York: Charles Scribner's Sons, 1953.
Lasswell, Harold D., Nathan Leites, et al. *Language of Politics:*

Studies in Quantitative Semantics. New York: George Stewart, 1949.

Lawton, George. *John Wesley's English: A Study of His Literary Style.* London: Allen & Unwin, 1962.

Lazarsfeld, Paul, and Morris Rosenberg. *The Language of Social Research.* Glencoe, Ill.: Free Press, 1955.

Leavis, F. R. *New Bearings in English Poetry: A Study of the Contemporary Situation.* London: Chatto & Windus, 1932.

————. *Revaluation: Tradition and Development in English Poetry.* London: Chatto & Windus, 1936.

Lee, Vernon. *The Handling of Words, and Other Studies in Literary Psychology.* London: John Lane, 1923.

Leed, Jacob, ed. *Computers and Literary Analysis.* Kent, Ohio: Kent State University Press, 1966.

Lees, R. B. *The Grammar of English Nominalization, International Journal of American Linguistics,* 26, suppl. (1964).

Lehmann, W. P. "Contemporary Linguistics and Indo-European Studies." *PMLA,* 87 (October 1972): 976–993.

————. "Converging Theories in Linguistics." *Language,* 48 (June 1972): 266–275.

Levin, Harry. *The Power of Blackness.* New York: Alfred A. Knopf, 1958.

Levin, Kurt. *Field Theory in Social Science.* New York: Harper and Brothers, 1951.

Levin, Samuel R. *Linguistic Structures in Poetry.* The Hague: Mouton & Co., 1962.

Levine, George, and William Madden, eds. *The Art of Victorian Prose.* New York: Oxford University Press, 1968.

Levi-Strauss, C., R. Jakobson, C. F. Voegelin, and T. A. Sebeok. *Results of the Conference of Anthropologists and Linguistics.* Baltimore: Johns Hopkins University Press, 1953.

Lewis, C. S. *Studies in Words.* Cambridge: At the University Press, 1960.

Lily, William. *A Shorte Introduction of Grammar.* New York: Scholars' Facsimiles, 1945.

Long, Ralph B. *The Sentence and Its Parts.* Chicago: University of Chicago Press, 1961.

Longinus on the Sublime and Sir Joshua Reynolds' Discourses.

Trans. Benedict Einarsson, with an Introd. by Elder Olson. Chicago: Packard, 1945.

Lovejoy, Arthur. *Essays in the History of Ideas*. Baltimore: Johns Hopkins University Press, 1948.

————. *The Great Chain of Being: A Study of the History of an Idea*. Cambridge: Harvard University Press, 1936.

Lowenthal, Leo. *Literature, Popular Culture, and Society*. Englewood Cliffs, N.J.: Prentice-Hall, 1961.

Lowes, John Livingston. *Convention and Revolt in Poetry*. Boston: Houghton Mifflin Co., 1924.

Lowth, Robert. *A Short Introduction to Grammar*. London, 1762, 1775.

————. *Lectures on the Sacred Poetry of the Hebrews*, 2nd ed. London, 1816.

Lukács, George. *Realism in Our Time*. New York: Harper & Row, 1966.

Lunt, H. G., ed. *Proceedings of the Ninth International Congress of Linguists, Cambridge, Mass.*, 1962. The Hague: Mouton & Co., 1964.

Lyons, John. *Structural Semantics*. London: Oxford University Press, 1963.

McKeon, Richard. *Thought, Action, and Passion*. Chicago: University of Chicago Press, 1954.

Macksey, Richard, and Eugenio Danto, eds. *The Languages of Criticism and the Sciences of Man: The Structuralist Controversy*. Baltimore: Johns Hopkins Press, 1970.

MacLuhan, Marshall. *Understanding Media*. New York: McGraw-Hill Book Co., 1965.

Madden, John F., and F. P. Magoun. *A Grouped Frequency Word-List of Anglo-Saxon Poetry*. Cambridge: Harvard University Press, 1957.

Malkiel, Yakov. "Etymology and General Linguistics," *Word*, 18, nos. 1 and 2 (April–August 1962): 198–219.

Man, Paul de. *Blindness and Insight: Essays in the Rhetoric of Composition*. New York: Oxford University Press, 1970.

Martin, Harold, ed. *Style in Prose Fiction*. "English Institute Essays," 1958. New York: Columbia University Press, 1959.

Martini, Fritz. "Personal Style and Period Style: Perspectives on a Theme of Literary Research." In *Patterns of Literary Style*, ed. Joseph Strelka. University Park: Pennsylvania State University, 1971. Pp. 90–115.

Matthews, R. J., and W. Ver Eecke. "Metaphoric-Metonymic Polarities: A Structural Analysis." *Linguistics*, 67 (1971): 34–53.

Maxim, Hudson. *The Science of Poetry and the Philosophy of Language*. New York: Funk & Wagnalls, 1910.

Mead, George. *Movements of Thought in the Nineteenth Century*. Chicago: University of Chicago Press, 1936.

Medewar, P. B. *The Future of Man*. New York: Basic Books, 1960.

Mentré, François. *Les Générations Sociales*. Paris: Editions Bossard, 1920.

Merleau-Ponty, Maurice. *In Praise of Philosophy*. Trans. John Wild and James Edie. Evanston: Northwestern University Press, 1963.

———. The Primacy of Perception. Ed. James Edie, et al. Evanston: Northwestern University Press, 1964.

Messing, Gordon M. "The Impact of Transformational Grammar upon Stylistics and Literary Analysis." *Linguistics*, 66 (1971): 56–73.

Meyer, Leonard. *Music, the Arts, and Ideas*. Chicago: University of Chicago Press, 1967.

Meyerhoff, Hans. *Time in Literature*. Berkeley and Los Angeles: University of California Press, 1955.

Miles, Josephine. *Continuity of Poetic Language: Studies in English Poetry from 1640's to 1940's*. Berkeley and Los Angeles: University of California Press, 1951; New York: Octagon Press, 1966.

———. Emerson. Minneapolis: University of Minnesota Press, 1964.

———. "American Poetry, 1965." *Massachusetts Review*, 7 (spring 1966): 321–335.

———. "English: A Colloquy: or, How What's What in the Language." *California English Journal*, 2 (winter 1966).

———. "Review of Concordances." *Victorian Studies* (March 1965): 290–292.

———. "Emerson's Wise Universe." *University of Minnesota Review*, 2, no. 3 (spring 1962): 305–313.

———. "A Poet Looks at Graphs." *Michigan Quarterly Review*, 4, no. 3 (summer 1965): 185–188.

————. *Eras and Modes in English Poetry.* 2nd rev. ed. Berkeley and Los Angeles: University of California Press, 1964.

————. "Language of *Lycidas.*" *Lycidas.* Ed. Dean Patrides. New York: Oxford University Press, 1961.

————. *Pathetic Fallacy in the Nineteenth Century: Study of Changing Relation Between Object and Emotion.* Berkeley and Los Angeles: University of California Press, 1942; "University of California Publications in English," vol. 12, no. 2. New York: Octagon Press, 1965.

————. "Poetry of Praise." *Kenyon Review,* 23, no. 1 (winter 1961): 104–125.

————. "Reading Poems." *English Journal,* 52, nos. 3, 4 (March-April 1963).

————. *Renaissance, Eighteenth-Century and Modern Language in English Poetry.* Berkeley and Los Angeles: University of California Press, 1960.

————. "What We Compose." *College Composition and Communication,* 15 (October 1964).

————. "Wordsworth and Glitter." *Studies in Philology,* 15, no. 4 (October 1943): 552–559.

————. *Wordsworth and the Vocabulary of Emotion.* Berkeley and Los Angeles: University of California Press, 1942: "University of California Publications in English," vol. 12, no. 1. New York: Octagon Press, 1965.

Milic, Louis. *The Style of Swift.* New York: W. W. Norton & Co., 1966.

Minnis, Noel, ed. *Linguistics at Large.* London: Victor Gollancz, 1971.

MLA International Bibliography of Books and Articles on the Modern Languages. New York: Modern Language Association of America, 1973.

Moerk, Ernest L. "Quantitative Analysis of Writing Styles." *Journal of Linguistics,* 6 (1970): 223–230.

Monk, Samuel. *The Sublime: A Study of Critical Theories in Eighteenth-Century England.* New York: Modern Language Association, 1935; new ed., Ann Arbor: University of Michigan Press, 1961.

Moore, George, ed. *Anthology of Pure Poetry.* New York: Boni and Liveright, 1925.

Morris, C. W. *Varieties of Human Value.* Chicago: University of Chicago Press, 1956.

Mosteller, Frederick, and David Wallace, eds. *Inference and Disputed Authorship: The Federalist.* Reading, Mass.: Addison-Wesley, 1964.

Muller, Herbert J. *Science and Criticism: The Humanities Tradition in Contemporary Thought.* New Haven: Yale University Press, 1943.

Munro, Thomas. *Scientific Method in Aesthetics.* New York: W. W. Norton & Co., 1928.

Murray, Gilbert. *The Classical Tradition in Poetry.* Cambridge: Harvard University Press, 1927.

Murray, Roger. "A Case for the Study of Period Styles." *College English,* 33 (1971): 139–148.

Murry, J. Middleton. *The Problem of Style.* London: Oxford University Press, 1936.

Nicolson, Marjorie Hope. *Mountain Gloom and Mountain Glory: The Development of the Aesthetics of the Infinite.* Ithaca, N.Y.: Cornell University Press, 1959.

Nida, Eugene A. *A Synopsis of English Syntax.* Norman: University of Oklahoma Press, 1960.

Niebuhr, Reinhold. *The Self and the Drama of History.* New York: Charles Scribner's Sons, 1955.

Nowottny, Winifred. *The Language Poets Use.* London: University of London Press, 1962.

Ogden, C. K., and I. A. Richards. *Meaning of Meaning: Study of Influence of Language on Thought and of Science of Symbolism.* London: Kegan Paul, 1926; with Supplementary Essays by B. Malinowski and F. G. Crookshank, 2nd rev. ed. New York: Harcourt, Brace and Co., 1927.

Ohmann, Richard M. *Shaw: The Style and the Man.* Middletown, Conn.: Wesleyan University Press, 1962.

————. "Speech, Action and Style." In *Literary Style: A Symposium,* ed. Seymour Chatman. London: Oxford University Press, 1971. Pp. 24–59.

Ong, Walter J. S. J. *The Presence of the Word.* New Haven: Yale University Press, 1967.

Osgood, Charles, George J. Suci, and Percy Tannenbaum. *The*

Measurement of Meaning. Urbana: University of Illinois Press, 1957.

Panofsky, Erwin. *Meaning in the Visual Arts*. New York: Doubleday and Co., 1955.

Parkinson, Thomas. *W. B. Yeats: Self-Critic*. Berkeley and Los Angeles: University of California Press, 1951.

———. *W. B. Yeats: The Later Poetry*. Berkeley and Los Angeles: University of California Press, 1964.

Pater, Walter. *Appreciations: With an Essay on Style*. London: Macmillan & Co., 1920.

Paul, Anthony M. "Figurative Language." *Philosophy and Rhetoric*, 3 (1970): 225–247.

Payne, Stanley. *The Art of Asking Questions*. Princeton, N.J.: Princeton University Press, 1951.

Pearson, Karl. *The Grammar of Science*, 1st ed. New York: Charles Scribner's Sons, 1892.

Peirce, Charles Sanders. *Philosophical Writings*. Selected and edited by Justus Buchler. New York: Dover, 1955.

Peltola, Niilo. *The Compound Epithet and Its Use in American Poetry from Broadstreet through Whitman*. Helsinki, 1956.

Pepper, Stephen C. *World Hypotheses*. Berkeley and Los Angeles: University of California Press, 1942.

Peyre, Henri. *Writers and Their Critics: A Study of Misunderstanding*. Ithaca, N.Y.: Cornell University Press, 1944.

Piaget, Jean. *The Language and Thought of the Child*. Trans. M. Worden. New York: Harcourt, Brace and Co., 1926.

Pike, Kenneth L. "Implications of the Patterning of an Oral Reading of a Set of Poems." *Poetics*, 1 (1971): 34–45.

———. *Language in Relation to a Unified Theory of the Structure of Human Behavior*. 2 vols. Glendale, Calif.: Summer Institute of Linguistics, 1954–1955.

Platt, Joan. "Development of English Colloquial Idiom During the Eighteenth Century." *Review of English Studies*, 2, no. 5 (January 1926): 70–81; 2, no. 6 (April 1926): 189–196.

Pollock, Thomas Clarke. *The Nature of Literature: Its Relation to Science, Language, and Human Experience*. Princeton, N.J.: Princeton University Press, 1942.

Pool, I. de Sola, ed. *Trends in Content Analysis*. Urbana: University of Illinois Press, 1959.

Pope, Alexander. *The Art of Sinking in Poetry*. Ed. Edna Steeves. New York: King's Crown Press, 1952.

Pottle, Frederick A. *The Idiom of Poetry*. Ithaca, N.Y.: Cornell University Press, 1941.

Pound, Ezra. *Letters*. Ed. D. D. Page. New York: Harcourt, Brace and Co., 1950.

————. *The ABC of Reading*. Norfolk, Conn.: New Directions, 1951.

Prall, D. W. *Aesthetic Analysis*. New York: T. Y. Crowell, 1936.

Puttenham, George. *The Arte of English Poesie*. Ed. Gladys Willock and Alice Walker. Cambridge: At the University Press, 1936.

Pyles, Thomas. *The Origins and Development of the English Language*. New York: Harcourt, Brace and Co., 1964.

Quayle, Thomas. *Poetic Diction: A Study of Eighteenth Century Verse*. London: University of Liverpool Press, 1924.

Quine, Willard. *Word and Object*. Cambridge: M.I.T. Press, 1960.

Radin, Mats. *Word-Order in English Verse from Pope to Sassoon*. Uppsala, 1925.

Rainolde, Richard. *The Foundacion of Rhetorike*. New York: Scholars' Facsimile and Reprints, 1945.

Randall, Henry John. *The Creative Centuries: A Study in Historical Development*. New York: Longmans, Green, 1945.

Ransom, John Crowe. *The New Criticism*. Norfolk, Conn.: New Directions, 1941.

Rapoport, Anatol. *Science and the Goals of Man*. New York: Harper & Brothers, 1950.

Read, Herbert. *Form in Modern Poetry*. London: Sheed & Ward, 1932.

Reichenbach, Hans. *Experience and Prediction: An Analysis of the Foundations and Structure of Knowledge*. Chicago: University of Chicago Press, 1938.

Revzin, Izaak. "Generative Grammars, Stylistics and Poetics." In *Sign, Language and Culture*, ed. A. J. Greimas et al. The Hague: Mouton, 1970. Pp. 558–69.

Richards, I. A. *The Philosophy of Rhetoric*, London: Oxford University Press, 1936.

————. *Practical Criticism*. New York: Harcourt, Brace and Co., 1930.

Riffaterre, Michael. *Essais de stylistique structurale*. Ed. Daniel Delas. Paris: Flammarion, 1971.

Roberts, Paul. *English Syntax*. New York: Harcourt, Brace and Co., 1964.

Rosenzweig, Mark R. "Comparison Among Word-Association Responses in English, French, German, and Italian." *American Journal of Psychology*, 74, no. 3 (September 1961): 347–360.

Røstvig, Maren Sofie. *The Background of English Neo-Classicism, with Comments on Swift and Pope*. Oslo: Universitetsprag, 1961.

——. *The Happy Man: Studies in the Metamorphoses of a Classical Ideal*. 2 vols. Oslo, 1954; Oxford: Blackwell, 1958.

Rubel, Veré L. *Poetic Diction in the English Renaissance*. New York: Modern Language Association of America, 1941.

Ruesch, Jurgen, and Weldon Kees. *Non-Verbal Communication. Notes on the Visual Perception of Human Relations*. Berkeley and Los Angeles: University of California Press, 1956.

Russell, Bertrand. *An Inquiry into Meaning and Truth*. New York: W. W. Norton & Co., 1940.

Ruwet, Nicholas. "L'Analyse structurale de la poésie." In *Linguistics*, no. 2. The Hague: Mouton & Co., 1963.

——. "Linguistics and Poetics." In *The Languages of Criticism and the Sciences of Man: The Structuralist Controversy*, ed. Richard Macksey and Eugenio Danto. Baltimore: Johns Hopkins Press, 1970. Pp. 296–313.

Rylands, George. "English Poetry and the Abstract Word." In *Essays and Studies*, 16, ed. H. J. C. Grierson. London: Oxford University Press, 1931.

——. *Words and Poetry*. New York: Payson and Clarke, 1928.

Sachs, Curt. *The Commonwealth of Art*. New York: W. W. Norton & Co., 1946.

——. *Rhythm and Tempo*. New York: W. W. Norton & Co., 1953.

Saintsbury, George. *History of Criticism and Literary Taste in Europe from Earliest Texts to the Present Day*. Edinburgh: W. Blackwood, 1902–1906.

Sampson, H. *The Language of Poetry*. London: Cranton, 1925.

Santayana, George. *The Sense of Beauty: Outlines of Aesthetic Theory*. New York: Charles Scribner's Sons, 1896.

Sapir, Edward. *Language, An Introduction to the Study of Speech.* New York: Harcourt, Brace and Co., 1921.
——. *Culture, Language, and Personality: Selected Essays.* Berkeley and Los Angeles: University of California Press, 1956.
de Saussure, F. *Cours de Linguistique Générale.* Ed. Charles Bally. Paris, 1922; 2nd ed., Paris: Payot, 1949. Trans. Wade Baskin. New York: Philosophical Library, 1959.
Sayce, R. A. *Style in French Prose: A Method of Analysis.* Oxford: Clarendon Press, 1953.
Scheuerwegs, Gustave. *Present Day English Syntax: A Survey of Sentence Patterns.* New York: Longmans, Green, 1959.
Schucking Levin L. *The Sociology of Literary Taste.* Trans. E. W. Dickes. New York: Oxford University Press, 1944.
Schopenhauer, Arthur. *The Art of Literature.* Trans. T. Bailey Saunders. London: Swan Sonnenschein & Co., 1891.
Searle, John. *The Philosophy of Language.* London: Oxford University Press, 1971.
Sebeok, Thomas A., ed. *Style in Language.* Cambridge: M.I.T. Press, 1960.
Selvin, Hanan Charles. *Effects of Leadership.* Glencoe, Ill.: Free Press, 1960.
Shapiro, Karl, and R. Beum. *Prosody Handbook.* New York: Harper & Brothers, 1965.
Sheldon, W. H. *Process and Polarity.* New York: Columbia University Press, 1944.
Sherman, L. A. *Analytics of Literature.* Boston: Ginn and Co., 1893.
Skinner, B. F. *Verbal Behavior.* New York: D. Appleton, 1957.
Smith, Adam. *Lectures on Rhetoric and Belles Lettres.* Ed. John Lothian. New York: Thomas Nelson, 1963.
Smith, Gregory, ed. *Elizabethan Critical Essays.* 2 vols. Oxford: Clarendon Press, 1904.
Spence, Joseph. *Anecdotes, Observations, and Characters of Books and Men,* 2nd ed. Ed. S. W. Singer. London, 1858.
Spingarn, J. E. *Critical Essays of the Seventeenth Century.* Oxford: Clarendon Press, 1908.
——. *The New Criticism.* New York: Columbia University Press, 1911.
Spitzer, Leo. *Linguistics and Literary History: Essays in Stylistics.* Princeton, N.J.: Princeton University Press, 1948.

Sprat, Thomas. *The History of the Royal Society of London*, 3rd ed. London: Samuel Chapman, 1722.

Staton, Walter, Jr. "The Characters of Style in Elizabethan Prose." *Journal of English and Germanic Philology*, 57 (1958): 197–207.

Stebbing, William. *Some Verdicts of History Renewed*. London, 1887.

Stein, Gertrude. *Lectures in America*. New York: Random House, 1935.

Stein, Leo. *The ABC of Aesthetics*. New York: Boni and Liveright, 1927.

Steiner, George. "Linguistics and Literature." In *Linguistics at Large*, ed. Noel Minnis. London: Victor Gollancz Ltd., 1971. Pp. 111–136.

————. "Linguistics and Poetics." *TriQuarterly*, 20 (1971): 73–97.

Stevenson, Charles L. *Ethics and Language*. New Haven: Yale University Press, 1944.

Steward, Julian H. *Theory of Culture Change*. Champagne: University of Illinois Press, 1955.

Stewart, George R. *The Technique of English Verse*. New York: Henry Holt and Co., 1930.

Stouffer, S. A., L. Guttman, et al. *Measurement and Prediction*. Princeton, N.J.: Princeton University Press, 1950.

Strelka, Joseph, ed. *Patterns of Literary Style*. University Park: Pennsylvania State University Press, 1971.

Surtz, Edward L. "Epithets in Pope's *Messiah*." *Philological Quarterly*, 27, no. 3 (July 1948).

Symons, Arthur. *The Symbolist Movement in Literature*, rev. ed. New York: E. P. Dutton Co., 1919.

Sypher, Wylie. *Four Stages of Renaissance Style: Transformations in Art and Literature, 1400–1700*. New York: Doubleday & Co., 1955.

————. *Rococo to Cubism in Art*. New York: Random House, 1960.

Tate, Allen, ed., Phillip Wheelright, Cleanth Brooks, I. A. Richards, and Wallace Stevens. *The Language of Poetry*. Princeton, N.J.: Princeton University Press, 1942.

Taylor, Henry. "Poetical Essays on Poetry." *Works*, vol. 5. London: Kegan Paul, 1878.

Teggart, F. J. "Causation in Historical Events." *Journal of History*, 3, no. 1 (January 1942).

————. *Processes of History.* New Haven: Yale University Press, 1918.

————. *Prolegomena to History.* "University of California Publications in History," vol. 4, no. 3. Berkeley: University of California Press, 1916.

Temple, Ruth Zabriskie. *The Critics' Alchemy: A Study of the Introduction of French Symbolism into England.* New York: Twayne Publishers, 1953.

Theory and Practice in Historical Study. "A Report of the Committee on Historiography," Bulletin no. 54. New York: Social Research Council, 1946.

Thomas, Owen. *Metaphor and Related Subjects.* New York: Random House, 1969.

Thompson, John. *The Founding of English Metre.* London. Routledge & Kegan Paul, 1961.

Thorndike, Edward L. *The Teacher's Word Book.* New York: Columbia University Press, 1921.

Thorne, James P. "Stylistics and Generative Grammars." *Journal of Linguistics,* 1 (1965): 49–59.

Thurstone, L. L. *Vectors of Mind: Multiple-Factor Analysis for the Isolation of Primary Traits.* Chicago: University of Chicago Press, 1935.

Tobin, James. *A Bibliography of Eighteenth Century English Literature and Its Cultural Background.* New York: Fordham University Press, 1939.

Todorov, Tzvetan. "Meaning in Literature: A Survey." *Poetics,* 1 (1971): 8–15.

Toulmin, Stephen, and June Goodfield. *The Discovery of Time.* New York: Harper & Row, 1965.

Trager, George L., and Henry Lee Smith. *An Outline of English Structure.* Norman: University of Oklahoma Press, 1951.

Trapp, Joseph. *Praelectiones Poeticae,* 2 vols. Oxford, 1711–1715.

Trench, Archbishop Richard Chenevix, D.D. *On the Study of Words.* Ed. A. S. Palmer. London: Routledge, 1913.

Trimpi, Wesley. *Ben Jonson's Poems: A Study of the Plain Style.* Stanford, Calif.: Stanford University Press, 1962.

Tucker, Susie. *English Examined: Two Centuries of Comment.* Cambridge: At the University Press, 1961.

Tuve, Rosemond. *Allegorical Imagery: Some Mediaeval Books and*

Their Posterity. Princeton, N.J.: Princeton University Press, 1966.

———. *Essays by Rosemond Tuve: Spenser; Herbert; Milton*. Ed. Thomas P. Roche, Jr. Princeton, N.J.: Princeton University Press, 1970.

———. *Elizabethan and Metaphysical Imagery: Renaissance Poetic and Twentieth Century Critics*. Chicago: University of Chicago Press, 1947.

———. *Images and Themes in Five Poems by Milton*. Cambridge: Harvard University Press, 1957.

———. *A Reading of George Herbert*. London: Faber & Faber, 1952.

———. *Seasons and Months: Studies in a Tradition of Middle English Poetry*. Paris: Librairie Universitaire, 1933.

Tuveson, Ernest. *Millennium and Utopia*. Berkeley and Los Angeles: University of California Press, 1949.

———. *The Imagination as a Means of Grace: Locke and the Aesthetics of Romanticism*. Berkeley and Los Angeles: University of California Press, 1960.

Tyler, L. *Psychology of Human Differences*. New York: Appleton-Century-Crofts, 1956.

Uitti, Karl. *Linguistics and Literary Theory*. Englewood Cliffs, N.J.: Prentice-Hall, 1967.

Ullman, Stephen. *Language and Style; Collected Papers*. New York: Barnes & Noble, 1964.

———. *The Principles of Semantics*, 2nd ed. New York: Philosophical Library, 1957.

Urban, Wilbur M. *Language and Reality: The Philosophy of Language and the Principles of Symbolism*. London: Allen & Unwin, 1939.

Ushenko, Andrew Paul. *The Field Theory of Meaning*. Ann Arbor: University of Michigan Press, 1958.

Valéry, Paul. *The Art of Poetry*. "Bollingen Series," vol. 45. New York: Pantheon, 1958.

Vallins, G. H. *The Pattern of English*. London: Deutsch, 1956.

Vangelisti, P. "Semantics of Literary Form," *Language Quarterly*, 9 (1970): 45–48.

Vendryes, J. *Language: A Linguistic Introduction to History*. Trans. Paul Rodin. New York: Alfred A. Knopf, 1925.

Vossler, Karl. *The Spirit of Language in Civilization.* Trans. Oscar Oeser. London: Kegan Paul, 1932.

Wallace, K. R. *Francis Bacon on Communication and Rhetoric.* Chapel Hill: University of North Carolina Press, 1943.

Wallerstein, Ruth. "The Development of the Rhetoric and Metric of the Heroic Couplet, Especially in 1625–1645." *PMLA,* 50, no. 1 (March 1935): 166–209.

————. *Studies in Seventeenth Century Poetic.* Madison: University of Wisconsin Press, 1961.

Warren, Alba H. *English Poetic Theory, 1825–1865.* Princeton, N.J.: Princeton University Press, 1950.

Wasserman, Earl. *The Subtler Language: Critical Readings of Neoclassic and Romantic Poems.* Baltimore: Johns Hopkins University Press, 1959.

Watson, George. "The Language of the Metaphysicals." In *Literary English Since Shakespeare,* ed. George Watson. New York: Oxford University Press, 1970.

————, ed. *Literary English Since Shakespeare.* New York: Oxford University Press, 1970.

Weaver, W. "Probability, Rarity, Interest and Surprise." *Scientific Monthly,* 14, no. 2 (1948): 390–392.

Webber, Joan. *Contrary Music: The Prose Style of John Donne.* Madison: University of Wisconsin Press, 1963.

Weissenberger, Klaus. "The Problem of Period Style in the Theory of Recent Literary Criticism: A Comparison." In *Patterns of Literary Style,* ed. Joseph Strelka. University Park: Pennsylvania State University Press, 1971. Pp. 226–64.

Welby, V. *What is Meaning? Studies in the Development of Significance.* London: Kegan Paul, 1903.

Wellek, René. *Concepts of Criticism.* Ed. Stephen G. Nichols. New Haven: Yale University Press, 1963.

————. *A History of Modern Criticism, 1750–1850.* New Haven: Yale University Press, 1955.

Weyl, Herman. *Symmetry.* Princeton, N.J.: Princeton University Press, 1952.

Whately, Richard. *Elements of Rhetoric.* New York: Harper & Brothers, 1860.

Whatmough, Joshua. *Language: A Modern Synthesis.* New York: St. Martin's Press, 1956.

Wheat, Leonard B. *Free Associations to Common Words.* New York: Bureau of Publications, Teachers College, Columbia University Press, 1931.

Wheelwright, Philip. *The Burning Fountain: A Study in the Language of Symbolism.* Bloomington: Indiana University Press, 1954.

White, Lancellot Law, ed. *Aspects of Form.* London: Humphries, 1951.

Whorf, Benjamin Lee. *Four Articles on Metalinguistics.* Washington, D.C.: Department of State, 1950.

———. *Language, Thought and Reality: Selected Writings.* Ed. John B. Carroll, Cambridge: M.I.T. Press, 1956.

Wilhelm, Helmut. *Change.* Trans. Cary Baynes. New York: Pantheon, 1960.

Williams, C. B. *Style and Vocabulary: Numerical Studies.* London: Griffin, 1970.

Williamson, George. *The Proper Wit of Poetry.* Chicago: University of Chicago Press, 1961.

———. *The Senecan Amble: A Study in Prose from Bacon to Collier.* Chicago: University of Chicago Press, 1951.

Wilson, Edmund. *Axel's Castle: A Study in the Imaginative Literature of 1870–1930.* New York: Charles Scribner's Sons, 1931.

Wilson, F. P. *Seventeenth Century Prose.* Berkeley and Los Angeles: University of California Press, 1960.

Wilson, Thomas. *Arte of Rhetorique, 1560.* Ed. C. H. Mair. Oxford: Clarendon Press, 1919.

Wimsatt, W. K., Jr. *The Verbal Icon.* Lexington: University of Kentucky Press, 1954.

Wimsatt, William Kurtz. *The Prose Style of Samuel Johnson.* New Haven: Yale University Press, 1941.

Winters, Yvor. *Anatomy of Nonsense.* Norfolk, Conn.: New Directions, 1943.

Wölfflin, Heinrich. *Principles of Art History.* Trans. M. D. Hottinger. New York: Dover Publications, 1932.

Wright, George T. *The Poet in the Poem.* Berkeley and Los Angeles: University of California Press, 1962 [c. 1960].

Wyld, Henry Cecil. *Some Aspects of the Diction of English Poetry: Three Lectures.* Oxford: Basil Blackwell, 1933.

Wyler, Siegfried. *Die Adjektive des mittelenglischen Schoenheits-feld.* Zurich, 1944.

Young, Agnes Brooks. *Recurring Cycles of Fashion, 1760–1937.* New York: Harper & Brothers, 1937.

Youngren, William H. *Semantics, Linguistics, and Criticism.* Consulting ed. Richard Ohmann. New York: Random House, 1972.

Yule, G. Udny. *The Statistical Study of Literary Vocabulary.* Cambridge: At the University Press, 1944.

Zipf, George Kingsley. *Human Behavior and the Principle of Least Effort.* Cambridge, Mass.: Addison-Wesley, 1949.

Zoltán, Szabo. "The Types of Stylistic Studies and the Characterization of Individual Style: An Outline of Problems." *Linguistics,* 62 (1970): 96–104.

Zwerdling, Alex. *Yeats and the Heroic Ideal.* New York: New York University Press, 1965.